JEREMIAH JOYCE

Jeremiah Joyce was one of the accused in the famous Treason Trials of 1794 which marked the suppression of radical agitation in Britain for the ensuing twenty years. He was a political radical who imbibed the traditions of the 'commonwealthman' and actively campaigned for a more democratic and representative state. Through the early 1790s he acted as the metropolitan political agent for his patron the Earl of Stanhope and he liased between radical groups whilst also distributing radical literature including Tom *Paine's Rights of Man*. He was one of the very few artisans at the end of the eighteenth century adopted by the literary and scientific intelligentsia and was unique in training to become a Unitarian minister at the age of 23 after serving a seven-year trade apprenticeship and having worked as a journeyman.

This work traces the legacies, traditions and visions of the English Enlightenment as they are expressed through Joyce's life and literary production. It explores the evolution of these traditions against the threatening background of the French revolution and the developing imperatives for education in general, and science education in particular. By tracing the linkages between political, educational, scientific and publishing cultures, it reflects on the issues of late eighteenth century patronage, the literary forms of popular science and the evolution of the metropolitan book trade. In so doing the book recovers the life of a hitherto much neglected science writer and political activist and contributes to the histories of politics, education, science and the developing discipline of book history.

About the Author

John Issitt teaches in the areas of philosophy, history and educational studies for the University of York and the Open University, UK. His research interests are in the history and politics of knowledge. He holds a National Teaching Fellowship through which he develops innovative approaches to learning and supports students in collaborative writing.

Science, Technology and Culture, 1700–1945

Series Editors

David M. Knight
University of Durham

and

Trevor Levere
University of Toronto

Science, Technology and Culture, 1700–1945 focuses on the social, cultural, industrial and economic contexts of science and technology from the 'scientific revolution' up to the Second world War. It explores the agricultural and industrial revolutions of the eighteenth century, the coffee-house culture of the Enlightenment, the spread of museums, botanic gardens and expositions in the nineteenth century, to the Franco-Prussian war of 1870, seen as a victory for German science. It also addresses the dependence of society on science and technology in the twentieth century.

Science, Technology and Culture, 1700–1945 addresses issues of the interaction of science, technology and culture in the period from 1700 to 1945, at the same time as including new research within the field of the history of science.

Also in this series

Hewett Cottrell Watson
Victorian Plant Ecologist and Evolutionist
Frank N. Egerton

The Genius of Erasmus Darwin
Edited by C.U.M. Smith and Robert Arnott

Science and Dissent in England, 1688–1945
Edited by Paul Wood

JEREMIAH JOYCE

Figure 1: Portrait of the Reverend Jeremiah Joyce. Published 11 Nov. 1794, by B. Crosby. Stationer's Court, Ludgate Street, London. National Portrait Gallery.

Jeremiah Joyce
Radical, Dissenter and Writer

JOHN ISSITT
University of York, UK

LONDON AND NEW YORK

First published 2006 by Ashgate Publishing

Reissued 2018 by Routledge
2 Park Square, Milton Park, Abingdon, Oxon OX14 4RN
605 Third Avenue, New York, NY 10017

First issued in paperback 2021

Routledge is an imprint of the Taylor & Francis Group, an informa business

© John Issitt 2006

John Issitt has asserted his moral right under the Copyright, Designs and Patents Act, 1988, to be identified as the author of this work.

All rights reserved. No part of this book may be reprinted or reproduced or utilised in any form or by any electronic, mechanical, or other means, now known or hereafter invented, including photocopying and recording, or in any information storage or retrieval system, without permission in writing from the publishers.

A Library of Congress record exists under LC control number: 2006000575

Notice:
Product or corporate names may be trademarks or registered trademarks, and are used only for identification and explanation without intent to infringe.

Publisher's Note
The publisher has gone to great lengths to ensure the quality of this reprint but points out that some imperfections in the original copies may be apparent.

Disclaimer
The publisher has made every effort to trace copyright holders and welcomes correspondence from those they have been unable to contact.

ISBN 13: 978-0-815-38992-7 (hbk)
ISBN 13: 978-1-351-15508-3 (ebk)
ISBN 13: 978-1-138-35823-2 (pbk)

DOI: 10.4324/9781351155083

Contents

List of Illustrations vi
Acknowledgements viii
Abbreviations for References ix
Series Editor's Preface x
Foreword xii
Cast of Principal Characters xvi

PART 1: JOYCE THE POLITICAL RADICAL

1. Early Life in Cheshunt 3
2. Apprentice Painter of Glass in Georgian London 12
3. Hackney College – Radicalism and Dissent 26
4. Metropolitan Political Agent 32
5. Political Notoriety and the Charge of Treason 45
6. Release and Reception 58

PART 2: JOYCE THE UNITARIAN DISSENTER

7. Politics and Education 65
8. Life and Death, 1795–1816 69
9. Joyce in the Unitarian World 78
10. Respectable Sermons 92

PART 3: JOYCE THE SCIENCE WRITER

11. Patronage, Education and Writing 99
12. A Literary Apprenticeship 107
13. Learning to Present Science: Publishing with Joseph Johnson 118
14. Publishing with Sir Richard Phillips 136
15. Publishing with the House of Longmans 156
16. Publishing with Sherwood Neely and C.J. Barrington 170
17. Overview of Joyce's Works 173

Conclusion 175

List of Joyce's Published Works 180
Index 183

List of Illustrations

1. Portrait of the Reverend Jeremiah Joyce. Published 11 Nov. 1794, by B. Crosby. Stationer's Court, Ludgate Street. National Portrait Gallery London. ... ii

2. Frontispiece from the 1860 edition of Joyce's *Scientific Dialogues*, published in Halifax by Milner and Sowerby. ... xiv

3. Map of Cheshunt in 1800. Drawn by Henry Crawter, Cheshunt Public Library. ... 5

4. Woolcombing. This illustration appears as the first trade described in *The Book of Trades* which Joyce compiled and wrote in 1804 published in London by Benjamin Tabert. By permission of the British Library. Shelfmark 012806.de.11 ... 7

5. The Noble Sans-Culotte by H. Humphreys, 3 May 1794. ... 36

6. Extract from the Unitarian version of the *New Testament*, 1808. Opening page of St John's Gospel. Copyright Dr Williams's Library, London, reproduced by kind permission of the trustees. ... 84

7. Extract from 'Preliminary Considerations' the opening sections of Paley's *Evidences* (1794) compared with Joyce's edited and abbreviated version in his *Analysis of Paley's Evidences* (1795). ... 112

8. Illustration from *Shakespeare's Seven Ages of Man Illustrated* (H. D. Symonds, 1800). Drawn by Thomas Stothard and engraved by William Bromley 1799. Copyright Dr Williams's Library, London, reproduced by kind permission of the trustees. ... 117

9. Illustrations from Joyce's *Dialogues on the Microscope* published by Johnson, 1812. By permission of the British Library. Shelfmark 7005.a.3. ... 128

10. A view of Tabart's shop from a plate appearing in *Visits to a Juvenile Library* by Eliza Fenwick, Vol. 1 (Phillips, 1805), p. 43. ... 137

11. 'Economy of Time and Labour exemplified in a Chinese Waterman', from *Geography Illustrated on a Popular Plan* (Phillips, 1803). By permission of the British Library. Shelfmark 571.b.6.   141

12. 'The Luminous space in the sword of Orion', from *Wonders of the Telescope*. (Phillips, 1805). By permission of the British Library. Shelfmark 7801–862.   147

13. Orang Outang. Illustration and entry from *Kendall's Pocket Encyclopedia*. 2nd Edn., corrected (Longmans, 1811) Vol. 4, p. 280. Shelfmark 270 g.387–390. Reproduced by kind permission of the Bodleian Library, University of Oxford.   164

14. 'Structure and Functions of Man', from *Systematic Education* (Longmans, 1815). By permission of the British Library. Shelfmark 1031.i.5   168

Acknowledgements

I would like to thank Mike Bartholomew, Geoffrey Cantor and David Knight for their help and guidance in the production of this work. I would also like to thank the Library staff of the Dr Williams's Library, Harris Manchester College Oxford, the British Library and the Brotherton Library in Leeds, all of whom have been most helpful over the years.

I would like to thank the subject of this work, Jeremiah Joyce. Joyce, who as the reader is about to find out, is an illusive character and has occupied me in various ways for ten years. Along the way I have learnt quite a lot about him and a great deal about myself, for which I am deeply grateful.

Most importantly, I would also like to thank my wife Patricia, my children Theo and Georgia and my parents Margaret and Ken for all their tolerance and warm support.

Abbreviations for References

MCO	Manchester College Oxford
DNB	Dictionary of National Biography
PRO, T.S.	Public Records Office. Treasurer's Solicitor's Papers
DWL	Dr. Williams's Library
TUHS	Transactions of the Unitarian Historical Society
BJHS	British Journal of the History of Science

Series Editor's Preface

In the history of science and technology, we are accustomed to meeting the giants. Galileo, Newton, Franklin, Lavoisier, Humboldt, Brunel, Faraday, Edison, Darwin and Einstein feature over and over, and although their work still invites scholarly scrutiny, there is no problem in finding out facts about them. But we do not learn science from such people as these, and nor did our ancestors. We read children's books, popular writings, and school textbooks; we go to lectures; we look things up in encyclopaedias; and we watch television, where our grandparents had magic-lantern shows. Those who get science across in these ways will mostly never be famous, and yet without them there would have been nobody to encourage and take note of the giants. To understand how science and technology have developed, we need to know more about the sometimes elusive and often forgotten people who have popularised it.

Jeremiah Joyce, whom we encounter in this very personal biography by John Issitt, is just such a figure. Son of a woolcomber, active in the years of what has been called the 'Second Scientific Revolution', the decades either side of 1800 when the Industrial Revolution got under way and science began to become a career rather than a hobby, his life was caught up in the political excitement and world war that followed the French Revolution of 1789. Like the great chemist Joseph Priestley, he was both a political radical and also a faithful, committed Unitarian minister (trained at the Dissenting Academy in Hackney), though it was only at the end of his life that Joyce was called to a regular ministry. Again like Priestley, he spent some years as tutor and sidekick in the household of a left-wing nobleman; but as reaction to Robespierre's Terror in France reached its height in 1794, Priestley fled to the USA, and Joyce was arrested with others on charges of treason and confined in the Tower of London.

Though the treason trials in that war on terror collapsed, Joyce and his fellows were branded 'acquitted felons' and shunned by right-thinking persons. He made his way by writing; but like Hollywood radicals in the McCarthy era, he had to do most of it anonymously or pseudonymously. His *Scientific Dialogues* were indeed famous and successful, but John Issitt has demonstrated that this book was only a small fraction of what he wrote, much of which has not been credited or attributed to him. This was a time of rapid expansion in literacy, the March of Mind, with monitorial schools run by churches, with cheaper books printed in longer runs, and a hunger for knowledge fed by entrepreneurial publishers. This biography opens up that world, where a jobbing writer, a craftsman of letters, could operate across different levels and publishing worlds, compiling, abstracting and rewriting in clear and workmanlike prose – and all the time emphasising Design, as befitted an optimistic member of the religious left.

We learn a great deal about publishing and publishers who could do extremely well out of works written, edited or compiled by Joyce and other writers, who by comparison earned a pittance. Nevertheless, Joyce did earn enough to live on (rather as his contemporaries Davy and Dalton did from the practice of science), and must be accounted one of the first professional popularisers of science. The reader will meet collaboration, plagiarism, the appearance of publishers' series (and of complementary educational texts, reinforcing each other), and evidence of costs, receipts and profits in the new world of children's and popular books and compendia. We find Joyce keeping up to date on the whole, aware of progress across the sciences and of new inventions, while avoiding controversial and uncertain science as far as possible. It is all too easy to suppose that truth is mighty and will prevail, without going into how this might happen, or has happened. Looking at Joyce's career helps us to see how the work of those giants of science and technology became known to our forebears; and John Issitt has performed an important resurrection job, which casts new light on an interesting and congenial man, living in a politically murky period.

David Knight
October 2005

Foreword

Trying to write the life of Jeremiah Joyce was like trying to put clothes on an invisible man. Through archives, record offices, the biographies of Joyce's contemporaries and hundreds of reference works, I found only scraps that record the passage of his life and I had to squeeze every last drop of information from the sources I did find. My detective instincts were simultaneously frustrated and excited when I discovered that many notices of Joyce had been ***deliberately*** removed. It seemed that my efforts to assemble his biography were dogged by a kind of historical eraser that had been used to rub out his life, his actions and his work. In places where I felt sure I would find some information on him, I found only the fingerprints of his friends and associates as they removed any record of their contact. As I excavated the leads and turned every stone, I found that most of his friends kept very minimal records of him, that many groups with whom he had contact did not even acknowledge him and that communications I knew Joyce had actually had, had been destroyed. The aura of deliberate silence surrounding him became even more profound when I discovered that Joyce himself had willed that all his papers should be burnt when he died.

I also discovered that it wasn't just Joyce's contemporaries who had failed to write him into history. I knew that Joyce had achieved an amount of fame and notoriety and that he lived through that most crucial of periods in European history – the period of the French Revolution and the Napoleonic Wars, which had so many powerful effects on British life. He was a prolific writer, he was one of those charged with treason in the famous treason trials of 1794 and he was a friend to some famous personalities in the history of radical politics. Surely I would find records of his actions in the scholarly outpourings of historians. Yet the history of literature signally fails to acknowledge him and the history of political radicalism hardly fares better – only giving very minor and descriptive notices of his role as a political activist.

The reasons why Joyce had been 'edited out' soon became clear. He was a political radical and a supporter of the French Revolution with whom any evidence of contact was quite literally dangerous for those around him – thus records were destroyed. He was from a working class background distasteful to many intellectuals placed further up the social ladder. He wrote educational books for children – a genre not recognised or celebrated as valuable by the literary elite then or now. Furthermore, a large number of the books he wrote for children were not published under his own name but under pseudonyms and concocted brand names designed to exploit the growing markets for children's books. These were four powerful reasons why Joyce had become a historical unknown.

I became gripped by the figure of a political radical alienated from society by an elite class culture and subsequently rubbed out of history by very similar forces. I became obsessed with the endeavour to discover the real man, the textures and qualities of his world and the impulses which led him to act as he did. I revisited many of the archives and re-examined all the sources for a second, third and sometimes a fourth time with meticulous attention to detail. I searched for anything that would lead me on and anything that I could triangulate with another source. When I exhausted the obvious, I began to use hunches, guesses and wild speculations. I trawled through vaguely related sets of letters, through indexes and through journals and newspaper reports. In a strange way the scarcity of sources actually did me a favour as I had to treat every tiny nugget of information like a prize. I had to assemble the very basic clues about his life and wring every last possibility out of the smallest and seemingly inconsequential detail. This involved hours and hours pursuing half leads that generally led nowhere but sometimes led to a new archive or a new set of possible connections.

I began to feel like a cross between Sherlock Holmes and Hercule Poirot. But the close attention to detail forced a healthy development in my own approach. I had to become very practical and let go of some of the pompous and redundant intellectualising my life as an aspiring academic involved. I had to work over the facts of the size of Joyce's house, who lived next door, how far it was from his brother's tallow chandlery to his place of worship, what the date of a particular printing of one of his books was, how many were printed and how he was paid. It was this sort of detail that got me closer to the man and it was this sort of detail that offered some windows on his life.

One fact, however, provoked a sense of caution in me and made me mindful of the responsibilities of the historical researcher. Joyce's last directed act on this world was the requirement, in his will, that all his papers be burned – he was therefore complicit in his own 'editing out' of history. Two hundred years later, was I violating his wishes by compiling and writing his life's story? If he were here to read it, would it bring him pain, embarrassment and shame and would he curse me? The historical distance between me and him clearly gives me an advantage as that account can never be settled, but the cautionary lesson was useful as it really did urge a humility in the study of a life lived. Furthermore, as I hope to show, Joyce was a decent man ill-treated by both historical circumstances and literary convention, and his story deserves to be told.

Over ten years I assembled everything I could. As the clues to his life slowly increased, I began to see continuity and coherence in his life. I began to feel that I would recognise this man if I met him in the street and I increasingly began to feel that this was an honourable man to whom history had been unfair. This was a man who needed recovering. He had traversed the class structures, he had fought the establishment, he had put his life on the line for what he believed, he had created a way of living for himself when there were very few willing to work with him. He had been a political activist, he had been in the Tower and had played his part in the development of the democracy we enjoy today. These were reasons enough for me to feel justified in writing his life.

There was another cautionary moment in my work to excavate Joyce's life. I was writing up the story to submit as a doctoral thesis when my supervisor asked me if

I was identifying too much with Joyce. Despite the two hundred years between us, both me and Joyce were from working class but aspiring backgrounds, we were both drawn to the same sort of radical politics, we were both teachers, we both shared an anarchic disregard for establishment in all its forms, we had both lived a number of lives and filled a number of social personas, we had both worked with our hands and our brains and we were both unable to shake off the feeling of being alienated from the social worlds in which we lived. Was I writing the history of myself transferred on to the history of Joyce? The question certainly put a temporary brake on my work and made me think hard. I realised that in a small way I had, in the business of trying to get under Joyce's skin, identified with him, but I also realised, thankfully, that I had a firm grip on myself and the work in which I was engaged.

Figure 2: Frontispiece from the 1860 edition of Joyce's *Scientific Dialogues*, published in Halifax by Milner and Sowerby.

I first encountered Joyce on a shelf in an obscure library in Leeds. In an 1860 edition of a work he first published in 1800 *Scientific Dialogues Intended for the Instruction and Entertainment of Young People*, an intriguing engraving used as the frontispiece (Figure 2).

The figures were from an earlier age than the date of publication and seemed to invoke a classical eighteenth century image. The engraved plate may simply have been one the print shop had available when it put the book together and its only reason for being there was the attempt to entice a well meaning parent into a purchase, but its classical imagery led me to explore the book's history and to try to find out more about its author. I found that this book had been published throughout the nineteenth century. It had been translated into several languages and produced all over the world in literally hundreds of editions by over 20 publishers. I estimated that over a period of one hundred years, millions of people would have held a copy of this work in their hands and it had probably been more successful in extending scientific knowledge than many of the very difficult volumes by scientific heroes such as Isaac Newton and Antoine Lavoisier.

From the first and minimal biographical notices I encountered, I began to develop an intriguing and in some ways contradictory set of images of Joyce. He had been a political radical in London in the early 1790s and had been imprisoned in the Tower on a charge of treason in 1794, but after he was acquitted he had given up overtly political activities. Despite coming from a working class background he became tutor to the children of an aristocrat who was the brother-in-law of the Prime Minister. He had started his working career by serving a seven-year apprenticeship as a painter of glass but he had then trained as a minister of a dissenting – Unitarian – church and had eventually became a reasonably successful writer. These facts alone generate an image of a life of contrasts, of multiple social worlds, of wilful action, of shifting visions and, most importantly for me, of genuine interest.

Joyce's notoriety was established in the period just after the French Revolution in the 1790s which became known as 'Pitt's terror years' – in the years when a defensive government tried to stamp out any hint of the radical goings-on and democratic potentials that came from across the channel. Acres of print have been devoted to account these years and to evaluate the revolutionary potential of their emergent radical politics and culture shifts of the period. Many brilliant historians have trawled, sifted and weighed the evidence in the context of a developing liberal democratic and modern British state. Such is the importance of the 1790s that generally only the professorial grandees of academic history have been able to pronounce on the relevance of the actions and the players. The treatment I offer does not seek to compete with such accounts. It does not seek to contribute another voice to the canon or to place my name in the list of historians pronouncing on the 1790s. My concern is to recover the life of a man who has been overlooked by so many. Simple as that.

Cast of Principal Characters

Robert Aspland	1782–1845	Leading Unitarian minister
Benjamin Flower	1755–1829	Radical Cambridge publisher
William Godwin	1756–1836	Radical philosopher
George Gregory	1754–1808	Writer and Prebendary of St Paul's
Thomas Hardy	1752–1832	Radical leader of the London Corresponding Society
Joseph Johnson	1738–1809	Radical Unitarian publisher
Jeremiah Joyce	1763–1816	Radical, Unitarian, writer
Hannah Joyce	1796–1858	Daughter of Jeremiah
Joshua Joyce	d 1816	Radical, tallow chandler, brother of Jeremiah
Theophilus Lindsey	1723–1808	Leading Unitarian minister
Thomas N. Longman	1771–1842	Publisher
William Nicholson	1753–1815	Science writer
Thomas Pysche Palmer	1747–1802	Unitarian minister. One of the Scottish Martyrs sent to Botany Bay
Richard Phillips	1767–1840	Radical publisher
William Pitt	1759–1806	British Prime Minister
Richard Price	1723–1791	Philosopher and Arian minister
Joseph Priestley	1733–1829	Leading Unitarian minister, scientist and radical
Abraham Rees	1743–1825	Dissenting Minister and encyclopaedist
William Shepherd	1768–1847	Unitarian minister and Liverpool politician
Charles Stanhope	1753–1816	Aristocrat, radical
Hester Stanhope	1776–1839	Daughter of Charles, traveller
John Horne Tooke	1736–1812	Radical, Leader of the Society for Constitutional Information
Hugh Worthington	1752–1797	Arian divine

PART 1
Joyce the Political Radical

Chapter 1

Early Life in Cheshunt

Dissenting Origins

The modern bustling town of Cheshunt in Hertfordshire is situated twenty five miles north of London just beyond the M25 circular. Cheshunt has a long and important history unknown to most drivers as they hurtle past. The Roman Ermine Street ran between York and London and is one of the earliest tracks through the Cheshunt area, but the present main road became the principal trade route communicating the North-east with London in the twelfth century. Kings and Queens had hunted there from the time of Henry VIII when the feudal manors developed into enclosed parks. The Royal palace of Theobalds which became the largest estate in the area was a regular venue for the travelling royal court in the seventeenth century. It was at these palace gates that Charles I was proclaimed King and from where he began his journey to Nottingham to raise his standard in the Civil War. From 1725, when the road through Cheshunt was significantly improved by a turnpike trust, the speeding royal mails from Edinburgh as well as the local mail coaches transporting the *Cambridge Telegraph* and the *Hertford Rocket* thundered through, often only stopping to quickly change horses at one of the many coaching inns in Cheshunt and nearby Waltham Cross.[1]

Fifty percent of the Pilgrim Fathers who set sail to America to escape religious persecution in the 1640s, came from Hertfordshire and the surrounding counties of Suffolk and Essex and the area is still heavily populated by non orthodox church-goers. Quakers, Independents, Baptists, Congregationalists and Methodists have all been present in large numbers in Cheshunt. In the eighteenth century however, the largest percentage of religious dissenters were Presbyterians.

English Presbyterianism changed dramatically in a relatively short time span. From the Elizabethan period, when Presbyterians represented one of the most conservative elements of the Christian Church in terms of doctrine, theology and practice, they became by the end of the eighteenth century, one of the most radical, unorthodox and critical voices in matters of theology, politics and science, on the English civil and political landscape.[2] Following the 1662 Act of Uniformity

---

1 For the history of Cheshunt see Edwards, J. (1974), *Cheshunt in Hertfordshire*, Cheshunt Urban District Council. Archer, C. (1923), *Historic Cheshunt*, The Cheshunt Press.

2 The classic study of English Presbyterianism and a truly wonderful book is Olive Griffiths, O. (1935), *Religion and Learning: A study in English Presbyterian thought from the Bartholomew Ejections (1662) to the foundation of the Unitarian Movement*, Cambridge University Press.

requiring every minister to declare assent to the Book of Common Prayer and the administration of the Church of England before St Bartholomew's Day, Jeremiah Joyce's great grandfather, the Reverend John Benson along with 150 other ministers from neighbouring areas, rather than commit what they saw as an act of perjury, decided to accept ejection from the Church. At considerable personal cost Benson, a former Deacon at Norwich and a minister at Little Leigh in nearby Essex, became a dissenting preacher.

The Joyce family were well known as leading Presbyterian dissenters. Among the many notices of the family's clashes with civil authorities now held in local records offices and archives is the case in 1688 of Joyce's great uncle William and his wife, who were arraigned before an ecclesiastical court in Cheshunt for refusing to conform to the rituals of the Established Church.[3] Religious dissenters were subject to many draconian social restrictions which served to limit their personal horizons. Officially they were excommunicated from the Established Church and therefore all the aspects of society which depended in some way on religious affiliation or on making oaths of allegiance, were debarred from them. They could not be directors of the East India Company, the Bank of England or any joint stock company. They could not hold high office in civic and military worlds and could not go to the universities of Oxford and Cambridge and they had no political representation in parliament. Until the Acts of Indemnity in 1727, they could not sue in a court of justice, act as a guardian to children or receive any legacy or gift. Some of these restrictions were lifted over the course of the eighteenth century but it wasn't until 1813, after a lengthy campaign, that they finally received equal and official citizenship and it wasn't until the mid twentieth century that it is safe to say that they no longer experienced significant social discrimination.

Presbyterian dissenters clearly gained great strength from their own communities. Indeed it was because of their social exclusion and oppression that their communities became so strong and distinct. In many ways their sense of social aspiration was heightened and refined through their sense of critical judgement over the affairs of a social and political world from which they were excluded. As a breeding ground for intellectual reflection, for religious understanding and for political mission, the social world of the dissenter was very rich. Their communities developed their own church 'meetings' and they developed their own system of schooling with a curriculum that reflected their interests and needs. Many middle class dissenters travelled to universities in Scotland and the Low Countries, where they could obtain a higher education and where they were exposed to different cultures and ideas. Their communities offered a distinctive sense of identity born from the experience of injustice and driven by a claim of moral legitimacy. Furthermore, with a clear ceiling placed on their social aspirations in the establishment world, many dissenters were able to focus their efforts on trade. As a result their communities were firmly

---

3   There are numerous entries for the Joyce name in the Cheshunt area from 1688 in Urwick, W. (1884), *Nonconformity in Herts*, Hazell, Watson and Viney, London.

structured by the ethos of trade and economic independence which in turn nurtured a culture of success, achievement and endeavour.

Joyce's Father – A Master Woolcomber

Cheshunt was a centre of the wool trade. For several generations from at least 1699, Joyce's immediate family had held a significant property 'by free deed of the manor'. Situated close to the centre of Cheshunt at an intersection of roads communicating the local area with the main road south to London, the Joyce family operated their business of woolcombing. Their plot of land was about an acre in size on which stood a house, outhouses and a barn and it was here that Joyce was born on 24 February 1763.

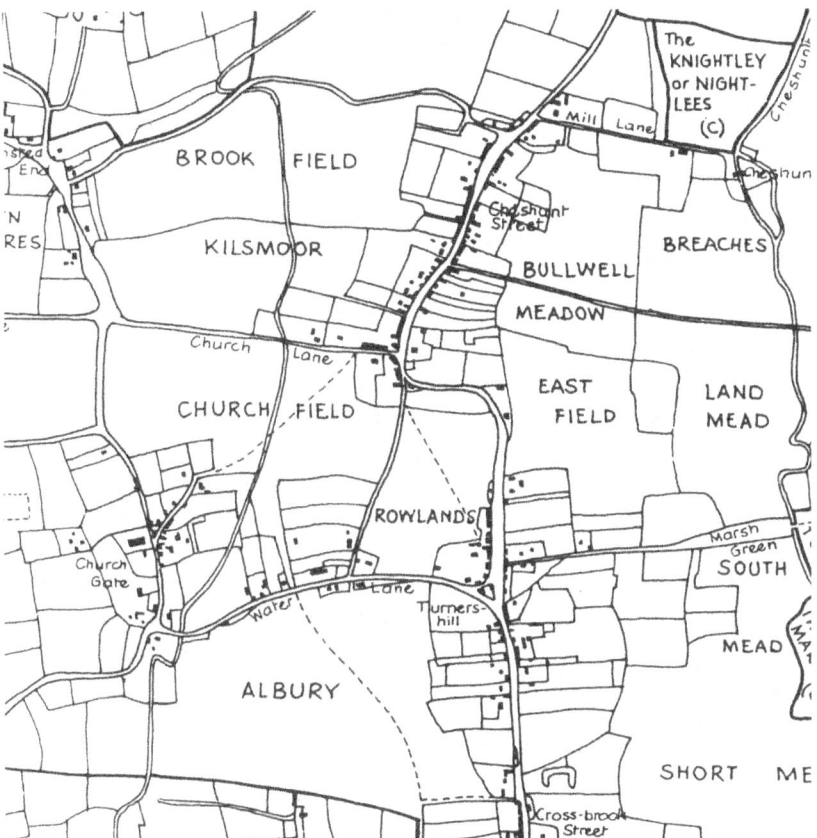

Figure 3: Map of Cheshunt in 1800. Drawn by Henry Crawter, Cheshunt Public Library. The Joyce property was situated on 'the lane leading from Turners Hill to Churchgate South'.

Perhaps not unsurprisingly there is very little record of Joyce's mother and therefore very little can be said about her. Born Hannah Somersett (1726 – 1816), she was daughter of John Somersett of Mildreds Court in the Poultry district of London where she spent her early years. Her family had many contacts in Hertfordshire and at the age of twelve she went in-service to a family in Cheshunt.[4] Clearly a very pious woman, at the age of nineteen she joined the local Presbyterian congregation and this was probably where she met Joyce's father, then active in the Presbyterian meeting.[5] She must had a very strong constitution as she lived until the grand age of 90 and was 37 when she gave birth to Jeremiah, the third child of four children surviving infancy – Joshua (eldest), Sarah, Jeremiah and a younger sister Elizabeth.

Much more can be said about Joyce's father whose activities are recorded in several contexts. Joyce senior (1718–1778), also named Jeremiah, worked as a master-woolcomber and had a business resembling a small factory where he purchased and processed raw wool. The cottage industry of woolcombing involved combing the raw wool from shorn sheep using oil and heated metal combs, and selling on the finished wool for manufacture. He employed a number of journeyman woolcombers working at his property, but he also 'put out' work to other domestic combers working at their own properties. Situated so near London, Joyce senior could exploit both the extensive sheep farming in the area and the existence of a ready market for prepared wool to be made into woollen products and either sold in London, or shipped for export. Whilst woolcombing was his main business he was also engaged in other aspects of the wool trade as he regularly bought worsted yarn (spun from the combed wool which he also supplied) from Cheshunt Workhouse out of which he produced woollen garments including the parish Beadle's coat.[6]

Woolcombers were much in demand in the mid-eighteenth century before the introduction of more mechanised systems of wool manufacture and production in the 1790s. They were highly politicised workers whose sense of independence was profound and reached its peak during the period of Joyce's upbringing. Their trade was necessary for the production of all woollen goods and placed them in a position of relative power in labour relations leaving them able to demand substantial wages. They had become powerful and organised with a strong sense of guild identity and a history of strained relations with employers. In order to maintain their position the guild restricted their own numbers and no woolcomber was allowed to take an apprentice other than his eldest son – therefore excluding Joyce who had an elder brother Joshua.

---

4   DNB, Joyce entry.

5   Joyce, J., Obituary notice of Hannah Joyce *Monthly Repository* 11, (1816), p. 110.

6   Hertfordshire Record Office, Parish of Cheshunt: Workhouse Minutes, 1753–1799, 4 July 1763. A Beadle was an official who kept order at parish functions and acted as a kind of local policeman.

Figure 4: Woolcombing. This illustration appears as the first trade described in *The Book of Trades* which Joyce compiled and wrote in 1804, published in London by Benjamin Tabert.

As a child Joyce imbibed the woolcombers' political talk and their sense of responsibility for their fellow workers stayed with him throughout his life. In 1804 he compiled an edition of *The Book of Trades* in which the first trade he described was that of woolcomber and where he described the political ballads woolcombers posted on the walls of their shops and their communal practice of giving woolcombers 'on the tramp' who were looking for work 'a penny from the common stock raised by the men' if there was no work available.[7]

As a guild member, a tradesman and an employer as well as a businessman, Joyce's father had to negotiate a number of levels of society and was therefore in a position to develop an understanding of the local commercial world. It was this sense of social perspective that fuelled his sense of social conscience and responsibility and he held a number of civic positions in Cheshunt: as an overseer of the poor, an administrator of the parish workhouse, a churchwarden (which was a civic, rather than a religious, duty in this period), as well as being a subscriber and contributor to the local dissenters' school.[8]

Joyce's early childhood was therefore cast against the background of religious dissent, powerful and well articulated artisan values, a sense of social responsibility and the aspiration to independent commercial success. Such a mix of traditions inevitably placed his family, and his father in particular, in positions of having to respond to contradictory concerns. For example, on the one hand the American War of Independence had serious negative effects on woolcombing as it reduced trade and probably brought economic hardship to the Joyce family, yet on the other hand his dissenting affiliations with many Americans led Joyce senior to have sympathy for their cause. It was the culture and perspective of religious dissent that provided a resolution to this and other dilemmas and Joyce senior maintained his support for the cause of the American War, arguing that it represented the right to self-determination – consistent with the religious right to adopt dissenting religious practice. This was one of the most influential events of Joyce's early teens and Joyce's father's staunch support for the American's cause left its mark on Joyce who later wrote that his father had developed his 'attachment to the principle of freedom' through his support for the colonists.[9] The war also functioned, symbolically at least, to align the themes of religious dissent with the themes of parliamentary reform.[10]

---

7   For a history of woolcombing see Burnley, J. (1889), *History of Wool and Woolcombing*, Sampson Low, London. For an interesting insight into the life of a woolcomber see E.P. Thompson's classic (1972) *The Making of the English Working Class*, Penguin, London, pp. 311-313, in which Thompson's account of the woolcombing trade is partly based on *The Book of Trades* (1804) Tabert, London, which, unbeknown to Thompson, was compiled by Jeremiah Joyce.

8   Hertfordshire Record Office, Parish of Cheshunt: Workhouse Minutes, entries for 1759 & 1763; and *Dissenters' Charity School Record, 1764-1798*, entries for 1766 and 1767. Note that the office of a churchwarden was more of a civic than a church role at this time.

9   Joyce, J. (1794), *An account of the author's arrest for "Treasonable Practices"*, printed for the author, p. 13.

10   Webb, R.K. (1980), *Modern England*, Allen & Unwin, London, p. 94/5.

Joyce's father's commercial aspirations required that he implement the often harsh realities and values of the market place in terms of the prices and wages paid to his employees. Yet as a guild member and as a religious dissenter he was urged to resist external agencies and forces of economic and political control. As a child Joyce would therefore have witnessed and felt some of the inevitable ambiguities, problems and compromises resulting from his father's position. It was the fundamental principle of independence that grounded the mindset of the Protestant dissenter and driven by the experience of civil and religious persecution that provided the resolution to many of these dilemmas. This principle of independence which originated from the demand for religious and theological independence, also translated into a guiding principle for action on economic, social and personal levels. Joyce senior, armed with both a coherent ethics and deeply held religious principles, was therefore able to provide his son with a model of human decency in the face of sometimes quite harsh social opposition and ugliness, by living out his sense of Christian morality through his active concern with civic duty and social paternalism and his engagement with worthy and non profit-making activities.

Joyce's Family Life

Joyce's close working associate and friend Robert Aspland's memoir of Joyce records Joyce's family as 'in humble life but of truly respectable character'.[11] By Aspland's middle class standards, Joyce's was a humble upbringing, but the socio-economic values and circumstances of Joyce's early years were those of independent industry, the economic and commercial realities of a small manufactory, and a sense of civic duty and social responsibility. To many Cheshunt citizens, the Joyces may well not have been considered 'humble'. Furthermore, Joyce's developing sense of self-identity and worth was not created from the experience of growing up as a member of the very lowest ranks of the social order. In a letter to his sister Elizabeth written in July 1783 when Joyce was twenty, he thanked divine providence for allowing his family to be brought up 'in a medium state, I mean free from poverty not prey to the snares of lichor'.[12] A more accurate positioning of Joyce in terms of eighteenth century economic ranking would be to see his family as upper working class/lower middle class at the point where artisans moved up to occupy the position of small businessmen and employers. Aspland's description therefore, has to be treated with caution and as expressing Aspland's own middle class and early nineteenth century perspective wherein 'respectable' reflected an aping of middle class values and social deportment, rather than the rather older puritan meaning of 'respectability' more applicable to Joyce's family, which signified the ability to maintain oneself without the aid of charity and with a sense of self respect and independence, obtained from engagement in a respectable occupation. Joyce's early home life, exposed as it was to

---

11 Robert Aspland, 'Memoir of Jeremiah Joyce', *Monthly Repository* 12, December 1817, pp. 697–703.

12 MCO, Shepherd MSS, Vol. 6, No. 13.

the civic and commercial concerns of his father and the dissenting religious flavours of pious devotion from his mother, provided a distinctive environment that nurtured Joyce's adult blend of religious conviction and social duty. While such influences may have had a different impact on his persona as perceived by the various social groups he moved in, in general Joyce held tightly to the lessons of his childhood and he lived out his parents' values to the full.

The aspiration for social progress, the political demand for freedom from the social and religious penalties of the Test and Corporation Acts which dogged and restricted the lives of dissenters in so many ways, and the entrepreneurial commercialism of free enterprise were therefore simultaneous impulses which shaped the thinking and sentiment of the young Joyce. The perspectives of Presbyterian dissent offered a closely interwoven religious and political understanding which provided a rhyme and a reason for the contradictions of the human condition and offered a vision of the future.

Joyce's Schooling

In Cheshunt, the Presbyterian chapel united with the Congregationalist chapel in 1733 and a substantial dissenters' meeting, known as Crossbrook St Chapel, survived there throughout the eighteenth century.[13] A charity school attached to the chapel, originally run by Independents, was founded in 1719 with the support of Sir Thomas Abney and the famous hymn writer and poet Isaac Watts, who lived close by. Ministers would perform the role of teacher and the Reverend Samuel Worsley (1741–1800) who was pastor from 1765 to his death in 1800, was Joyce's teacher. There is no record of the school curriculum when Joyce studied there but there is a record of the rules of the school which give some insight into the context of Joyce's school experience.

> The chief Design of ye School is to teach poor children (who are very numerous in these parts and very ignorant) to read their bible, that by readg. they might be acquainted with ye things of religion; & that they might be a little civilised & made fitter to get their own Livg.: & all other Things were contrived & adjusted as far as possible to answer this Design without raising them above ye rank of Life in which Providence has placed them.[14]

The rules predate Joyce's attendance at the school by fifty years, but the theme of civilising poor children and fitting them to their social position through inculcation of appropriate competencies and religious knowledge, was as much an imperative of the second half the eighteenth century, as it was of the first. The rules were built from 'Methods of Management...corrected and improved for ye good of ye learners',

---

13 Urwick, p. 513.

14 Peter Rooke, a local historian in Cheshunt wrote an introduction to *Dissenters Charity School* Record, 1764–1798 which he has transcribed and is now held in Hertfordshire Record Office.

reflecting the traditions of benign patronage and the educational mission of dissenters and puritans that goes back to the sixteenth century and beyond. That 'Providence' was the origin of social station and that the goals of education should work to maintain a hierarchical social order was taken for granted. However, the focus on nurturing independence 'to get their own livg', reflects the dissenting emphasis on independence and self-reliance – imperatives urged upon dissenters both by their religious views and their by alienated social and political status.

The school was well established during Joyce's time and whilst ostensibly for dissenters, it admitted children from the Established Church and, unusually, admitted girls as well as boys. The school rules prescribed that:

> The boys, besides their reading, are taught also to write a plain hand, & they learn arithmetic so far as addition subtraction and multiplication, that they may be able to make up a small bill of parcels suited to ye lower affairs of life. The girls are taught, besides reading, to knot, to work plain work, & to mark: & here and there one is instructed to write upon some just reason given by their parents.

Joyce's teacher, Worsley, had been educated at the famous Daventry Academy under Caleb Ashworth. This was an academy catering for dissenters debarred as they were from Oxford and Cambridge and where Worsley met his fellow student the scientist and religious dissenter Joseph Priestley. In dissenting academies the curriculum was very different from the great public schools and Oxbridge. Students studied history, experimental philosophy and biblical criticism and there was a dedicated focus on mathematics. We can do no more than speculate about what Worsley actually taught Joyce, although it is likely that he taught elementary versions of some the subjects he had studied at Daventry. What is clear though is that that it was through Worsley that Joyce gained his life-long interest in mathematics.

Chapter 2

Apprentice Painter of Glass in Georgian London

Chemistry, Art and Craft

Joyce's daughter Helen recorded that at the age of 14 in 1777 her father was placed as apprentice to a 'Mr. Willis, Painter and Glazier, in the Strand'.[1] A 'painter and glazier' was really a fine painter whose canvass was the transparent medium of glass and whose trade had more in common with a portrait or landscape artist than the trades we recognise today as painting, decorating or glazing. The painter of glass, rather like the engraver, was an elite craftsman whose commerce was with the artistic and elevated ends of society and who operated at a high level of articulation and aesthetic appreciation. Joyce's chosen trade is particularly emblematic of the age of 'Enlightenment' as it dealt in the controlled passage of light and produced not just religious imagery for the church or for civic buildings, but figures, scenes and designs that lit up the porches, doorways and stairwells of wealthy households. Situated so prominently in the Strand Joyce was working at the high end of decorative arts which towards the end of the eighteenth century benefited from the emergent taste for gothic – a style that particularly suited the medium of light through glass. Joyce's master Willis – who later became the master of the guild of painters and glaziers – was therefore well placed to exploit the growing market for expensive decoration in an ever-expanding Georgian London.

Painter's of glass needed all the skills of the artist but also needed to understand the passage of light through arrangements of both stained and painted glass.[2] They needed to follow the sometimes secret chemical recipes for the production of stains and enamel paints and they needed to understand the process of firing painted glass at particular heats in particular sequential order in high temperature kilns. Before the Reformation most stained glass windows were literally built from an arrangement of different coloured 'pot metal' glass largely brought from France and produced by monks. From 1636, when the source of glass was cut off, the techniques of using stains which would permeate clear glass and the application of translucent paints which would fix to the surface, began to develop in Britain. Amongst historians

---

1 MCO, Shepherd MSS, Vol. 10, No, 89, 1846, Helen Joyce to Hannah Joyce.
2 Great care has to be taken with the term 'arts', particularly at this point in the eighteenth century. The modern distinction between arts and crafts is not directly applicable to Joyce's context, when the term 'arts' indicated practical knowledge.

of glass there are arguments over what really counts as stained glass with some purists arguing that stained glass should really be understood as the older pre-Reformation type in which the figures are radiant with light created though a skilful arrangement of coloured glass, rather than a painting transferred from a non-transparent to a transparent canvass and which simply serves to demonstrate the painter's virtuosity.[3]

The main type of glass used for stained glass windows was 'Crown glass', which was blown and spun into a disc from which sheets were cut and had been produced in London from 1678.[4] By the eighteenth century the quality of glass was quite good and clear glass could be bought in regular sized sheets. Willis's shop would have been the eighteenth century equivalent of a modern household decoration shop in a fashionable area of the city. Existing catalogues show that wealthy customers chose from a ready-made off-the-shelf selection of designs, portraits or landscapes. Prices were worked out through a combination of the size of the window and the complexity and ingredients of the production process – for instance how many colours were used and how many firings were required. Customers could pay twelve to thirty guineas for portraits of bulls, dukes or bowls of fruit or less for simple border designs but they could pay over a hundred guineas for commissioned bigger windows and large church windows could run into thousands of pounds.

By 1777, when Joyce commenced his apprenticeship, the market had become intensely competitive. Shops would claim their colours as the most gorgeous and the most radiant and trumpet the skill of their painters. Many of the painting techniques and technologies used for glass painting were adapted from those developed in the pottery industry and were jealously guarded as they held a potential advantage in the market. All the substances used had to be oxides of metals or minerals such as gold, silver and cobalt that would become brilliant after firing. Producing such stains and paints was highly skilled work and the secret recipes had to be followed with precision, meticulous care and cleanliness to avoid contamination and the possible waste of expensive materials. The recipes involve reducing metals to powder by solvents and mixing with a flux which also had to be carefully prepared for particular colours and stages of production. The recipes appear almost alchemical, especially as they produced the almost magical effect of coloured light. The following is one of the more simple recipes for the production of a ruby red paint from gold.

Mix 8oz of nitre mixed with 2oz of sal ammoniac to produce aqua regia. Take 4oz of this mixture and add ½ oz of gold and heat for a few hours. Mix some of the remaining aqua regia with tin filings and heat until dissolved. Put 20 drops of gold solution plus 20 drops of tin solution into spring water. The gold is reduced to a red powder. Rinse and dry carefully.[5]

---

3   Moore, P. (ed.) (nd), *Crown in Glory*, Jarrold and Sons Ltd, Norwich, p. 60.
4   For information on glass visit http://www.londoncrownglass.co.uk
5   Whittock, N. (1827), *The Decorative Painters and Glaziers Guide*, G. Virtue, London, p. 287.

Other paints were created from copper which produced dark red, tin produced white, iron produced dark red and flesh colour, cobalt and zaffre produced shades of blue – all of which had to be reduced to powder through different chemical processes.

Stains were equally hard to produce and had to be very carefully applied. A recipe for an orange stain is:

> Take 2 part virgin silver and 1 part crude antinomy, Mix heat grind and sieve and then keep in a sealed container. To use mix with 6 parts common Venetian red and mix with water to produce cream. When using, float the stain on the glass with a swan quill or camel hair brush and leave to dry for 14 hours.[6]

An extensive range of stains from lemon green to opaque black to citrus yellow and dark blue, was available but each painter of glass preserved particular variations on the recipes which might give them a commercial advantage. Joyce would have had to grind materials with mortars and pestles, measure out small amounts, apply heat, separate mixtures and store materials carefully before mixing to a solution immediately prior to use – all procedures similar to those found in a laboratory. He would have prepared soft fluxes from common flint glass, pearlash, sea salt and borax which mixed with the paint in such a way that the mixture became fluid and fixed to the panel but didn't run into other colours. He would know how impurities could endanger the process or reduce the lustre of the final paint. He would know how important it was to keep instruments clean and he would observe the chemical reactions as substances were reduced and recreated into other forms usable as paint. He would have observed the transformations of substances under the influence of heat and chemical treatment. He would have experienced the difficulties and frustrations that anybody who has worked in a laboratory will have experienced – that of making the experiments and processes actually work.

The earliest years of Joyce's seven year apprenticeship would have been largely concerned with the preparation for firing the kiln. Large amounts of wood, coal coke and charcoal wood have to be bought and stored in preparation for a firing. It might take two days to get the kiln up to temperature and once it was full of painted sheets the heat would have to be maintained for long periods as the sheets would have to be re-arranged several times to different heights with the kiln.

As a first year apprentice his tasks would have been relatively menial but as he progressed through his seven years he would have gained experience of the full range of techniques. Many windows were literally copied from the works of masters or from cartoons by contemporary artists. Much copying could be done by literally placing the original behind the sheet of glass and tracing the outlines, but for the painter of glass this is very often a stage process: parts of the pane would have to be fixed and fired before the next stage could be started. Joyce's early panes would probably have been simple border designs and background preparations for later finer work. He would then have very likely moved to heraldry before tackling figures, portraits and landscapes. Many painters of glass went to drawing school

---

6   Ibid., p. 290.

where they would learn about perspective and architectural styles. They would have to be familiar with Ionic and Corinthian columns and know Greek, Roman and Gothic styles. They would have to learn to paint the folds of robes, beards, hands and faces of saints. They would have to understand proportion and shading and learn how to produce these effects without the full palette of the normal painter, but with the more restricted range of colours that could survive the firing process and remain translucent. To complete his apprenticeship Joyce would have to have mastered all these skills.

A Growing Political Consciousness

Joyce's radical politics were fuelled during his time as an apprentice. Whilst he personally operated at the more prestigious end of the manual trades, he would have witnessed at first hand the harsh and sometimes abusive nature of employment relations in the building industry. Commissions for large windows would have to be assembled in the shop and reconstructed in situ where individual panes would have to be leaded together and fixed to a system of supporting iron bars. Joyce would have to visit and work on building sites where he witnessed the hardships and realities of the lives of his fellow craftsmen – masons, carpenters, plasterers and painters. He would have seen how constancy of work and the seasonal fluctuations of daylight created affected their lives – in the summer they would have to work for 13 or 14 hours per day to make up for the short days of the winter. He would have seen how they were affected by the vagaries of the London social season which restricted the time available for re-fitting and decorating the residencies of the wealthy, and how many regularly suffered long periods of unemployment.[7]

Joyce's metropolitan position offered him a set of resources which formulated and developed his political consciousness. London's glaziers of the period are recorded as being 'a truculent lot' and there is a long tradition of London's apprentices taking an oppositional stance to the decrees of Parliament.[8] At the age of 21 in 1784, on the completion of his apprenticeship, Joyce became a freeman of the city of London entitling him to ply his trade as journeyman in the city and conferring on him membership of the Common Council of London.[9] It was the ability of London's free journeymen to form their own committees and petition Parliament through the Common Council, armed with the latent threat of striking, that protected them against some of the worst effects of bad harvests and unemployment felt in the provinces.[10] Joyce imbibed the social, political and economic impulses in his guild's involvement in local government, which attempted to resist external power and oligarchic leadership and therefore became highly politically literate – aware of the

---

7   George, M.D. (1965), *London Life in the Eighteenth Century*, Penguin, London, pp. 263 and 166.

8   *London's Livery Companies* (1931), Sampson Low, London, p. 285.

9   Shepherd MSS, Helen Joyce to sister Hannah, 1846.

10 Rude, G. (1971), *Hanoverian London*, Secker and Warburg, London, p. 204.

potentials of economic, political and social pressure and conscious of the power of organisation. As a youth and as a young, strong and no doubt at times angry, man he may have railed at the abuses of arbitrary power and the undemocratic constitution of government.

London life had many contrary and poignant lessons to offer the young Joyce. In 1780 (Joyce was 17), the anti-Catholic Gordon Riots in London exhibited some of the uglier sides of civil protest and discredited the extra-parliamentary associations.[11] Joyce could not avoid the violent spectacle, which continued for six days throughout the centre of London and whose violence was, initially at least, part-promoted by some of his fellow London apprentices. He would have experienced the dangers and volatility of the Mob, witnessed the incompetence of the civil authorities, and seen the accusations made in the media attributing the cause of the riots to 'foreign plot' or to the anarchic intentions of the political opposition to bring down the government.[12] There is no record of Joyce's sentiment over this event but the Gordon Riots delivered the lesson to many reformers, that the general population could not be relied upon to act with reason and sentiments of justice.

Essex Street Chapel

The day-to-day reality of a painter of glass was only one feature of Joyce's mid and late teenage years. Joyce was both physically and intellectually placed at a fountainhead of aspiration for social, religious and political reform. As a youth, then a young man, he lived and worked very close to one of the key meeting places of the dissenting intelligentsia – Theophilus Lindsey's Essex Street Unitarian Chapel. The chapel was situated on the same site as the current headquarters of the British Unitarian ministry, which is less than a hundred metres from the Old Bailey. This area circumscribed the majority of Joyce's physical and social geography through these years as he worked just around the corner on the Strand and his elder brother Joseph owned and ran a tallow chandlery literally next door to the Chapel. It is very likely that Joyce stayed with his brother and from there began to be involved with Lindsey's chapel which he attended from his arrival in London in 1775.[13]

Lindsey was in his sixties when he founded the Essex Street Meeting. He was a former Anglican minister who had rejected the teachings of the orthodox ministry and, encouraged by a group of Protestant dissenters, he took the provocative step of placing his ministry at the heart of London life not far from St Paul's. Partly sponsored by Joseph Johnson the Unitarian publisher, Lindsey had arrived in London three years earlier than Joyce in 1774 and had taken rooms in Essex Street. Both Lindsey, a radical theologian and Johnson, a radical publisher, were to figure

---

11 Baglione F.M. (1997), 'Gordon Riots', in *Britain in the Hanoverian Age, 1714–1837*, Garland, London, p. 296.

12 Hibbert, C. (1959), *King Mob*, Longmans, London, p. 136.

13 Joyce, J., 'On Unitarianism' *Monthly Repository*, 10 (1815), p. 260.

significantly throughout Joyce's subsequent career. It was to be mainly through them that Joyce gained access to the intellectual worlds of highly articulate dissenters and to the distributive networks of dissenting and radical literature.

As an artisan situated in Essex Street, Joyce was part of an influential 'social substratum' of rational dissent which fuelled the radicalism that would appear most vividly ten years later in the 1790s.[14] This substratum was constituted not simply from the intellectual elite. It stretched from the aristocratic heights of the third Earl of Stanhope, who would later become Joyce's employer and an important player in Joyce's life story, to the intellectuals of the Bowood circle which included the moral philosopher Richard Price and the radical philosopher scientist Joseph Priestley, and down to the skilled artisan classes of which Joyce was a member. It was the contact between these groups that facilitated the transmission and progress of ideas of democracy throughout many levels and into many corners of society and it allowed Joyce, who was at its lowest social level, to connect with those above him in the social hierarchy. Importantly, this substratum was significantly composed of two social groups that would nurture and facilitate Joyce throughout his life – dissenting ministers and publishers.

Essex Street Chapel connected Joyce with a rising political consciousness and pressure for reform. The 1770s and 1780s marked a distinctive change in the level and type of public political consciousness, particularly in the city authorities of the metropolis which developed a heightened self-conscious awareness of its own political power and of its influences on national politics in the period of Joyce's apprenticeship.[15] Such London-based political consciousness links to the more general rise in extra-parliamentary pressure on politics which was becoming increasingly visible and organised through the activities of John Wilkes and the Middlesex electors, and Christopher Wyvill and the Association movement. London-based groups such as the Society for Supporters of the Bill of Rights (1769) and the Society for Constitutional Information (1780) which resisted the power of government, all had connections with the Essex Street Chapel. Many reform leaders attended the chapel and many had similar religious persuasions. Major John Cartwright and John Jebb, for instance were important figures of the reform movement and both were Unitarian in theology.[16] Jebb frequently attended Lindsey's Chapel, and Cartwright had many connections with other radical leaders who attended – the moral philosopher Richard Price, the MP Thomas Hollis and the radical dissenter Capell Loftt – all of whom knew Joyce.[17]

---

14 Philp, M. (1985), 'Rational religion and political radicalism in the 1790s', *Enlightenment and Dissent*, 4, 35–46 (p. 41).

15 Sutherland, L. (1956), 'The City of London in eighteenth–century politics' in R. Pares and A.J.P. Taylor (eds), *Essays presented to Sir Lewis Namier*, Macmillan, London, p. 55.

16 Holt, R. (1932), *The Unitarian Contribution to Social Progress in England*, Lindsey Press, London, p. 88.

17 NB article on Jebb; Osbourne, J. (1972) *John Cartwright*, Cambridge University Press, p. 25; Robbins, C. (1961), *The Eighteenth–Century Commonwealthman*, Harvard University

The area of London in which Joyce was living had become a centre for many groups of reformers in the tradition of liberal thought. Joyce's intellectual inheritance lies in the tradition of the 'Commonwealthman', which links the Levellers of the puritan revolution through several generations to the reformers of Joyce's period, and provided much of the impulse for the radicalism of the 1790s.[18] The Grecian Tavern in Devereux Court was just off Essex Street and had been the meeting place for Mathew Tindal, John Molesworth and his friends who were the early eighteenth century generation of Commonwealthmen.[19] The last generation of such men met and worshipped in Lindsey's Essex Street Chapel. Inalienable rights, freedom to worship, resistance to oligarchic government, the application and use of reason, the empirical investigation of the natural world and the belief that the wealth of society should be held in common by its members, were all powerful elements of the tradition of the commonwealthman. Public discussion of political issues was an imperative among such men and they insisted on candid and rational exposition of ideas in discussion and debate.[20] As a member of the Essex Street congregation, and living in an area resonant with the history of reform Joyce was exposed to a wide-ranging diet of political, scientific and theological ideas.

After completing his seven year apprenticeship Joyce spent a year and a half working as a journeyman before he 'quit mechanical employments', and commenced training for the Unitarian ministry at Hackney College in 1786.[21] This was a highly unusual career aspiration in the 1780s. To move from being an artisan who got his hands dirty, to a minister – a profession ring fenced by the middle and upper classes – represented a major elevation on the social ladder. This move presented him with the stark realities and barriers of social class – realities he never wholly overcame. Throughout his life Joyce was never to be fully accepted into the community of middle class dissenters and remained perpetually alienated from the community surrounding him.[22] His social position was constantly maintained by the history of his working class origins and his trade apprenticeship. Whilst Joyce never tried to hide or distance himself from his origins, the society in which he moved would never let him forget it.

Early Theological Training

Joyce remained aloof from the baser affairs and distractions of Georgian London. In his spare time he acted as an apprentice minister with Hugh Worthington, the Arian

---

Press, p. 369.
   18 Robbins, pp. 3–21.
   19 Ibid., p. 7.
   20 Philp, p. 37.
   21 Joyce, J., 'Obituary notice of Joshua Joyce' *Monthly Repository*, 11 (1816), p. 244.
   22 Seed, J., 'Jeremiah Joyce, Unitarianism and the Vicissitudes of the Radical Intelligentsia', *TUHS*, 17, 3 (April 1981), pp. 97–108.

divine who preached at Salters Hall. Joyce was clearly a deeply religious young man and at the age of twenty in 1783 he wrote to his younger sister Elizabeth, then recovering from a serious illness, in the preaching tones and metre no doubt gained though his study with Worthington. The letter carries both the flavours of brotherly concern and the youthful zeal of an apprentice minister:

> To mind and love religion now whilst we are young. To respect and reverence the command of God. To adore the grace of Jesus. To delight in public worship and private devotion. Not to go to the house of God merely to have this or that doctrine displayed but to go there with this determination to go home again and practise the important duties of Christianity.[23]

The letter also expresses one of the main qualities expected of a Unitarian minister – that of the practical application of religious understanding. It wasn't enough to understand theology; it was necessary to live out the precepts of a religious understanding in day-to-day action.

Worthington had a special appeal to the youthful Joyce who referred to him as his 'favorite preacher', whose sermons he felt were 'instructive, plain, scriptural and adapted to the young'.[24] Worthington had a charisma and a personal style that maintained Joyce's affection for him despite later theological disagreements. Worthington had written *The Progress of Moral Corruption.... A Sermon* (1778), which urged constant personal vigilance and religious duty.[25] Joyce quoted at length from this sermon in his memoir of Worthington and he selected colourful passages exhorting the listener to love God and warning that without the proper form of devotion the

> 'agency of his holy spirit is withdrawn and a man is left to struggle by himself, admidst the tossing waves of appetite, and the dreadful rocks of temptation – like a ship torn from her cable'.[26]

Worthington's evangelical effort exhorted his congregation to consider immediate Christian concerns in their worldly engagements and he made his appeal particularly to a young audience. One of the most vivid features of London in 1780s was the swelling population due mainly to the migration of workers seeking employment. Such an increase included large numbers of children many of whom were underfed and poorly clothed. They presented a very visible social problem and a spectacle of human and social need. Such need appealed to dissenters who ascribed the cause of social need, in part, to current and unjust social structures. For many dissenters the progress of society necessitated care of its most vulnerable members and attention

---

23 MCO, Shepherd MSS, Vol. 6, No. 13, Joyce to sister Elizabeth, 21 July 1783.

24 Joyce, J., 'Memoir of the Rev Hugh Worthington', Vol. 8 (April 1813), pp. 561–577.

25 Worthington, H. (1778), *The Progress of Moral Corruption. A Sermon*, Johnson, London.

26 Joyce's 'Memoir of Worthington', p. 574.

to the perceived needs of the youth of the metropolis, prey to the ever present distractions of drink and gambling. Worthington was not alone in recommending increased biblical knowledge amongst children and young people as the solution.

Joyce was himself a vulnerable young man who had recently arrived in London and was a target of Worthington's concern. From Worthington he inherited the paternalistic attitudes of the ministry in trying to guide the path of youth away from the social evils and temptations present in abundance in London, and towards a model of upright and moral citizenship. Joyce spoke passionately of Worthington's endeavours to provide moral instruction and guidance:

> He studied the human heart, and was quick in the application of his knowledge to the purposes of moral instruction. Hence he was perpetually urging those just embarked on the dangerous ocean of life, to mark with a firm and steady opposition allurements intended to draw from the path of rectitude: to be satisfied with such pleasures as were simple, innocent and manly.[27]

Worthington's endeavour to guide the vulnerable clearly left its mark on Joyce, who, throughout his life, saw his educational efforts in terms of 'guiding the steps of the young into the temple of knowledge'.[28]

Joyce was not the only apprentice minister Worthington had under his wing. Thomas Taylor (1758 – 1835), who became known as Thomas Taylor the Platonist, was also co-aspirant for the dissenting ministry and studied with Worthington at the same time as Joyce. Little is known about Taylor in this period except that he gave lectures on Platonism at Flaxman's House in the 1780s, that he was an influence on William Blake, and that he translated many works from Greek.[29] It is unclear whether Joyce had contact with Taylor beyond the Worthington connection, but it is clear that Taylor instructed Joyce in mathematics and had a considerable effect on him.[30] An 1816 biographical entry describes Joyce as 'A dissenting teacher of the Unitarian persuasion, taught by Mr Taylor the noted platonist'.[31] Taylor was five years older than Joyce and, like Joyce, had nonconformist and artisan origins. Their shared efforts and aspirations, combined with their social origins may well have promoted their friendship. It is not surprising that Joyce found platonism or mathematics interesting as these were themes reflected both in his early education and in the rational focus of Presbyterians. The famous exhortation at the gates to Plato's ancient academy was that entry was given only to those who had studied mathematics – seen as prerequisite to gaining true knowledge of the universe.

---

27 Ibid., p. 577.

28 Ibid.

29 Raine, K. and Harper, G. (1969), *Thomas Taylor the Platonist*, Routledge, London, p. 3.

30 Aspland, R. (1817), 'Memoir of Jeremiah Joyce', *Monthly Repository*, 12, December 1817, pp. 697 – 700 and DNB Joyce entry.

31 Watkins and Shoberl, (1816), *Universal Biographical Dictionary*, Longman, London,, Joyce entry.

The tradition of the ministry was in Joyce's background. With the encouragement of Worthington, through the mid 1780s the option of studying for the ministry began to take shape. The plans for a dissenters' academy in Hackney, which would both provide for the educational needs of London's dissenting commercial and professional community and provide a supply of dissenting ministers, were in hand in 1784 and Hugh Worthington was a member of the governing body. Joyce's candidature was justified through his connections with Worthington and Lindsey and by his record of private study of mathematics and platonism. Furthermore, in the eyes of the rational dissenting ministry, raising and training an artisan to the position of minister, fulfilled their image of social progress – Joyce clearly fitted the bill!

From Arian to Unitarian

Joyce's religious and political perspectives were intimately woven from the conceptual matrix of 'rational dissent'. This was a label self consciously adopted by the social group centred around the dissenters Richard Price, Theophilus Lindsey, Joseph Priestley and the Essex Street Chapel. Its organising themes were the demand for the civil and religious liberty to worship according to one's conscience, the promotion of reason-based biblical criticism, and the requirement for personal deportment characterised by independent thought, candour and piety. This web of ideas was held together by the essentially religious concern for a spiritual life which placed theological argument prior to political argument.[32] Rational dissenters both engaged and studied the social and the natural world, with an assumption of a spiritual metaphysics and the claim of reason-based creation. Many rational dissenters wrote prolifically to promote the precepts of rational dissent and many of these outpourings were designed to lead the reader to accept and follow the Unitarian vision. Joyce was to be intimately and actively involved in this publication effort and it was through Lindsey's Essex Street Chapel that the propaganda of rational dissent was promulgated.[33]

The tradition of rational dissent stood squarely in the broader theme of Protestantism that tried to read current and future events in terms of biblical prophecy. This was the theme of millenarianism which offered an optimistic anticipation of the future and was one of the important religious ideas that underpinned the aspiration for social progress. The promise of a second coming in which injustice would be vanquished – an essentially religious idea – clearly linked to the promise of a more just social world – an essentially political vision. The effort to prepare for a second coming therefore could be interpreted as justification to prepare for a more equitable social world which in turn justified radical social action. The line

---

32 Fitzpatrick, M. 'Science and Society in the Enlightenment', *Enlightenment and Dissent* 4, (1985), 83–105 (p. 84).

33 Ditchfield, G. (1968), 'Some Aspects of Unitarianism and Radicalism 1760 – 1810', unpublished doctoral thesis, University of Cambridge, p. 253.

of descent of millenarianism most influential on Joyce goes through Isaac Newton to William Whiston and from David Hartley to Joseph Priestley. The millenarian thread will be examined more closely in the next chapter in relation to views of the French Revolution, which, for many millenarian dissenters, was prophecy realised.[34] However, it is important to note that millenarianism was an important feature of rational dissent and, thus one of the influences upon the young Joyce.

Unitarianism was the exemplar of rational dissent, but Unitarian theology was largely a progression from the earlier theology of Arianism, and like many other Unitarians Joyce during his period of training with Hugh Worthington – an avowed Arian – moved through an Arian phase before becoming a Unitarian. Arian doctrine originates from the Greek theologian Arius (AD ?250–336), who asserted that Christ was not of one substance with the Father, but a creature raised by the Father to the dignity of the Son of God. Christ was not therefore literally the son of God and therefore neither God nor of God. The doctrine had powerful implications that quickly put church authorities on the defensive and was immediately challenged by Athanasius (AD ?296–373), patriarch of Alexandria, and pronounced heretical at the first council of Nicaea (AD 325). The doctrine was largely unvoiced until it was revived first by the Italian Faustus Socinius and some early eighteenth century Anglicans – notably Samuel Clarke, and William Whiston, as well as by Presbyterian dissenters and once again it quickly drew the fire of the church. The dangerous and controversial implications of the Arian argument were that if Christ was not a person of the Trinity then the doctrine of atonement was meaningless as Christ was not God's son and could not 'atone' for our sins. A further implication had distinctly political potential: with no inherited original sin, man was not in need of redemption and therefore man could be understood as essentially good and capable of organising himself. A yet further implication, again with a political echo and guaranteed to provoke a defensive response from the church, was that if Christ did not possess absolute and divine authority, the notion of apostolic succession which provided the overall legitimacy of the church and which was understood as coming from Christ through St. Peter and then through the church to its ministers, was null and void. This obviously challenged the church at its most fundamental level and implied that dissenting ministers had as much claim on religious truth as did any other minister.[35]

However, the relatively short time span over which Arianism held sway as a theological doctrine and its subsequent replacement by Unitarianism, reflects the weakness of its overall explanatory power. While Arianism promoted critical scrutiny of orthodox Trinitarian doctrine, it also produced an hierarchical and problematic theological framework with God at the top, man at the bottom and Jesus and the

---

34 Garrett, C. (1975), *Respectable Folly: Millenarians and the French Revolution in France and England*, John Hopkins University Press, p. 225.

35 Clark, J. (1985), *English Society 1688–1832: Ideology, Social Structure and Political Practice during the Ancien Regime*, Cambridge University Press, p. 281.

Holy Ghost somewhere in between.[36] Arianism solved the major theological problem of whether or not there was a time when Christ did not exist, by making him divine but a subordinate creation of the Father. But the doctrine also left the vital Christian attributes of mercy and forgiveness to Jesus, who was not God but who served as a mediator between man and God and therefore implied that these attributes were not divinely inspired.

Arianism therefore presented a confusing theology which invited analysis and reworking in the interests of simplicity, clarity and consistency. The powerful natural philosophers Nathaniel Lardner and Joseph Priestley whose thinking dominated the rational dissenting world, applied just such an analysis and they developed a more coherent theology. Both Lardner and Priestley had been Arians but rejected it as a doctrine in favour of a Unitarian position in which there is one God and Jesus was explicitly accepted as not divine – he was a man to whom God spoke directly. Joyce shared in this same Arian to Unitarian progression and he became a Unitarian in 1786, the year that Priestley's *History of Early Opinions concerning Jesus Christ* exhaustively recounted the origins of Trinitarian and Arian doctrines, and posited Unitarianism as the true and primitive theology.[37]

Theology and Politics

The radical theological ideas of the mid eighteenth century were partly responsible for the emergence of radical politics in the 1790s.[38] The progressive and symbiotic links between a challenge to the theological orthodoxy and a challenge to the political orthodoxy are clearly made in the traditions of rational dissent. Establishment and Tory sentiment held that civil government was the ordinance of God, as much as ecclesiastical government was the ordinance of the church. Unitarians therefore presented a powerful challenge to these foundational establishment views. They denied the Trinity, rejected the Book of Common Prayer and crucially posited Jesus as a man. They therefore challenged the ecclesiastical establishment at the same time as they challenged the civil establishment.

This dissenting theological challenge was mirrored by a fundamental political argument over the manner in which liberty was claimed and secured within society. Establishment sentiment held that liberty was the product of the equilibrium of forces which had to be maintained by a complex of laws and which denied, via the

---

36 Griffiths, O. (1935), *Religion and Learning: A study in English Presbyterian thought from the Bartholomew Ejections (1662) to the foundation of the Unitarian Movement*, Cambridge University Press, pp. 36/7.

37 Priestley, J. (1786), *History of Early Opinions concerning Jesus Christ*, For the Author, Birmingham,

38 Waterman, A.M.C.'The nexus between theology and political doctrine in Church and Dissent', in K. Haakonssen, (1996), *Enlightenment and Religion*, Cambridge University Press, pp. 193–218.

Test and Corporation Acts and the oaths of allegiance, equal citizenship to anyone who would not subscribe to the Established Church. Dissenters on the other hand, took a largely contractarian view of government following the political philosophy of John Locke. They argued that the authority invested in the state could remain only as long as the individual had a claim on social justice.[39] As dissenters were denied equal citizenship, they saw themselves as subject to unacceptable social injustice.

For the dissenter, the authority of the state was bestowed by the individual on the state. As individual conscience was not bestowed by the state, and civil society effectively discriminated against dissenters who exercised their individual conscience in their choice of worship, civil polity violated their rights and was inconsistent with dissenting views of the founding principles of government.[40] The appeal on the behalf of dissenters for freedom to worship was, from their point of view, an appeal to the state to give back something that had been taken away from them through the corrupt practices of the Established Church and current and previous governments. The appeal seen from the position of the early reform movement, was really an appeal to the candour, to the honesty of those in government, to give back something that had been taken away.

To the disappointment of the dissenting community, in 1773 the Feathers Tavern petition and the subsequent bill for the relief of dissenters, was thrown out by the Lords. From that point the language of dissent, equipped with John Locke's notions of natural and inalienable rights and articulated by reformers like Price and Priestley, became more vociferous and oppositional.[41] This was the period of Joyce's teens and the development of his political ideas. His growth as a political radical took place in the crucial passage of radical perspectives which began with a demand for the return of rights taken away in the 1770s and developed the demand for universal rights that would be later seen most vividly in the works of Thomas Paine in the 1790s.

On the wider stage of intellectual ideas, a utilitarian philosophy was developed in Adam Smith's *Wealth of Nations* and Jeremy Bentham's *A Fragment on Government*, which were both published in the same year (1776). For both writers, the proper goal of government was to seek the greatest happiness for the greatest number, although they disagreed on how to achieve that goal. Whilst Smith proposed minimum interference from government, which, led by 'an invisible hand', would inevitably bring good, Bentham preferred the deliberate use of legislation on the principle of felicity, as a means of procuring maximum happiness.[42] These contrasting ideas, which represent two co-ordinates of eighteenth century liberalism, fed directly into the themes and motifs of rational dissent. Smith's social science and his 'invisible hand', and Bentham's project to develop government based on reason, contributed

---

39 Henriques, U. (1961), Routledge, London, p. 97.

40 Saunders, A., 'The state as highwayman: from candour to rights', Haakonssen, p. 246.

41 Thomas, D. (1977), *The Honest Mind: The Thought and Work of Richard Price*, Clarendon Press, Oxford, p. 284.

42 Webb, R.K. (1980), *Modern England*, Allen & Unwin, London, p. 124.

vital intellectual tools with which to bring scientific methodology to religious, social and political life. Such scientific methodology was the concern of Joseph Priestley, who drew many of his political ideas from the Wilkite agitation and the Association movement, and developed a utilitarian perspective.[43] Joyce imbibed these 'Enlightenment' themes and built them into his religio-political perspective.

---

43 Hoecker, J., 'Joseph Priestley and Utilitarianism in the age of reason', *Enlightenment and Dissent*, 3 (1984), p. 55.

Chapter 3

Hackney College – Radicalism and Dissent

Such was the suspicion and hostility that Hackney College provoked that when it closed in 1796, a writer for the *Gentleman's Magazine* claimed that the 'slaughterhouse of Christianity' had fallen.[1] Hackney's reputation as a hotbed of radicalism peaked in the years immediately following the French Revolution when the radicals Joseph Priestley and Gilbert Wakefield were tutors, when the writers William Godwin and William Hazlitt were students and when any criticism of the government could be construed as treasonable. Hackney students were very visible to London society as potential political radicals and made their presence felt in the gallery of the House of Commons on 2 March 1790 when Charles James Fox gave his celebrated speech against the Test and Corporation Acts. The College's physical proximity to London became provocative to the houses of metropolitan power and presented a challenge to the establishment. This sense of visibility to more orthodox London society and Church of England circles is reflected in the references made to the College in Humphrey's and Cruikshank's cartoons of the period which linked Hackney College, 'old Phlogoston' (Joseph Priestley) and the Crown and Anchor (meeting place of the London Societies).[2] General support within the College for the Republican cause is shown by the 'republican suppers' held there. It is also clear that both students and tutors openly welcomed the French Revolution; news of the fall of the Bastille was greeted with applause and satisfaction by students as the first word of it was brought to England by one of the college tutors – George Cadogan Morgan.[3]

Hackney College was one in a line of short-lived eighteenth century dissenting academies catering both for the educational needs of the commercial class of dissenters debarred as they were from the universities of Oxford and Cambridge, and for the supply of ministers to serve the dissenting community. The College had been planned by a group of dissenters and in January 1786 it was opened by a committee

---

1 Quoted in Stephenson, H.W., 'Hackney College and William Hazlitt', *TUHS*, 4, 3 (1929), 219–247, 376–411 (p. 235).

2 See George, M.D. (1942), *Catalogue of Personal and Political Satire*, British Museum, Vol. 7.

3 McLachlan, H. (1929), 'The Old Hackney College', *TUHS*, 3, 3 pp. 185–205, p. 199/200.

which included Joyce's mentor and teacher, Hugh Worthington.[4] Joyce was one of the first intake of four students in October 1786, with Thomas Broadhurst, Michael Maurice and Joseph Towers.[5] Joyce was a divinity student and he secured a College 'foundation' provided through the trustees of the Presbyterian Fund, which meant that he didn't have to pay the considerable sixty guinea sessional tuition and board fees. Despite this bursary and a £200 patrimony he received after the death of his father, Joyce was still not financially comfortable and had to pay his living and other costs through working in the College Library cataloguing books for which he received 10 guineas a year.[6]

The college authorities appear to have interpreted their regulations very flexibly in respect of Joyce. The rules governing both entry and the appropriate period of study state that in addition to being 'well recommended both as to conduct and qualifications', lay students should be aged between 15 and 18 and the general expectation was that all new students, including those training for the ministry, should be in their teens.[7] Joyce was 23 when he entered. Furthermore, the normal course of study for a divinity student was five years yet Joyce stayed only three and a half years – probably because the time he had previously been studying with Worthington was taken into consideration.

The first sessions were given in the Dr Williams Library, Red Cross Street before the College moved to its permanent home – the stately mansion of Homerton Hall, set in 18 acres in Hackney. The college rules, 'For Family Government and Order', outlined a regime for the running of the College and gave clear instructions as to how students should behave.[8] Teaching was over six days and students were required to attend morning and afternoon services at some place of public worship on the Sabbath. The rules detail how and when students should arise, the appropriate rota for ringing the bell to awaken them, the calling of registers, punishments for late arrivals and for neglect of duties. No 'Games for money' were allowed, 'no removal of candles from the common hall', no 'intercourse between the students and the kitchen or those parts of the house appropriate to the use of the Servants' (rule XI). Despite these rules, some of the students clearly took advantage both of the liberal ethos of the college and the distractions of nearby London and the level of indiscipline in the College was a notable and consistent feature of college life.[9]

---

4   For Hackney see Watts, R., 'Revolution and Reaction: 'Unitarian' academics, 1780–1800, *History of Education*, 20, 4 (1991), pp. 307–323; Stephenson, H.W.; Steinhof, A. 'New College, Hackney – A Dissenting Academy 1786 – 1796' (MA Dissertation, Leicester, 1978); McLachlan, 'The Old Hackney College'.

5   DWL, *Hackney College Minute Book*, 1785-1791.

6   Aspland, Memoir of Joyce, p. 697 & DWL, College Minute Books, p. 93.

7   DWL, 'Terms of admission into the New Institution' provided as appendix to Steinhof.

8   DWL and Steinhof, appendix.

9   Watts, p. 311; McLachlan, p. 253.

In academic terms, Hackney offered a much richer, more varied and more intellectually challenging educational experience than that found in the two English universities. It nurtured a sense of critical enquiry consistent with the themes of liberal education and it demanded engagement with non-traditional subjects including experimental philosophy and biblical criticism.[10] Critical study of the bible served to subvert some powerful orthodox assumptions as it led to careful evaluation of foundational doctrines such as original sin, the immaculate conception, the atonement and the existence of Satan.

Hackney's intellectual resources were impressive. Of the six lecturing staff who taught Joyce, the ministers Abraham Rees who taught Hebrew, ecclesiastical history, maths, astronomy and modern geography;[11] Andrew Kippis, who taught ancient geography, universal grammar and the principles of government; and Richard Price, who lectured in moral science and higher mathematics were all Fellows of the Royal Society (FRS) as well as being active political campaigners. The college environment was also quite intimate, never having more than 50 students and, for the greater part of Joyce's stay, fewer than 20. The ratio of 6 lecturers which included 3 FRS, to 20 students therefore offered an enviable teaching provision by anybody's standards and provided a rich learning environment. As part of the training for aspiring ministers, students were required to give regular (monthly) orations on provocative subjects such as 'The evil and wickedness of war, especially of that in which we have been and are now fatally engaged' and 'Discourse on the best method of the education of youth'.[12] Such orations required students to sharpen and craft their use of argument and rhetoric and developed their abilities to perform in the dramatic setting of the pulpit. At Hackney Joyce therefore gained not only an academic education but also a training in public speaking.

Joyce was significantly older than many of the others and was from an artisan background. In the first years of his study his hands would have been rough from his years of physical labour and his manners would have reflected the working class culture of his upbringing and early life. His social deportment no doubt clashed with the middle class and refined sensibilities of the sons of wealthy dissenters he encountered. Throughout his life he was alienated to some degree from the middle class intellectual set and this sense of a cultural distance was brought into stark relief through his experience at Hackney college.

Clearly some of the tutors did not stick rigidly to the curriculum. Thomas Broadhurst – one of Joyce's contemporaries – recorded that the moral philosopher Richard Price would wander into issues of philosophy and politics when he should have been teaching maths.

---

10 McLachlan, p. 254.

11 Rees, A. (1819), *The Cyclopedia; or Universal Dictionary of Art, Science and Literature*, Longmans et al., London.

12 Steinhof, p. 38.

The good doctor [Price] had only three pupils to attend upon him, Mr David Jones, Mr Jeremiah Joyce and myself, these three being the only students then in the College sufficiently advanced to attend Dr Price's lectures which were given in Jebb's *Excerpta*, from Newton's *Principia* and Dr Thomas Simpson's *Treatise on Fluxions*. Dr Price, however, gave but very few lectures at all while in his situation of Professor at Hackney College, both tutor and pupils being better pleased to fill up their lecture hours in agreeable conversation on philosophy or on politics, rather than employ it in difficult and abstract calculations.[13]

Joyce's earlier study of mathematics with Thomas Taylor the Platonist, probably aided his mathematical proficiency and as a result brought him to Price's attention. It may have been through these conversations that Price first formed a favourable impression of Joyce – an impression sufficient for Price to recommend Joyce to the hugely wealthy aristocrat the Earl of Stanhope, as private secretary and as tutor to his children – discussed in the next chapter.

Given Joyce's later reputation as a notorious radical and 'acquitted felon', gained largely through his time in the Tower under the charge of treason, one might have anticipated numerous accounts of him as a revolutionary leader of the academy that Edmund Burke saw as 'the new arsenal in which the subversive doctrines and arguments were formed'.[14] Yet the silence that surrounds Joyce is profound and there is only one rather oblique comment relating to Joyce's political views in this period and this from the twentieth century historian H.W. Stephenson who does not give his source. According to Stephenson, Joyce's 'political views were such as to make it inadvisable for them to be too freely advertised', which meant that they were probably pro-French and republican.[15]

Joyce was not taken into the new dissenting academy as an embryonic political radical. He was taken in as an aspirant minister who was hard working and religiously committed. The fact of his lowly social origins may well have flattered the progressive and liberal values held by some of the members of the committee and may exemplify a minor 'rapprochement' between the radical intelligentsia and the lower artisan classes.[16] But Joyce was clearly an exception. There were no other students from a similar background in the college in which the general ethos was to provide an education for the dissenting middle and upper classes. Joyce's place was gained not through a tendency for radicalism, but by virtue of his compliance with the values of the middle class metropolitan dissenting community.

Positioned so close to London, the college offered accessible higher education and enabled its tutors, who were mainly ministers, to teach at the college at the same time as carrying on their regular duties. The annual spring College sermons were all delivered to, and printed for, London congregations and were addressed to 'the

---

13 Broadhurst, T. *The Christian Reformer*, 4 (March 1848), p. 172.

14 Burke, E. (1808), 'Appeal from the new to the old Whigs', *Works*, Rivington, London, Vol. 6, pp. 69–268 (p. 225).

15 Stephenson, p. 381.

16 Seed, p. 107.

supporters of a New Academical Institution'.[17] The sermons included a description of what the curriculum contained, why the College was necessary and what benefits it offered to the laity. They also pointed out the need for the proper training and provision of ministers and argued that the dissenting community should support the College. The sermons acted as an advertisement, a request for financial support and a means of reporting to the subscribers and they exhibit the social and economic links between the London dissenting community and the College. In his 1789 sermon Hugh Worthington outlined the importance of a rounded education:

> Every institution calculated to afford COMPLEAT instruction to youth designed for the ministry, must be of essential importance to the advancement of religious knowledge, and to the extension of religious candour. If young ministers are but half educated, how can they be the means of diffusing these blessings in the church and the world? Can a man give what he has not? If the blind lead the blind, both shall fall into the ditch.[18]

The distinctive strength and cohesion of the social network of the London Dissenting community was created partly in response to the external social pressures and the discrimination to which dissenters had been subjected. The forging of links between the ministry and the laity through a shared educational experience in the same College, was important not least because it nurtured friendships upon which the ministry depended for financial support. The role of the educator in delivering the lessons of scripture was one of the key linkages in this social network and was highly valued within the dissenting community.

Joyce's theological perspective developed considerably through his time at Hackney and his critical studies of the bible were also applied to his own Arian stance. With the empiricism of David Hartley's associationist psychology, the works of the Arians turned Unitarians Nathaniel Lardner, and Joseph Priestley's arguments which demanded that there should be no theological or metaphysical constructs other than those based on reason and evidence, the complex theological position of Arianism became untenable for Joyce. His rejection of Arianism was not without its personal difficulties and he became estranged from Hugh Worthington, who remained an Arian and who was quite vehement in his opposition to the development of Unitarianism.[19] Joyce gradually lost confidence in the Arian position and eventually fell out with his former tutor, recording that Worthington no longer spoke to him after he had challenged Worthington on the issue of the existence of a devil.[20] Such theological differences however did not force a divide between camps within rational dissent – famously Richard Price an Arian, and Joseph Priestley a Unitarian, remained firm friends. Joyce adopted the view that the evidence of a creator was manifest in the design of the natural world and, in particular, in the form and functions of the

---

17 Holt, pp. 171–178.

18 Worthington, H. (1789), *A sermon .. To the Supporters of a New Academical Institution among Protestant Dissenters*, T. Cadell and J. Johnson, London, p. 45/6.

19 Joyce, 'Worthington Memoir', p. 573.

20 Joyce, 'On Unitarianism', *Monthly Repository*, Vol. 10, (1815), p. 745.

human mind and body. Joyce's adoption of rational and empirically based reasoning, following Isaac Newton and John Locke, re-enforced his denial of the supernatural elements of the theology of the Trinity and promoted him to see the single unity of the godhead as creator, provider, designer and judge. On the basis of such an account the connection between the act of creation and the purposes of a creator was obvious. A creator must have had a purpose in designing the human form and giving human beings reason, as everything is infused with design and purpose. For Joyce, such purpose could be recognised by correct application of reason based on an empirical examination of the natural world.

Joyce's Unitarian theology and the epistemology that went with it, provided the fundamental justification for his political radicalism. For Joyce, to explain the hidden mechanisms behind the phenomena of the physical world, it was necessary to apply reason. The demand for reason in matters of interpreting the physical world transferred to the demand for reason in matters of the socio-political world. The status of reason as an intellectual standard within the religious world view of rational dissent cannot be overestimated. For Unitarians of the period unjust social action in the form of discrimination against dissenters acting according to their conscience, was a contravention of reason and therefore a contravention of the will of God. Reason was the action of God and deciphering the rational plan of the world through the exercise of reason, was both consistent with the religious perspective of rational dissent and a fulfilment of the reason-based divine plan. Natural philosophy, the methodology of science and individual political rights were therefore the logical extensions of the Unitarian religious programme. This classic set of Enlightenment associations – of reason, science and rights – drew the fire of the traditional majority and from government and church authorities who reacted defensively to a programme that undermined their fundamental assumptions and attempted to subvert their social position.[21]

Joyce was 26 when he reached the end of his stay at Hackney in 1789 – the year of the French Revolution. He was equipped with a powerful intellect, influential friends and first hand experience of the world of the working man. He was devout, pious and a potential champion of dissent. He was immersed in a community that had strong social connections and that looked to highly educated ministers to provide its leadership. He might have expected to join an established ministry for a number of years before taking charge of a congregation himself. He might have expected his efforts to be focused on the pastoral and on the soterial roles of a dissenting minister in which education had a vital but secondary role. However, it wasn't in a public ministry that Joyce first found employment but with the politically radical Earl of Stanhope, ostensibly at least, as tutor to his children.

---

21 Watts, R., pp. 307–323 (p. 308).

Chapter 4

Metropolitan Political Agent

The French Revolution in the summer of 1789 drastically changed the course of history. In the first months after the Revolution, many British intellectuals welcomed the overthrow of a despotic regime and imagined that a British style parliamentary system would naturally emerge as a replacement. One of the most vocal figures of this pro-revolutionary sentiment was Joyce's tutor – Richard Price. It was Richard Price who publicly welcomed the Revolution as heralding 'the dominion of reason and conscience' at a high profile meeting of the Reform Society in November 1789, and it was Richard Price who, probably in the same month, recommended Joyce to the radical aristocrat the Third Earl of Stanhope.[1]

The support of Whigs concerned to limit the power of the crown such as Stanhope, was actively sought by activists in the dissenting community. Such support offered a source of political influence in their attempt to overthrow the laws and statutes which oppressed them. The winter of 1789 and the period up to March 1790, when their third attempt to repeal the Test and Corporation Acts eventually failed, was a period of heightened agitation by the dissenting community which had been campaigning hard and was hopeful about its chances of success.[2] Stanhope was associated with many of the political and religious groups to which Richard Price and other Hackney College dissenters belonged. He attended the Hackney Gravel Pit meeting where Price was minister and he provided just the sort of political connection the dissenters sought.

A recommendation from Price at a moment when the effects and potentials of the French Revolution dominated the intellectual, political and social climate was not simply a fortuitous introduction to landed society for an up-and-coming young minister. It was a political act that publicly connected Stanhope to the Unitarian community via Joyce.[3] The linking of a lower class dissenter trained at the notorious and radical Hackney College with a Whig member of the House of Lords, in a

---

1   Price, R. (1789), *The Discourse on the Love of our country*. Delivered 4 November 1789 to Revolution Society in the London Tavern. In Claeys, G. (1995), *Political Writings of the 1790s*, 8 Vols, Pickering, London, 1995, pp. 3–23. Numerous sources confirm Price's recommendation to Stanhope including Butler, M. (1984), *Burke, Paine, Godwin and the Revolution Controversy*, Cambridge University Press, p. 4.

2   The classic account of the movement for repeal of the Acts is given in Goodwin, A. (1979), *The Friends of Liberty*, Hutchenson, London, pp. 65–98.

3   Newman, A. (1963), *The Stanhopes of Chevening*, Macmillan, London, p. 190.

climate of growing fear of a French-style revolution happening in England, was a political connection that London society could not have missed.

On 20 January 1790, Joyce presented his compliments to the Hackney College Committee, and took up employment with Stanhope.[4] Joyce was employed ostensibly as tutor to Stanhope's eldest son Mahon, but given Joyce's artisan background it is hard to imagine that he was employed to educate Mahon in the fine points of the social graces expected from the first son of a hugely wealthy aristocrat. The accountancy records of the firm of Mr George Wilson, Stanhope's banker, show that Joyce was employed from 25 of January 1790 as 'Tutor to Lord Mahon' (who would later become the Fourth Earl Stanhope), at the princely sum of £200 per year.[5] The fact that Joyce was paid directly from the bankers' rather than through the household accounts from which household servants were paid, indicates Joyce's employment as a contracted agreement between gentlemen.

Joyce clearly had to fulfil a number of social personas. At one extreme, he was a high-status servant where his social function and position were confined to the tutoring of Stanhope's children. At the other extreme, he was a confidante, privy to Stanhope's political dealings, visible to society as an intellectual equal, and as a representative of the Unitarian community active in radical politics. Those around Joyce clearly judged his social position in these different ways. He is referred to as 'tutor to Stanhope's children' by Robert Aspland in his memoir of Joyce, but as his 'secretary' by both the spy Gosling in his report to the government on 9 May 1794, and by Ghita Stanhope, the Earl's granddaughter.[6]

Joyce's appointment with Stanhope therefore can primarily be seen as a deliberate act that established a mutually profitable connection between the politically active dissenting community and Stanhope the liberal peer. Yet his appointment cannot simply be considered as expressing political motivations on the stage of London politics. From Stanhope's perspective Joyce presented attractive credentials. He was highly educated, pious, a supporter of the Revolution and, unusually, from a lower class background. His career to that point expressed social aspiration and flattered the vision of liberal reform. Joyce was clearly a serious scholar who had the requisite academic qualifications for the position. He was advanced in mathematics, knew Latin, was trained as a minister and therefore possessed the right moral and spiritual qualifications. Stanhope was also therefore employing a teacher for the education of his son and heir, and as a man of considerable intellect himself, he would have been unlikely to employ someone who he felt did not have sufficient intellectual capacity and the requisite skills.

---

4 DWL, *Hackney College Minutes* 1785–1791, p. 127.

5 Centre for Kentish Studies. Maidstone Record Office, Stanhope MSS, U.1590. A.103, *Account of Mr. Geo Wilson with Charles Earl Stanhope.* 1786–1793.

6 Spy Gosling's 'information' in Thale, M. (1983), *Selections from the papers of the London Corresponding Society 1792–1799*, Cambridge University Press p.155; Ghita Stanhope *The Life of Charles Third Earl Stanhope,* Longmans, 1914, p. 147.

Joyce had no independent income and needed employment urgently at the end of his college days. Yet employment with Stanhope may not have been his only option. He was trained for the ministry and might reasonably have expected a junior position in a London meeting with the prospect of a future ministry. In so far as it signals some willingness to comply with the established order, even if he had a longer term egalitarian vision in mind, Joyce's acceptance of a position with an aristocrat as tutor to the inheritor of considerable wealth indicates liberal reform rather than violent revolution as his political position, and suggests some distance from the extremes of the democratic and revolutionary aspirations of Thomas Paine.

Joyce's move into an aristocratic household presented him with a starkly contrasting environment to that of his previous world. The relatively large amount of £200 per year and the benefit of free board and lodging as a member of Stanhope's household represented a substantial increase from the approximately 3s a day and variable wages and conditions Joyce could expect as a journeyman glazier or the minimal funds of his student years.[7] His diet, his clothing, his daily life and his commerce with the people around him would have changed drastically as he operated his new station. He would have had to adapt his manners, learn new etiquette and become familiar with Stanhope's households.

Although Joyce was employed to tutor Stanhope's eldest son and future inheritor of the vast estates, Stanhope actually had six children and Joyce clearly taught them all at various times. These were children whose aristocratic pedigree was second only to that of royalty. The first three from his first wife Lady Hester Pitt (1755–80), sister to William Pitt the Prime Minister, were girls – Hester 14, Griselda 12 and Lucy 10. The second three were from his second marriage to Louisa Grenville (1758–1829) sister to Lord Grenville who was at different times both Home and Foreign secretary, and were boys Mahon 9, Charles 5, and James 2. There were very few such groups of aristocratic children, there were very few such situations and there were very few tutors who got to teach children in those circumstances. The uniqueness of Joyce's situation – a working class man teaching six of the most aristocratic children in Britain – cannot be overstated. It was from these unique opportunities and experiences that Joyce's life as a professional educator began to emerge and his educational activities with the Stanhope children are discussed in Part 2.

Stanhope's French Connections

Stanhope was an active supporter of the French Revolution. He adopted the convention of calling himself 'citizen' and he removed the crests from the gates of his mansion at Chevening in a symbolic act of support for the revolutionary cause. He was also a major conduit for the communications of the French National Assembly. The records show that Stanhope had extensive correspondence with the Marquis de Condorcet,

---

7   Philps Brown, H. and Hopkins, S. (1981) *A perspective of Wages and Prices*, Methuen, London, p. 11.

the Duc de la Rochefoucauld, Sir Francis d'Ivernois, G.A. de Luc, Charles Bonnet and numerous other Frenchmen in the early 1790s and clearly establish his support for the Revolution although many of the actual letters were deliberately removed due to their dangerous and embarrassing implications.[8]

Stanhope's London residence was a venue for French emissaries and for English supporters of the revolutionary cause. In the first years of the Revolution one powerful image of the new French constitution was that of a constitutional monarchy very similar to that of the English style tripartite balance of the three estates – monarchy, aristocracy and commons. As a member of the English nobility, Stanhope occupied a parallel social status to the Marquis de Condorcet and the Duc de la Rochefoucauld, both of whom were initial supporters of the Revolution and to whom Stanhope had a natural affiliation. Stanhope was also attractive to French politicians because he was brother-in-law of Prime Minister Pitt and married to the sister of Lord Grenville, and therefore had the ear of powerful politicians.

English views of the appropriateness of Stanhope's French connections varied. Following the storming of the Tuilleries and the fall of the monarchy, the Bishop of Llandaff implored Stanhope to approach his friends in France to try to save the Royal Family.[9] Considerable suspicion about his French connections began to develop and Walpole associated Stanhope with the Unitarian ministry in his comment, 'the horrors make one abhor Lord Stanhope and his priestley [sic] firebrands who would rain Presbyterian conflagrations here'.[10] As the situation worsened in 1792, Stanhope was involved in many attempts to preserve peace and he carried informal messages to Pitt and others. He was involved in the last attempt to preserve peace made by the Duc de Bassano Maret and he read letters to Parliament from Condorcet as part of their joint effort to prevent war.[11]

Stanhope became the focus of anti-French sentiment. He was lampooned in cartoons with such titles as 'The Anarcharsis Cloots' and 'The Noble Sans-Culottes', and cast as a French republican wearing a too-small bonnet-rouge and throwing off his breeches. Stanhope is portrayed by Gilray as a dotty and distracted fool verging on madness – a theme easily connected in the cartoon narratives and subtexts, to the notion of danger. He was seen as being the enemy from within and attracted considerable anti-Jacobin vitriol. A Mr Miles wrote an open letter to Stanhope which remonstrated with him for his support of the French Revolution and the impact that his support had on 'the misguided' who 'looked to him as their leader'.[12] This public letter articulates the fears held by many in the 1790s and shows how Stanhope – and therefore his recognisable employees – formed the focus of those fears:

---

8   Stanhope, G. (1914), *The Life of Charles Third Earl Stanhope*, Longmans, London,, pp. 87-153 (hereafter Ghita Stanhope) and Stanhope MSS, passim.
9   Ghita Stanhope, pp. 118/9.
10 Ibid., p. 96.
11 Ibid., p. 123.
12 *A letter from Mr. Miles* (1794), Cornhill, p. 2.

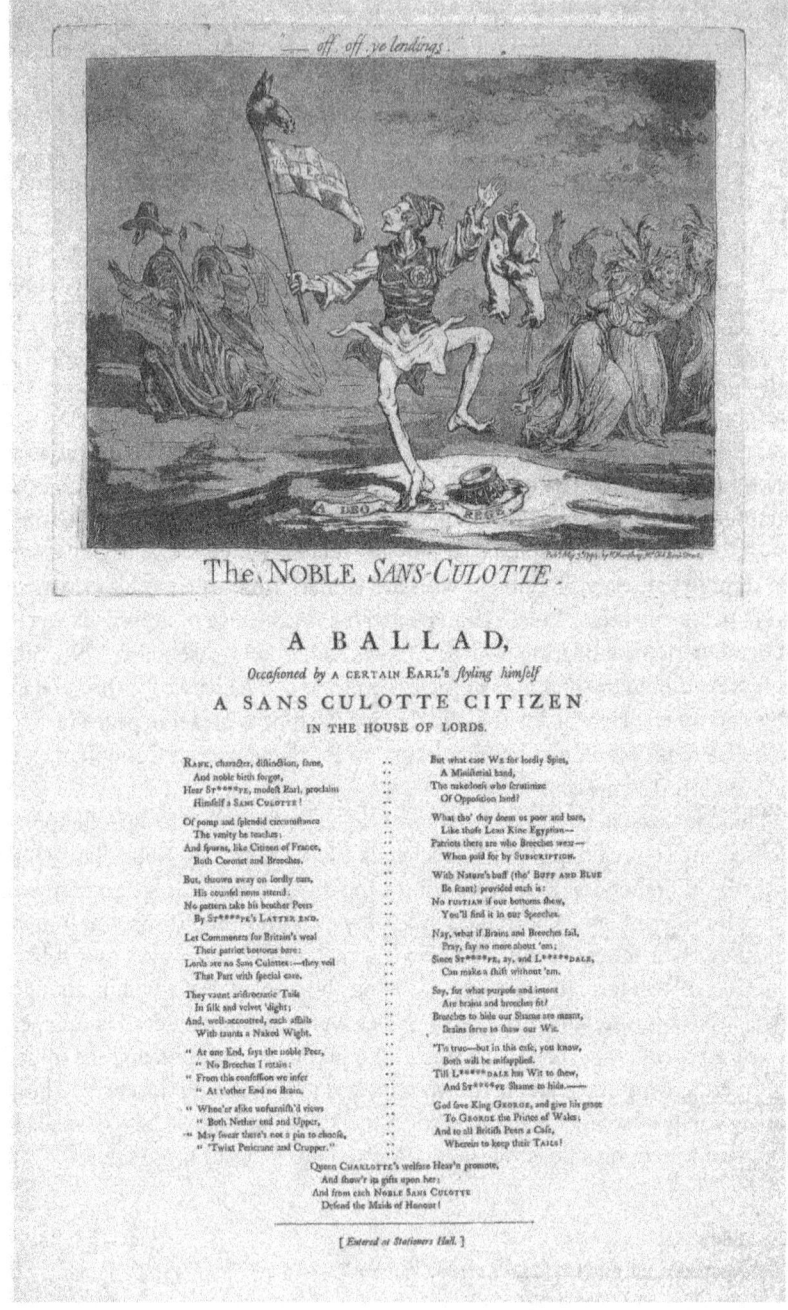

Figure 5: The Noble Sans-Culotte by H. Humphreys, 3 May 1794.

We have men ....artful and designing men, my lord, who bellow for *reform* but mean REVOLT, and would go to any lengths rather than relinquish their purpose. The object of the new clubs and associations which they introduce and endeavoured to establish in this country, was certainly meant to excite a ferment in the minds of the people: their object was to overcome Parliament and the Nation, and the tumult once begun, who can say where it would end, whose property would be secure, or whose life respected?[13]

Through his contact with Stanhope and his role in London radical societies Joyce would have been privy to many dangerous political communications with the French. There is one, untrustworthy, reference to him being a member of the 'British revolutionary club' and actually being present at one of their meetings in Paris in December 1792, but this cannot be verified.[14] Nevertheless, he must have met many French revolutionaries and, as a consequence, became known in London society as a pro-French political radical.

Joyce's Political Activities in London in the Early 1790s

Apart from major estates in Ireland, Derbyshire and elsewhere, Earl Stanhope's main residence was at Chevening, Kent, the family home where Joyce spent the greater part of ten years. Chevening House is located in the village of Chevening, which is near the intersection of the current M25 and the A21 near Sevenoaks and is now the official residence of the Secretaries of Foreign and Commonwealth Affairs which operates the British Government's programme of scholarships to foreign students.

In the early years of the 1790s however, Stanhope and his family were often in London. Joyce spent most of his official working time as secretary and as tutor, in Stanhope's central London residence in Mansfield Street just off Cavendish Square located in the most fashionable and expensive area of London. It was also from Stanhope's London residence that Joyce operated as a political radical, where he liaised between Stanhope and the politically active groups he was in contact with, and where he was eventually arrested in May 1794.[15]

Between 1790 and 1792, Joyce joined three metropolitan based societies, all of which pursued or reflected interests that were concerned with parliamentary reform.

---

13 Ibid., p. 12.

14 Alger, G. (1889), *Englishmen in the Revolution*, Sampson Low, London, p. 99.

15 Confusion over the place of Joyce's arrest was created by the variable and dubious recollections of the ailing Hester Stanhope one of Joyce's former charges, who told her physician Dr Meryon, that Joyce was arrested at Chevening (Ghita Stanhope, p. 147). In fact there are several newspaper reports that state that Joyce was arrested in Mansfield St (for example in the *Times*, 15 May 1794 reproduced in the next chapter) and given the journey time from Chevening in Kent to Whitehall in central London where Joyce was interrogated at 1.00 pm, it was impossible for him to have been arrested at Chevening and been transported to Whitehall in the time available. This fairly innocuous factual error has unfortunately been reproduced in nearly all the biographical notices of Joyce.

Joyce joined the London Revolution Society, the Unitarian Society and the Society for Constitutional Information, each of which had different agendas and memberships from different social backgrounds. Joyce, who clearly functioned to coordinate the different activities, concerns and agendas of these three radical groups, also became a secretary to the joint committee between the London Corresponding Society and the Society for Constitutional Information in 1794. The Society for Constitutional Information was predominantly concerned with political education, and reflected the political views of intellectuals in the older liberal tradition of commonwealthmen, whereas the London Corresponding Society emerged from the developing class structure of the Industrial Revolution, was distinctly working class and, under the influence of the works of Thomas Paine, was more concerned to directly address social and economic injustice. From the circumstances of his birth, Joyce might have been drawn to the London Corresponding Society, but his membership of the Society for Constitutional Information was more consistent with his now elevated social ranking, his ministerial position and his tutorship of an aristocrat's children.

Joyce's membership of three reform societies was unusual and involved considerable and potentially dangerous written communications and attendance at meetings. Given his employment by Earl Stanhope, with tutorial duties to his son, his residence in Stanhope's houses, and their mutual enthusiasm for reform and the French Revolution, Stanhope must have sympathised with Joyce's activities. Indeed it is clear that Joyce acted, to some degree, as Stanhope's political agent, involving himself in societies and radical politics which Stanhope broadly supported but did not feel it appropriate to join.

The Revolution Society

On 14 September 1790 Joyce and his elder brother Joshua were proposed as members of the London Revolution Society. This was one of many English societies created to celebrate the centenary of the English 1688 Glorious Revolution, many members were in contact with French political societies.[16] Made up largely of Protestant dissenters, the Revolution Society also included members from the Established Church and the higher ranks of society. They met on 4 November each year to celebrate William III's birthday and the 1788 meeting of the society made the following bold declaration of their political principles.

---

16 Emsley, C. (1979), *British society and the French wars 1793 – 1815*, Macmillan, London p. 13.

1. That all civil and political authority is derived from the people.
2. That the abuse of power justifies resistance.
3. That the right of private judgement, liberty of conscience, trial by jury, the freedom oft he press and the freedom of elections ought ever to be held sacred and inviolable.[17]

These were the classic principles of liberal reform and Old Dissent which claimed the Glorious Revolution as the basis of a fair constitution – a constitution which, members of the Revolution Society held, had become abused by imbalances in the tripartite estates of Commons, aristocracy and monarchy. To holders of such views the French Revolution expressed the just development of exactly their principles. The meeting of the London Revolution Society on 4 November 1789, chaired by Stanhope, was the occasion when Richard Price had delivered his famous sermon *Discourse on the love of our country*, which portrayed the French Revolution as an emulation of the 1688 English Revolution and as a continuation of the goals of the American Revolution. At the meeting Price moved that an address be sent to the French National Assembly expressing the support of the society and concluded:

> They [members of the society] cannot help adding their ardent wishes of a happy settlement of so important a revolution, and at the same time expressing the particular satisfaction with which they reflect on the tendency of the glorious example given in France to encourage other nations to assert the inalienable rights of mankind, and thereby to introduce a general reformation in the government in Europe, and to make the world free and happy.[18]

The address was signed by Stanhope and sent to the Duc de la Rochefoucauld requesting that it be presented to the National Assembly. Over following two years, there followed a series of communications from the Duke and others, many of which were addressed to Stanhope or to Price, and which were also published in 1792.[19] The prominence of the Society was increased at this time due largely to the effect that Price's sermon had in provoking Burke's *Reflections* (1790), which focused conservative reactions and vehemently condemned the Revolution and its English sympathisers.[20] Joyce therefore joined a highly political and high profile society that provided the stage for one of the most strident intellectual and reformist challenges to established government and had clear links with the new French government.

---

17 Quoted in Goodwin, p. 87.

18 Quoted in Ghita Stanhope, p. 87.

19 *The correspondence of the Revolution Society with the National Assembly, and with various societies of the Friends of Liberty in France and England* (1792).

20 Burke, E. (1790), 'Reflections on the revolution in France and on the proceedings in Certain Societies in London relative to that event. In a letter intended to be sent to a gentleman in France' in L.G. Mitchell (ed.) (1989), *The Writings and Speeches of Edmund Burke*, Clarendon, Oxford, Vol. 5, pp. 53–293.

Stanhope withdrew from the Revolution Society in the summer of 1790 on grounds that the decisions were being made without proper consultation.[21] Interestingly, this was just when Joyce was elected a member – a fact that may imply that Stanhope wished to maintain contact with the society but remain some distance from it. However, if Stanhope did wish to preserve a distance from metropolitan radicalism, he did not take great steps to distance himself from Joyce whose association with Stanhope is clearly recorded in his LRS membership entry which reads;

> 163. Jerem. Joyce. At Earl Stanhopes. Proposed by Christopher Harris and Sam. Travell.[22]

The Unitarian Society

Joyce's name appears in the list of members of the Unitarian Society in 1791 at its first meeting in the King's Head Tavern in the Poultry on 9 February. The links with Hackney College and 'Old Phlogiston' (Priestley) registered the Society as dangerously subversive on the political stage. At the meeting at which Joseph Priestley and Theophilus Lindsey and all the heads of the Unitarian church were present the Society expressed its political purpose and resolved to request that Charles James Fox move the repeal of statutes 9 and 10 of William III C.32 entitled 'An act for the more effective suppression of blasphemy' which licensed discrimination against dissenters. Joyce recorded in his final address to the Unitarian Society the climate of repressive tension in which the society was formed:

> They [the Unitarian Society] lay claim to the title as being the first society of the kind that ever existed in our much loved country; as daring to meet, for the purpose of propagating their opinions, at a time when every exertion subjected them to the severe and heavy lash of barborous laws; at a time when a mark of ignominy and reproach was attached to the name Unitarian.[23]

The demand for the right of freedom of worship provided only a thin cloak to the aspirations of its members to secure parliamentary reform. The consequence that the recognition of the rights of dissenters would necessitate social and political change was inescapable. However, the Society was generally concerned to present only its religious purposes to the wider public and keep the political aspirations of its members off its public agenda. The first entry in the Society's minute book is one of its few overtly political pronouncements. Further entries of the minute book show

---

21 Ghita Stanhope, p. 97.

22 London, Guildhall, Guildhall MSS, MS22.829. Membership list of the London Revolution Society.

23 Joyce, J. (1816), *The Subserviency of free enquiry and Religious Knowledge, among the lower classes of Society to the Prosperity and Permanence of a state*, For the author, London, p. 29.

both that political talk was not recorded and, particularly over the period of the Treason Trials (1794), the entries are minimal and no political issues are recorded at all. The lack of record of the political and reformist aspirations of the members of the Society who clearly had such aspirations, reflects both their nervousness about committing political sentiment and intentions to paper and the distance many of the members wished to place between the Society and the terrible events unfolding in France. Many members of the Society were considerably older than Joyce and represented the more traditional forms of dissent. Their reformist aspirations were not revolutionary and their concern was for a preservation of the harmonious and tripartite balance of the three estates. As events in France became uglier, many of the values of Old Dissent were violated and many Unitarians became embarrassed at the connection between their reformist aspirations and the French Revolution. This sense of embarrassment may also explain the relative distance between some of the older members of the Society and the younger and more radical Joyce, who was associated through Stanhope, with the French National Assembly and was heavily involved in metropolitan radical politics.

Unitarian disquiet was also fuelled by the relative social danger they faced. The accusations of Edmund Burke focused popular opinion on Unitarians as the public enemy. Burke characterised Joyce's friend Richard Price as 'a man much connected with literary caballers, and intriguing philosophers; with political theologians, both at home and abroad', and aimed his vitriol at Unitarians, the London societies and Hackney College.[24] Such public hostility was also fuelled by the common practice of the opening of Unitarians' mail by the Post Office, and the system of government spies set in place by the Home Office. There were, therefore, motives of personal security that urged Unitarians to make sure of a distance between themselves and pronounced and visible radicals. Joyce himself must have been forced to be on his guard despite the relative tolerance of the metropolis.

Not only were some of Joyce's most long standing friendships and connections forged through his contact with the Unitarian Society, but it was through his experiences with the Society that he was first introduced to the practical problems of producing literature for particular audiences. The Society was denominated 'The Unitarian Society for promoting Christian knowledge and the practice of virtue by the distribution of books', and many of the meetings of the society were held in the shop of the famous radical publisher and Unitarian Joseph Johnson, with whom Joyce had already had extensive contact.[25] At the 14 July 1791 meeting Joyce is recorded as a member of the committee which decided to print and place on the Society's catalogue 2000 copies of the *Family Instructor*, revised and corrected by Dr Kippis.[26] Joseph Johnson was to arrange the printing and undertake the sale and

---

24 Burke, in E.J. Payne, Vol. 2, p. 12.

25 London, Essex Hall MSS, item 4A, The Unitarian Society minute book started in 1791.

26 Andrew Kippis (1791) *Family Instructor* Unitarian Society, London. Original by Daniel Defoe.

delivery of the books to members of the Society. This was Joyce's first substantial effort to distribute books and was the beginning of a life-long involvement with the publishing industry. Joyce would later become a leading member and secretary of the Unitarian Society, although his name does not reappear in the society minutes until 1802 when the radical connotations of the French Revolution and the political activities of the early 1790s had slipped to some extent from the public memory.

The Society for Constitutional Information

In 1792 Joyce joined the rejuvenated Society for Constitutional Information founded by Horne Tooke and satired in political cartoons. The Society brought Joyce into contact with many interesting members of London's liberal society. The dramatist and writer Thomas Holcroft and the engraver William Sharp were from artisan backgrounds, but the membership also included members from the middle and higher ranks such as John Bonney the attorney, Romney the painter, John Richter, son of the artist Richter, and the famous Whig reformers John Horne Tooke and Major Cartwright.

Joyce was a committed member of the Society and he felt a duty to 'diffuse constitutional knowledge among my fellow citizens'.27 He described the role of the Society as a guardian of the constitution in which the interests of all Englishmen had a stake.

> In the venerable Constitution handed down to us through a long succession of ages, this must be the basis and vital principle, LAWS TO BIND ALL, MUST BE ASSENTED TO BY ALL. As every Englishman has an equal inheritance in those laws and that constitution which has been provided for their defence, it is, therefore necessary that every Englishman should know *what that Constitution is; when it is safe; and when it is endangered.* To diffuse this knowledge universally through the realm, to circulate it through every village and hamlet, and even to introduce it into the humble dwelling of the cottager, is the wish and hope of this Society.28

From the spring of 1792, the Society emerged as the effective leader of the whole democratic movement and took over from the Revolution Society the role as the chief communication channel between English radicals and their French counterparts.29 Through his membership of the Society and his employment with Stanhope, Joyce provided a major link between metropolitan radicalism, the French national government and pro-reform Liberals. He was also at the centre of a distribution network of radical literature. The surviving records of the Society show that he

---

27 Joyce, J. (1794), *A Sermon preached on Sunday, February the 23rd, 1794: to which is added an appendix containing an account of the author's arrest for treasonable practices*, Printed for the author, London, Nov. 1794, p. 43. Hereafter *Sermon* and *Account*.

28 Ibid., p. 44.

29 Goodwin, pp. 215/6.

received 100 copies of Thomas Paine's *Letter to Mr Secretary Dundas* (1792), and that Joyce's brother Joshua took 400 copies for distribution to Unitarians in Yarmouth, Ipswich, Shrewsbury and Canterbury in June 1792.[30] Living almost next door to the Essex Street Chapel, Joshua Joyce could readily supply the many Unitarians who visited. Joyce himself was afternoon preacher from 1793 and the brothers provided a major link between the Society and the Unitarian community across the country.

Joyce was heavily involved in the distribution of radical literature. On his arrest in May 1794, the authorities made an inventory of his papers which reveal that he had an extensive collection of radical literature.[31] As a regular attender at the monthly meetings of the Constitutional Society he was involved in the distribution of many political pamphlets and, notably, the first and second parts of Thomas Paine's *The Rights of Man*. From 1792 to 1794 the Society contributed to the distribution of 200,000 copies of part two, which it sold at the very low price of 6d and placed affordable anti-government literature in the hands of a much wider audience.[32]

To Unitarians, education was a crucial and meritorious endeavour that not only led society towards a more perfect state but was a source of liberty and virtuous action. The producers and distributors of political education in the 1790s had to negotiate the moral and legal censorship of powerful voices in society for whom political education was easily interpreted as seditious libel and who were quite likely to invoke the forces of law to resist what could be seen as a threat to the social order. From 1695, when the Act of Parliament which imposed a censorship of the press expired, anyone was, in theory, able to publish what they wished. In practice, if published material was deemed blasphemous, seditious, obscene or defamatory, the publisher could be answerable to a court of law.[33] Joyce, as an active member of societies considered subversive by the authorities, was therefore concerned with the publication of potentially seditious material.

Stanhope was active in the House of Lords and moved the second reading of the bill first put forward by Charles James Fox in 1792, which came to be known as the Libel Act. Prior to this act, in matters of libel, the official doctrine was that the only matter of fact to be decided by the jury was whether or not the publication meant what the prosecution said it meant.[34] The 1792 Act gave to the jury, rather than to the bench, the power of deciding the intention and nature of published matter in cases of seditious libel, and therefore made the jury the arbiter of the matter as well as of

---

30 Paine, T. (1972), *Letter to Mr Secretary Dundas*, PRO, Treasurer Solicitors Papers, 11/962. Issitt, J. (2003), 'A network for radical and political Education in the 1790s' *Journal of Publishing History*, 54, pp. 5–18.

31 PRO, T.S., 11/964.

32 Paine, T. (1792), *The Rights of Man*, Dent, 1944, Longmans, London; Ehrman, J. (1983), *The Younger Pitt: The Reluctant Transition*, Constable, London, pp. 114/5.

33 Aspinall, A. (1973), *Politics and the Press 1780 – 1850*, Home & Van Thal, London, p. 34.

34 Barrell, J. (1992), *The Birth of Pandora and the Division of Knowledge*, Macmillan, London, p. 127.

the fact.[35] The establishment, in its broadest sense, had therefore been protected from printed criticism by a section of its own membership – the judiciary. Such protection was seen by many Whigs and reformers as an unwarranted limit to the constitutional right of free speech and the legitimate right to petition parliament. The link between the legal power of the jury to decide matters of fact and the freedom to publish material hostile to the government was a crucial one in which Joyce would become intimately involved. The extension of the power of the jury at the expense of the judiciary became one of the critical points at issue in the *Treason Trials* (discussed below) as it came to symbolise the rights of Englishmen within the proper workings of a just constitution.

Stanhope was active in his support of Fox and wrote *The rights of Juries Defended; Together with authority of law in support of the rights and objections to Mr Fox's Libel Bill refuted* (1792). At the same time Joyce was active in the publication of texts, some of which were directly hostile to the government. One can view the actions of the two as a combined project: Stanhope active in ensuring that the people have authority over what is libel, and Joyce engaged in the production of potentially libellous material. With Pitt's decision to clamp down on opposition groups in 1792, Joyce's position became more and more dangerous.

---

35 Keir, D.L. (1968), *The constitutional History of Modern Britain since 1485* (Adam & Charles Black, London, p. 399; E.P. Thompson, *The Making of the English Working Class* Pelican, Harmondsworth, 1972, p. 135.

Chapter 5

Political Notoriety and the Charge of Treason

Introduction

Joyce's political activities through the 1790s took place in the face of rising surveillance and repression from William Pitt's government and increasing public hostility to any action that could be construed as pro-French. Church and King mobs burnt effigies of Joseph Priestley and Thomas Paine in the streets and the 'Association for the Preservation of Liberty and Property against Republicans and Levellers' founded by John Reeves, actively combated the Society for Constitutional Information.[1] Joyce could not avoid the hostility that he and all active radicals faced. His friend, William Shepherd, spelt out the dangers when he wrote to Joyce early in 1794 saying, 'I dare say Reeves has you on his books....beware of false brethren'.[2]

Such increased hostility and tension provoked a variety of responses amongst liberal intellectuals. It served to traumatise people and provoked them to develop personal and individual, rather than uniform, responses and positions. Furthermore, the political stage had been reshaped following the arrival of new voices – those of artisans against the government. The new politics recast the positions of activists on both sides of the political divide and resulted in the various actors becoming unsure of their individual roles.[3] Such personal and mixed responses to the French Revolution prompted most of those who had previously voiced demands for reform to either change their views or remain silent. Those, including Joyce, who retained their public opposition to the government clearly risked the accusation of seditious libel and/or treason.

Political tension had been significantly increased six months earlier following the case of the Scottish Martyrs with whom Joyce was to have extensive contact. On 30 April 1793 the second general convention of Scottish reformers (which became known as the 'British Convention') met in Edinburgh to campaign for radical parliamentary reform. By late summer four of the leaders were charged with sedition, found guilty and sentenced to transportation. Radicals and reformers across

---

1 Goodwin, p. 265.
2 PRO, T.S., 11/964. nd. Extracts from Joyce's papers.
3 Philp, M. (1991), *The French Revolution and British Popular Politics*, Cambridge University Press, p. 54; Ehrman, J. (1983), *The Younger Pitt: The Reluctant Transition*, Constable, London, p. 400.

Britain were enraged at what they saw as the brutal actions of the Scottish Judiciary and as the abuse of their fundamental right to seek representation.

The alarm and sense of urgency gripping the country and the House of Commons inevitably engendered action. The 'British Convention' held in Edinburgh had been organised by radicals and smacked of a French-style National Assembly, and the threatening spectacles of increasingly large public gatherings of lower class men in the meetings of the London Corresponding Society, brought Pitt and his government to act decisively against a perceived threat. In May 1794 Habeas Corpus was suspended and twelve London radicals were seized, interrogated by the Privy Council to be imprisoned in the Tower and eventually charged with treason. Joyce was one of those twelve.

The account of Joyce's involvement, as far as it can be traced given the fact that archival records have been heavily edited by those embarrassed or frightened by their connections with Joyce, reflects a heady mix of religious millenarianism, clandestine meetings, careful politicking, spies and legal wrangling. It was God's will, Joyce believed, that democracy and proper representative government be established on the road to the new millennium. His actions display personal bravery in the face of accusation, threat and interrogation and a strong sense of divine mission. As the following account seeks to demonstrate, in 1794 Joyce saw his own fate as an expression of God's will. His mission was to stand in the face of ignorant, selfish and repressive forces and open people's eyes to the inevitable will of the Creator.

The Sermon

From 1793 until 1804 Joyce was afternoon preacher at the Essex Street Unitarian Chapel, where he met and preached to many of the members of the liberal community including the MPs William Smith, Thomas Brand Hollis and James Martin. On Sunday 23 February 1794 Joyce delivered a sermon which was to be his first published work, although it was not actually published until November that year while Joyce was awaiting trial in Newgate prison.[4]

The sermon exhibits the links between the theological and political dimensions of Unitarian thought and the constellation of ideas that trace the pattern of Unitarian thinking as it moved from the religious to the secular realm. It has three interrelated arguments. First, that God has foreknowledge and that he imparted such knowledge to the prophets as commissions in the pursuit of his purposes. Second, that Christ was such a prophet and that his proclamations at the last supper that the twelve apostles would desert him in his hour of need was an example of such prophetic commission. Third, that the lessons of Christ on the cross trusting to God alone, secure in the knowledge of his kingdom and defiant in the face of danger and threats, was a lesson relevant to the current (1794) social and political situation. At a theological level, the sermon claims that a particular species of knowledge of the future exhibits the

---

4   Joyce, *Sermon* and *Account*, 1794.

hand of divine providence in the design of events. At a political level, the actions of the Scottish Martyrs, and the potential actions of Joyce's listeners, are configured as correct, moral and consistent with God's plan. The sense of the unfolding of momentous events and the need for firm, morally justified action that might lead to a form of martyrdom, is sustained by reference to the Scottish Martyrs recently sentenced and on board the *Surprize* transport to Botany Bay, whom Joyce refers to as 'some [who] are already suffering for their attachment to principles which they believed would tend to the happiness of the world'.[5] At the end of the printed edition of the sermon Joyce reproduced the address of the Society for Constitutional Information to the Scottish Martyrs which applauded their actions and assured them that 'the memory of your virtues shall never be effaced from our breasts', and promised 'the cause for which you struggled, is a glorious cause, the World that has witnessed your exertions, shall witness ours also'.[6]

On the stage of a central London pulpit, Joyce therefore delivered a sermon that cast contemporary political events in a way that arranged the forces of good (reformist) against the forces of repression (Pitt's government). In strongly portentous tones Joyce argued:

> It is not my province to sound the trumpet of alarm: "sufficient to the day is the evil thereof". One thing, however, is deserving of attention; that general expectation is looking for times of uncommon importance. The opinion that we are drawing near to an eventful period is almost universal. It may be, that danger and distress are standing at our doors; it is time, therefore, to consider whether we are to act our parts with patience and dignity. Whether we are ready to sustain every thing which *power* can inflict, rather than disgrace the cause in which we have embarked by a submission to base and servile motives. The signs of the times must present to every considerate person, an aspect as solemn and awful as the world ever witnessed.[7]

These forthright views, expressed within two miles of the seat of parliament, were only thinly veiled by the licence given to a religious sermon and carry the strong sense that Joyce felt that a major test of dissenting beliefs was imminent and that he might well have to play a testing role in the unfolding of divine providence himself.

The Arrest

Through the spring of 1794, Joyce coordinated the actions of a range of reform societies. On 4 April he represented the Society for Constitutional Information at the first joint conference with the London Corresponding Society, at which a motion was carried to pass all communications from reform societies throughout the country to the Corresponding Society, and that at the next meeting the delegates should

---

5 Ibid., p. 23.
6 Ibid., p. 25/6n.
7 Ibid., p. 22.

communicate all the information they had received.⁸ Joyce went to the house of the radical lecturer and member of the Corresponding Society John Thelwall, two or three days after this meeting where he met the dramatist Thomas Holcroft and other delegates.⁹ It was probably at this meeting that Joyce worked with Thomas Hardy, the leader of the Corresponding Society, to produce the letter of 7 April written by Joyce but signed by Hardy soliciting the assistance of the Whig group of the Society of the Friends of the People in organising 'a convention of the friends of freedom for the purpose of obtaining in a legal and constitutional method, a full and effectual representation'.¹⁰ The memory of their mutual project no doubt left its mark on Hardy who later wrote that Joyce was 'a man of great worth, and highly esteemed by all who knew him'.¹¹

The radicals were clearly working to organise a second British convention with the explicit intention of procuring a more democratic form of representative government. Joyce was a central player in this effort to coordinate and direct radical activity. As secretary to the Earl of Stanhope, he was a vital link between metropolitan radicals and a highly supportive Whig aristocrat, who was the brother-in-law of Pitt himself. He was an obvious target for a government on the defensive and anxious to repress any threat of revolution. Whether or not Joyce was trying to emulate Jesus's action in not avoiding or hiding from authorities who sought to imprison and charge him is not clear, but what is clear is that he did not minimise his profile as a radical. On 2 May at a point when tension was very high and when government action was likely and imminent, he acted as a steward at a Corresponding Society anniversary dinner at the Crown and Anchor Tavern – the venue for many meetings of the reform societies and a place where government spies were likely to be – when the band played the French revolutionary tunes 'CA IRA' and 'The Marseillaise'.¹²

From early May the government began to act swiftly and decisively. Early in the morning of 12 May the secretary of the Corresponding Society, Thomas Hardy and the secretary of the Society for Constitutional Information, Daniel Adams, were arrested by order of the King. On the same day Home Secretary Dundas presented a message from the King to the Commons saying that the King had received information that certain societies were planning to hold a convention, that they were involved in seditious practices and that he had ordered the arrest of the leaders.¹³ Joyce was arrested on 14 May on the pretext of an intercepted message he had written to Horne Tooke two days earlier asking 'is it possible to be ready by Thursday next'.¹⁴ The

---

8   Thale, p. 128.

9   PRO, Privy Council Record, Treason: Draft Minutes, 11.A.36B, 1794.

10 Thale, *Selections*, p. 130n.

11 *Memoir of Thomas Hardy written by himself* in D. Vincent (ed.) (1977) *Testaments of Radicalism*. Europa, London, p. 68.

12 Howell, T.B. (1818), *A collection of State Trials*, T.C. Hansard for Longmans, London, xxv (1794), p. 571.

13 Wharam, A. (1994), *The Treason Trials, 1794*, Leicester University Press, p. 98.

14 Ibid., p.5.

date, according to Joyce, was really a deadline for publication of a list of government sinecures that Tooke was to procure from the Court Calendar with the intention of exposing the corrupt practices of the government.[15] The authorities that intercepted the letter, however, interpreted it as a date for some form of insurrection.

Following the arrest of the secretaries of the societies in which Joyce was heavily involved, Joyce expected the authorities to come for him.[16] His fellow member of the Society for Constitutional Information, Horne Tooke, was arrested by a detachment of soldiers with a troop of Light Horse placed nearby – a fact that provides some measure of the level of government apprehension of a possible armed insurrection.[17] Yet Joyce's arrest was conducted by only two men – an under-secretary of state Mr King, and a King's messenger, Mr Ross, indicating that the authorities felt they should send a small but high-level deputation for Joyce and that they assumed that he would 'come quietly'. The authorities may have felt they had to treat Joyce – the employee of the brother-in-law to the Prime Minister – within the conventions of arrest afforded to members of the higher levels of society.

Joyce was arrested at Stanhope's London house on 14 May and the following appeared in the *Times* the next day.

> Yesterday morning at eight o'clock, Mr Ross Jun. One of his Majesty's Messengers in ordinance with proper assistants, went to the house of Earl Stanhope in Mansfield Street, Cavendish Square and took into custody, in virtue of a warrant granted to him by the two secretaries of state, the person and papers of the Rev. Jeremiah Joyce (private secretary to Earl Stanhope and tutor to the present Lord Mahon) for treasonable and seditious practices against his Majesty's government.[18]

Joyce's reputation as a notorious radical was sealed by the report which went on to reveal his 'revolutionary plottings'.

> The Rev. Mr Joyce was lately appointed Secretary to a meeting that was to be held in London in the month of June (intended to be called the British Convention) which was to consist of a Delegate deputed from all the different Jacobin clubs in the various parts of England, such as Sheffield, Norwich, Manchester, Birmingham &c. &c. This convention was to meet immediately on the prorogation of Parliament, when they thought to have found the Executive Government without the strong arm of Parliament – Luckily the plot was discovered before the completion of the plan.[19]

---

15 Aspland, R. (1850), *Memoir of the life, works and Correspondence of Robert Aspland* Whitfield, London, p. 701.
16 Joyce, *Sermon* and *Account*, 2nd ed. Jan. 1795, p. 3.
17 Wharam, p. 92.
18 *Times*, 15 May, 1794.
19 Ibid.

The Interrogation

On 16 May the committee appointed by the government to examine the papers of the societies, which included William Pitt and Edmund Burke, reported to the government. This report – *The first report from the committee of secrecy* – was printed as a pamphlet the following day and in the Stanhope archive there is a copy of the pamphlet annotated in Joyce's hand. Next to the following section Joyce made the comment 'They got this from the books':[20]

> ....the committee reflect on the leading circumstances, which they have already stated, of the declared approbation, at an early period, of the doctrine of the Rights of Man, as stated in Paine's publication; of the connection and intercourse with the French Societies; and with the National Convention, and, of the subsequent approbation of the French System; and consider that these are those principles which the promotion of a convention evidently make the foundation of their proceedings. They are satisfied that the design now openly professed and acted upon, aims at nothing less than stated in his Majesty's message, and must be considered as a traitorous conspiracy for the subversion of the established Laws and constitution, and the introduction of that system of anarchy and confusion which has fatally prevailed in France.[21]

The warrant for Joyce's arrest authorised the seizure of all books and papers related to the societies. In fact, the inventory of Joyce's papers taken by the authorities shows that many papers not explicitly covered by the terms of the warrant were also taken, as well as an extensive collection of radical literature.[22] Joyce had multiple copies of political speeches, trials of radicals, published letters of Joseph Priestley and Richard Price and the campaigning literature against the slave trade. He had six copies of the pamphlets *Two Pennyworth more of truth for a penny, or a true state of facts* (1793), and 20 copies of the pamphlet *Fast Day observed in Sheffield, to which is added a Hymn of Revolution* (1794), and many more. Those arresting him probably thought that this collection was evidence of Joyce's activities and the ownership of multiple copies further incriminated him in anti-government activities. Joyce later recorded that when he arrived at Mr Ross's house he refused, when asked, to acknowledge ownership of all the books and papers that had been brought from his accommodation on the grounds that they had been in the possession of a servant for some time. His concern was that they might have been tampered with and he could, by acknowledging ownership, find that he had given strength to charges against him.[23]

---

20 *The first report from the committee of secrecy* (1794) annotated Stanhope MSS, U1590, Doc Z94. An unannotated copy can be found in *Committee of Secrecy of the House of Commons respecting Seditious Practices. First Report* (16 May 1794), *Parl. Hist*, vol. 31, cols 475–97.

21 Ibid.

22 PRO, T.S., 11/964.

23 Joyce, *Sermon* and *Account*, 2nd ed. Jan. 1795, p. 3.

It soon became clear that it was a charge of treason, rather than sedition, that Pitt's government sought to bring against those they had arrested. The Privy Council conducted a series of individual interrogations in the council chambers of Whitehall. This was a powerful gathering of the most influential men in the country – William Pitt, Henry Dundas, Lord Hawkesbury, the Duke of Montrose, the Earl of Chatham, Lord Auckland, the Marquis of Stafford, the Lord Chancellor, the Attorney General and the Solicitor General. Such an interview was a significant and no doubt frightening experience for Joyce, who must have realised that the intention of those present was to indict him for treason and place him on trial. If they were successful, Joyce was facing at best deportation to Botany Bay, at worst the gallows. Joyce's record of the interrogation was published as *An account of the author's arrest for "Treasonable Practices"* (Printed for the author, 1794), and is fairly consistent with the official record.[24] Not surprisingly however, Joyce's account casts him as the hero and the Council as the villains. Joyce's account is longer and more detailed and includes what he interpreted as threats made by Council members. For example, after Joyce had refused to answer questions on grounds that it would harm the constitution, he recorded that Henry Dundas had said 'You had better leave the constitution to itself, and consider whether it will be in your interests to answer the questions which are put to you'.[25] This thinly veiled threat does not appear in the official version. Where Joyce records a lengthy series of questions and answers relating to his status as accused and his request for counsel, to which Dundas, Pitt and Lord Loughborough responded to with dark mutterings, the official version merely reports that 'Mr Joyce was told that he was certainly not bound to answer questions that might tend to accuse him.' Facing possible execution or transportation, Joyce would have been very sensitive to the implications of the questions put to him. His fuller record reflects his concern both to present his own performance as honourable and to expose the threatening implications of what was said.

Both accounts however, reveal Joyce's strategy in dealing with his interrogators – which was consistent with the responses of the other accused and was probably rehearsed.[26] He simply asked for counsel and when it was denied he refused to answer questions on the legal grounds that as an accused person he was not required to answer questions without counsel. When presented with a transcript of the Society for Constitutional Information's meeting of 11 April 1794 when he was in the chair and named as accepting the office of secretary to the joint committees of the societies, and when presented with a copy of his letter to Tooke, Joyce simply refused to answer.

Joyce was kept at Ross's house for five days until 19 May. He had been allowed to see his sister but was refused the use of pen and paper. He was informed that he could not see any member of the Stanhope household and that he was not to communicate with any other person. In the afternoon he was taken to the Tower

---

24 PRO, T.S., 11/963/3509.

25 Joyce, *Sermon* and *Account*, p. 37.

26 Wharam, pp. 94/5 and 101

under a warrant signed by most of the members of the Privy Council instructing the Governor of the Tower:

> ..in his Majesty's name, to authorise and require you to receive into your custody the body of the Reverend Jeremiah Joyce, herewith sent you for High Treason: and you are to keep him safe and close until he shall be delivered by due course of Law.[27]

Through the seven days 12 to 19 May, the arrests were the focus of the attention of the general public. Rumours of insurrection and connections with French societies stampeded public opinion against the radicals as broadsheet vendors sold sheets headed TREASON! TREASON! TREASON![28] Tension was further increased by debates over the introduction of a suspension of Habeas Corpus and the accidental discovery of a cache of pikeheads and battle-axes in Edinburgh was used by the government as evidence of insurrection.[29] Joyce was clearly implicated. To the public, the government and the judiciary, he could be vilified by his associations. As a Unitarian he was associated with the reformers Price, Priestley and Lindsey. As an employee of the Earl of Stanhope he was implicated with the French. As an active political radical who not only circulated seditious material, but who had been heavily involved in the coordination of radical groups, he was a dangerous plotter. Newly arrived in the Tower, Joyce must have viewed the future with trepidation.

The Tower, Newgate and the Trial

In the House of Lords on 22 May, Stanhope, whose sentiments were no doubt inflamed by the arrest of his secretary, opposed the measure to introduce the suspension of Habeas Corpus. He claimed that the move was designed to set up a Bastille and he strongly denounced the use of 'lettres de cachet' with which to arrest and imprison, without proof or reason and at the will of ministers.[30] In his account of his arrest and confinement Joyce gave a detailed description of his experiences. On his arrival at the Tower he was initially confined in the Yeoman Porter's house. Like the others arrested on the same charges, he was kept as a 'close' prisoner, which meant that a warder would stay with him in his cell, and a soldier guard his door. The warrant stated that the prisoners were not allowed to communicate with anyone, and were not permitted access to pen and paper without express order. After eight days Joyce was placed in one of the Tower cells overlooking the Tower wharf which offered him a good view but also subjected him to the insults of passengers, some of whom would taunt him with the epithets 'Jacobin', 'Democrat' and 'King Killer'. Bail was refused but by application to the Privy Council he was given pen and paper and, under supervision, he was allowed two two-hourly visits per week from his relations

---

27 Joyce, *Sermon* and *Account*, p. 10.
28 Thompson, p. 145.
29 Goodwin, pp. 335/6.
30 Ghita Stanhope, *The Life of Charles Third Earl Stanhope* (Longmans, 1914), p. 133.

and was allowed to walk on the Tower parapets, but he was not allowed to speak to any other prisoner. An indication of the level of anxiety felt by the authorities over the connections and persuasive power of the prisoners, is given in the Orders for the Warders of 4 August 1794 by Colonel Yorke, the deputy Governor of the Tower, which both required strict supervision of the prisoners but also instructed the warders that when they were outside the Tower 'they were not to go into any house either inhabited or empty, nor any of the armories, and that they return to their lodgings at retreat beating'.[31] Presumably the concern was that they might meet co-conspirators of the prisoners and therefore be persuaded to aid them.

The prisoners became a public spectacle and when they were allowed to take exercise on the Tower ramparts, crowds gathered to observe. William Shepherd, Joyce's life-long friend, records that he stood amongst the crowds watching the prisoners exercise, and tried to attract Joyce's attention.[32] They were kept in the public's eye by numerous references in newspapers. On 6 September *The Times* published 'a sketch of what would, in our opinion, be the daily matter of a Newspaper, conducted under a government, guided by maxims borrowed from the Revolutionary System of the French'.[33] This spoof constituted page 3 of the edition under the title 'The New Times' falsely dated Saturday 10 June 1800 (Bastille Day) in which the twelve accused, as well as other leading reformers, were parodied and caricatured. The lecturer and a leader of the London Corresponding Society, John Thelwell, was addressed as Telwell; Grosvenor Square was renamed Horne Tooke Square; everyone was addressed as citizen and a humorous report that a French brig laden with guillotines had arrived, was included. In the third column under the subtitle 'London', Joyce is caricatured as 'The Rev Citizen Joys'.

> This day, June 10th, at twelve o'clock the Rev. Citizen Joys, Minister of the National Church, will celebrate in the *Temple of Reason* (*ci-devant* ST PAUL'S CHURCH) a festival for the happy destruction of parliament.

The associations with the new French government were clear – the national church, the Temple of Reason and the title 'citizen' were all linked to the purpose of destroying parliament and served to present Joyce as a dangerous plotter. His Unitarian credentials combined with his association with Stanhope further served to fuel and colour the imagery served up to the public. As the period of imprisonment continued however, public sentiment began to swing a little more in favour of the radicals. Whilst he was in the Tower, Joyce began to notice that the abuse he was subjected to subsided and he became – in the eyes of the passers-by – an object of

---

31 Joyce, *Sermon* and *Account*, p. 12.
32 Ridyard. H. (nee Joyce) (1855), *A selection from the letters of the Reverend W. Shepherd*, Private Publication, Liverpool, p. 55.
33 *Times*, 6 Sept. 1794, p. 2.

pity.[34] Clearly there was some sympathy for the accused and they become known in some quarters as the 'twelve apostles'.[35]

On 24 October the prisoners were taken to Newgate and placed in uncomfortable and separate rooms about which many of them complained.[36] They were taken to the Sheriff's house in the Old Bailey the following day and arraigned on the charge of high treason. All the prisoners were individually asked the same questions and all replied with the routine formula for claiming trial by jury:

'Guilty or not guilty?'
'Not guilty.'
'How will you be tried?'
'By God and my country.'[37]

On the request of the accused, the court decided that they were to be tried separately and they were all taken back to Newgate to await trial. In the period between 25 of October and 1 December when Joyce was released, the trials of Thomas Hardy and Horne Tooke took place and received constant reporting in the press. To Pitt and the government's annoyance, the famous lawyer Erskine mounted a successful campaign and secured the acquittals of first Hardy then Tooke. As a result, the grounds of the charges against Joyce were also removed. Erskine had exposed the evidence of the prosecution as fraudulent, inconsistent and the product of government spies. In his effort he had been assisted by Joyce's brother Joshua who had helped in the examination of the circumstances of each of the 421 witnesses – 'sent to perplex and confuse the prisoners' on behalf of 'the minister'.[38] Erskine successfully convinced the jury that reformers were not crypto-republicans and that they had no other aims than universal suffrage and annual parliaments.[39] He managed to deflect the government's aim of stamping on radical activities and he turned the trials into a test of the British constitution and the rights of the individual both to campaign for reform and for proper trial by jury – a right seen by reformers as having been abused in the recent Treason Trials in Scotland. The government's case, exposed as contrived and badly directed, collapsed.[40]

---

34 Joyce, *Sermon* and *Account,* 2nd ed., p. 11.

35 *The Autobiography of Francis Place*, ed. by M. Thale, (1972), Cambridge University Press, p. 129n.

36 Wharam, pp. 142–146.

37 Ibid., p. 145.

38 Joyce, J., Obituary notice of Joshua Joyce *Monthly Repository*, 11 (1816), p. 244.

39 Goodwin, p. 349.

40 The accounts of these trials are familiar to most history undergraduates and there are shelves of treatments. The two classic accounts are those of E.P. Thompson and Albert Goodwin although there are many more. More recently, John Barrell has considered some of the linguistic and dramatic features of the trials in J. Barrell (1992), *The Birth of Pandora and the Division of Knowledge*, Macmillan, London and A. Wharam (note 13) explores some hitherto unknown details.

Joyce remained in Newgate until 1 December when he was brought to the bar with three of the other accused – Bonney, Holcroft and Kyd. The Attorney General announced that he did not propose to proceed further against them and they were released.

The Publication of the *Account of the Author's Arrest for Treasonable Practices*

When the trials had started in October they became a very public drama and the tropes of Christian martyrdom were incorporated into both the language of the media and the stagecraft of the major players.[41] The timing of Joyce's decisions to publish his engraved portrait and his own account of his arrest, shows a degree of tactical thinking. His engraved portrait, published on 11 November between the close of Thomas Hardy's trial and acquittal (5th) and the commencement of Horne Tooke's trial (13th), served to increase his public profile at a critical moment when the tide was turning in favour of the reformers. Tooke's trial had a successful outcome from the reformer's point of view as the government lost its claim to have exposed conspiratorial plottings and the issue in front of the public had become the rights of juries. Joyce published his *Account* on 23 November, the day after Tooke's trial had finished, when he anticipated that he would be one of the next to stand trial. In publishing his *Account* Joyce was therefore making a tactical appeal to the judiciary of the reading public.

While in the Tower Joyce had nearly completed a personal statement of his case in 'An appeal to his countrymen respecting his [Joyce's] political opinions and conduct' (of which there is no surviving record). However, following the prisoners' indictment for treason and with the impending prospect of a trial, Joyce abandoned his intention to publish such a personal statement and placed his trust in what he hoped would be an 'impartial trial'.[42] He did, however, publish, as a pamphlet in November, while in Newgate, *An Account of the Author's Arrest for Treasonable Practice*. The print run of 1000 of the first edition sold out in a few days and a second edition was issued shortly afterwards.[43]

Very soon after these first print runs, the *Account* then began to appear in a much more widely circulated pamphlet as it was placed as an appendix to Joyce's printed version of his February *Sermon*. A letter from Joyce's friend and leader of the Unitarian Church, Theophilus Lindsey, to the Dundee Unitarian Minister Robert Millar, dated 9 December 1794, confirms that the *Sermon* plus *Appendix* were printed

---

41 Wood, M. (1994), *Radical Satire and Print Culture: 1790–1822*, Clarendon, Oxford, p. 132.

42 Joyce, *Sermon* and *Account*, p. 1.

43 Aspland, *Memoir*, p. 704; Annotated copy of Joyce, *Sermon* and *Account*, 2nd ed., MCO Shepherd Papers, Vol. 8, No. 11, probably by Hannah Ridyard who was Joyce's daughter – saying 'the first edition sold 1000 v. quick'.

together as one publication while Joyce was in Newgate, but does not provide a date of sale.

> There has just come out a Sermon by Mr Joyce, one of the late state prisoners, printed while he was in Newgate with an Appendix....we know him well and esteem him, and so would you from this specimen of himself. We have taken 1/4 of a hundred to circulate. It is calculated to do much good at the same time as it gratifies the curiosity of the reader respecting the writer.[44]

Lindsey's letter is interesting because it is one of the few pieces of evidence of support for Joyce coming from the Unitarian Church. It is notable that entries in the Unitarian Society minute book are sparse in this period and contain no mention of Joyce or politics.[45] With Joseph Priestley recently departed for America and the general vilification and derision with which Unitarians were held, it would have been prudent to maintain silence on such political issues as a Unitarian minister accused of treason. Furthermore, it was rumoured that no fewer than 800 warrants against reformers, doubtless including many Unitarians, had been drawn up.[46] Had the government been successful in convicting Joyce and his co-defendants, the subsequent arrest of those suspected of radical activities or connected in any way with the accused may well have been widespread. For reasons of both personal security and the reputation of the Unitarian Church it was prudent for Unitarians not to signal their links with Joyce.

The government's main charge against Horne Tooke was that as leader of the Society for Constitutional Information, he was instrumental in the dissemination of the works of Paine. To some extent, therefore, it was the Society that was on trial.[47] Tooke's acquittal on 22 November removed the grounds upon which the government intended charging the other members of the Society, including Joyce, and his release could be realistically anticipated from that date. Therefore, with the prospect of his release, the heads of the Unitarian community may have felt more disposed to give public support to Joyce by supporting the combination of the *Sermon* with the *Appendix* and its publication as testament to the merit of one of their ministers and his recent actions.

The linkages between the content of the *Sermon* and that of the *Account* were not merely representative of the sanctions or sentiments of the Unitarian community. To Joyce there was clearly a chain of reasoning that traversed the worlds of religion, morality and politics and which easily shifted from divine direction to the realm of human and social action. To him, moral and political actions were those that were justified within the tenets of Unitarian thinking and were guided by the model of the man Jesus Christ who had received God imparted knowledge of the future, which Joyce had described in his *Sermon*. His *Sermon* had called on listeners:

---

44 DWL, MSS 12.46 (6). Lindsey to Millar. London, 9 Dec. 1794.
45 Essex Hall MSS, *Unitarian Minute Book*.
46 Thompson, p. 150.
47 Goodwin, p. 353.

to consider whether we are to act our parts with patience and dignity. Whether we are ready to sustain every thing which *power* can inflict, rather than disgrace the cause in which we have embarked by a submission to base and servile motives.[48]

The implication was that the listeners should, and that he would, defy the abuse of power. His *Account* offers a justification for his political action to do precisely that through the activities of the Society for Constitutional Information. He used extracts of the first report of the Society to state his democratic concerns:

to diffuse this knowledge [of the Constitution] universally through the realm, to circulate it through every village and hamlet, and even to introduce it into the humble dwelling of the cottager.[49]

The *Account* therefore described his activities in resisting the abuse of power as he had forecast from the pulpit in his *Sermon*. His own activities therefore lived up to his own demands for right and moral action as demanded in the *Sermon* and as lived out and described in the *Account*. There is one ironic parallel that may or may not have escaped Joyce. As Joyce had it, Jesus had known about the future course of events. The implication from the *Sermon* is that Joyce seems convinced about the future course of events. Was it Joyce's intention to imply that he himself had had some form of divine instruction? We may never know.

At the time of publication (late November/early December 1794), when Joyce's public profile was at its highest, it was the *Account*, published as supplementary material to the main body of the text – the *Sermon* – which detailed his experiences as a state prisoner that may have been the major selling point of the publication. The supplementary nature of an 'appendix' therefore was a contrivance to publicise his experience as an oppressed reformer and was another contribution to the pamphlet war between the government and radicals. From the Unitarian perspective the attachment of the *Account* to the *Sermon*, offered the support of the Unitarian community for the actions of one of its most radical members. From Joyce's personal perspective, the fortuitous turn of events meant that his activities as a political radical were vindicated and the linking of the *Sermon* with the *Account* affirmed the support of his own religious community, and confirmed for him at least the moral justification of his actions.

---

48 Joyce, *Sermon* and *Account*, p. 22.
49 Ibid., p. 14.

Chapter 6

Release and Reception

Joyce was released on 1 December. On the same day the government began proceedings against the lecturer John Thelwall. The jury returned a verdict of not guilty five days later and the last of the twelve accused were released on 15 December 1794. The trials were over and the government had suffered a considerable defeat. Back in May, on the strength of popular anti-French sentiment, Pitt might well have anticipated a repeat of the convictions in Scotland. In the event, the trials moved beyond the government's control and turned from the prosecutions of seditious and traitorous plotters, to a symbolic drama in which the rights of juries and the rights of Englishmen were at stake. After the trials medals were struck to celebrate the acquittals and there were many other celebrations. Joyce was kept in the public eye by the publicity given to the party given by Stanhope on Joyce's release. The village of Chevening was lit up, over 400 guests were invited and the revelries lasted all night. Joyce was presented on the arm of Hester Stanhope (Lord Stanhope's daughter), and there was a collection of emblematic figures standing behind a large notice reading THE RIGHTS OF JURIES. Even the *Gentleman's Magazine* which was generally no supporter of Unitarians or radicals, acknowledged in January 1795 that the celebration was a triumph of the cause of liberty.

> The acquittals they assembled to celebrate they considered as the triumph of truth and innocence, as an event which would give people confidence in the justice of our laws, the integrity of our juries and the independence of our judges, as an event which would perpetuate the rights of Englishmen and give vigour and stability to the constitution in King, Lords and Commons as by law established.[1]

Joyce published a second edition of the '*Sermon* plus *Account*' signed Chevening 15 January 1795, in which he added a further eleven pages. He used these pages to remonstrate with his accusers, expose the fraudulence of their case and respond to the group of politicians, including Edmund Burke and William Windham (MP for Norwich), who had claimed that the 12 accused were 'accused felons'. Joyce argued that throughout his imprisonment various 'alarms' were put out to 'excite the public' against the accused through the publication of hand bills and reports which were distributed, often free of charge. Joyce claimed that parliament's published declaration that there had been a traitorous conspiracy was really an attempt by the government to persuade the country and the grand jury of the guilt of the accused. Joyce claimed that this was propaganda that effectively usurped the cause of justice

---

1 *Gentleman's Magazine* 1 (1795), p. 73.

and the right to objective trial.² Joyce disputed many of the points raised in the various newspaper accounts and denied all knowledge of the spies who gave evidence. In particular, he gave a lengthy account of the intercepted note that he had sent to Tooke and which had been interpreted as the date of a potential insurrection but which, he claimed, was in fact an innocent note referring to a publication date.

In the debates of the House of Commons on 30 December, Windham had referred to Thomas Hardy as 'an acquitted felon' and contended it was 'by no means proved that [the twelve accused] were free from moral guilt'.³ Windham's claim that the accused in the *Treason Trials* were acquitted felons lingered in the public imagination and was used by Gillray in his famous 'New Morality' caricature which appeared three years later. As one who experienced this 'mark of moral guilt', Joyce responded that as there were no real charges against him and he had only received a *form* of a trial, he could not be shown to be legally guilty.⁴ He accused Windham of seeking to portray him as morally guilty because he could not substantiate the charge of legal guilt. Joyce hit back with the comment that he, due to his own relative lack of 'political guilt', could sleep better at night than Mr Windham and friends.⁵ In a reference to the French wars he accused Windham of having 'the innocent blood of unnumbered thousands', the 'misery of the cottager' and 'the mournful complaints of the disconsolate widow and helpless orphan' on his conscience, and he went on to claim that whilst Windham's ambitions were to make himself powerful and rich, his (Joyce's) motives were to 'increase knowledge' which he considered 'the best and surest fountain of virtue' and which he pursued in the interests of the 'rights of the people'.⁶

Joyce went on to rail against Pitt, whom he charged with reneging on former principles and having intended to strike 'a mighty and awful stroke aimed at every thing that was dear to the social interests of mankind'. He claimed that 'Justice had averted the blow' and the 'Liberties of the country will stand on a firmer basis than before'. Joyce tried to turn Windham's accusation round to accuse the ministers of being guilty of perpetrating a campaign in their own interests. Their real motive for publicly labelling the twelve as accused felons, he said, was 'an apology for their own conduct'. Obviously stung by the accusation of moral guilt, Joyce refuted the charge and claimed to prefer a public execution than live 'a suspected man'.⁷ In his closing comments Joyce made a statement that protested his innocence and depicted the evidence produced in the trials of plotting violent insurrection as the creation of spies. He claimed that the Society for Constitutional Information was only ever concerned with 'publicity' in the pursuit of parliamentary reform.⁸

---

2   Joyce, *Sermon* and *Account*, p. 18.
3   Goodwin, pp. 366/7.
4   Joyce, *Sermon* and *Account*, p. 27.
5   Ibid.
6   Ibid., p.27/8.
7   Ibid., p. 28.
8   Ibid., p. 30.

The role of publicity and publication is a crucial feature of the political events of the 1790s and represents one of most important arenas in which the government and radicals confronted each other. Anti-reform elements of the government could not win the support of the public through arguing simply for the restriction of free debate or for the restriction of the liberty of the press. Their line therefore was to accuse the leading members of reform groups of holding anarchic intentions. Their line of attack had to be essentially personal, as once cast into an arena in which principles dominated, they were hard pressed to justify what could easily be caricatured as unacceptable restrictions on liberty. For the radicals of the Society of Constitutional Information, however, the publications of Paine and such projects as Joyce and Tooke's attempt to publish lists of government sinecures could ostensibly be justified under the claim of the freedom of the press. Once generally released, such publications held the possibility of translating reformist intention into the potential for destabilisation of the current status quo and a consequent breakdown in social order. Both sides therefore deployed smoke screen tactics to cover their real motives and both claimed the moral high ground as their own. Over the period of building reformist pressure – essentially up to the mid 1790s and the introduction of the Gagging Acts in 1795 – the two sides shifted their positions to suit particular circumstances in order to give themselves the best purchase on the moral high ground.

It is in this process of contestation over the moral high ground in which Joyce's actions, and, in particular, the affixing of the *Sermon* to the *Account* are best understood. As a minister and using the moral platform of the pulpit, Joyce extended the older traditions of dissent associated with such older figures as the ministers Price and Priestley, into the confrontational arena of radical politics and he used the vehicle of popular publications, justified on the basis of moral and educational concern, to do so. Through linking the *Sermon* to the *Account* Joyce claimed that it was the providential hand of God that was introducing a new form of government which Joyce saw as based on a more equitable representation with better safeguards against abuse. From his ministerial and Unitarian standpoint Joyce claimed (in his *Sermon*) to have read God's intentions – as far as a human can – and justified his actions as a political activist (in the *Account*) on the basis of trying to aid the fulfilment of those intentions. In a telling letter from William Skirving, one of the Scottish Martyrs aboard a transport to Botany Bay, Skirving thanked Joyce for the consoling thought that 'he who at first commanded the light to shine out of the darkness, hath commenced his wonderful work'.[9] Joyce clearly thought God's providential hand was at work.

The Aftermath

Stanhope's support of Fox's Libel Act which secured final judgement in the hands of the jury rather than the judge, was vindicated in this episode: his own children's

---

9 PRO, T.S., 11/964. Extracts of Joyce's letters.

tutor was released on the basis of the Act he had helped to promote. Joyce was portrayed as a hero for the cause of liberty. He was offered the pulpit at several London meetings and became a sought after preacher. Shortly after the releases on 4 February 1795 a public celebratory dinner was held in the Crown and Anchor Tavern in the Strand at which Stanhope took the chair. After toasts including 'To the "swinish multitude" and may the honest hogs never cease to grunt, until their wrongs be righted' (a reference to Burke), and to a packed audience of 1300 and no doubt fired by anger over the way his employee had been treated, Stanhope praised the acquitted:

> Citizens, We have seen several of our best-intentioned fellow-citizens immured for many months in close confinement for crimes they never did commit nor dream of. We have seen several of them afterwards dismissed, without a single witness, or a single fact, or a single tittle of evidence (either written or parole) being so much as even produced against them. But, we have seen those worthy men dismissed without any species of indemnity; and also, without any kind of legal punishment having been inflicted (as yet) upon any one of their accusers.[10]

Stanhope went on to denounce what he saw as the abuse of power – no doubt taking a swipe at his brother-in-law Prime Minister Pitt – and, by implication, urged constitutional change.

> Citizens. Are certain courtly aristocrats and apostates never to cease trampling under foot the rights of their fellow citizens, the Liberties of their country and the justice of the Nation in this barefaced and unprecedented manner?[11]

Stanhope claimed that trial by jury was the first principle of proper government and was the 'citadel of the constitution', closely followed by the freedom of the Press as 'the palladium of the People's rights' and which used the art of printing to provide 'the new luminary' that would enlighten the 'gloomy night of ignorance'.[12] Stanhope's feeling of vindication resulted to a large extent from the actions of his employee Joyce, who had stood to lose his life. In extending the 'luminary' benefits of the art of printing Stanhope later developed his famous printing press and supported Joyce in many literary projects including the production of cheap distillations of Adam Smith's *Wealth of Nations* and William Paley's *Evidences of Christianity* (discussed in Chapter 4). Although it is impossible to ascertain the precise relationship between Joyce and Stanhope, from the evidence of Joyce's subsequent literary production after the affair of the *Treason Trials*, Stanhope came to function more as Joyce's patron than his employer, and may have felt to some degree indebted to Joyce whom

---

10 *Substance of Earl Stanhope's Speech Delivered from the Chair at a Meeting of Citizens at the Crown and Anchor on the 4th February 1795 to Celebrate the Happy Event of the Late Trials for Supposed High Treason* (1795) J. Burks, London, p. 5.
11 Ibid.
12 Ibid., pp. 8/9.

he might well have judged had borne the brunt of some of Pitt's fire that had really been intended for himself.

Joyce's subsequent political profile certainly mirrors that of Stanhope, who virtually withdrew from public politics shortly after the February celebrations, as did Joyce. The records of the Corresponding Society show that in the summer of 1795 Stanhope's support was sought for petitions to the King and that Stanhope was to some extent reluctant to offer it. The report from the spy Powell records that on 7 July, Richard Hodgson, a Corresponding Society member, reported to the Society's executive committee that 'he had seen Citizen Joyce who had told him that Lord Stanhope was going to sea in the Experiment ship which he had been so long in constructing and that therefore the society must give up presenting the Address to the king for the present'.[13] However, no doubt shaken by his experiences, Joyce, along with most of the members of the now disbanded Society for Constitutional Information, chose to maintain a considerably lower public profile and turned his attention to the education of Stanhope's sons and the production of several literary speculations.

---

13 Thale, *Selections*, p. 260.

PART 2
Joyce the Unitarian Dissenter

Chapter 7

Politics and Education

Political Reality

Awaiting trial and imprisoned in the Tower in the summer of 1794, Joyce wrote in his *Account*:

> ...a reform in the representation depends less upon argument, than upon the result of the impending trials. Should their termination be *unfavourable*, the public may take a long farewell to every principle of reformation. Reason and truth, in that case, must make way for the operation of power.

His acquittal and the collapse of the government's case in November 1794 may have suggested to him and to many other radicals and millenarians that reform and the cause of 'reason and truth' was indeed imminent. In the event, the outcome of the Treason Trials failed to confer public support for political reform. The government simply ignored the fact that they had lost the case and continued their use of spies to gain more evidence of revolutionary intent and brought in new legislation – the Gagging Acts – to stop the public meetings of radicals and the publication of radical political material. By the mid 1790s, radical agitation had largely stopped and millenarian hopes that the French Revolution signalled the beginning of a new and just political and social order were dashed.

The minor victory of the reformers in the 1794 Treason Trials was lost to the major victory the government had in removing any mechanisms for organised opposition. In 1795 the Society for Constitutional Information disbanded and the pressure Pitt exerted through the Gagging Acts quickly forced the London Corresponding Society to dissolve as well. The combination of political disillusionment and his frightening experiences in the Tower and Newgate no doubt urged Joyce to adopt a less prominent opposition to Pitt's government and he retired from the world of metropolitan radicalism. Like many other intellectuals and radicals, Joyce disassociated himself from the revolutionary implications of Paine's *Rights of Man* and withdrew his political aspirations to the safer ground of constitutional reform.

In Britain, pro-French radicals, reformers and Unitarians had to rethink their positions. They had to negotiate powerful arguments from Edmund Burke and friends which pointed to the consequences of an overthrow of the status quo taking place just across the English channel. The ideological capital made by conservative forces in the government grew in large measure from the arguments made by Burke in his highly influential *Reflections*. Burke's deeply pessimistic view of human nature led him to view people as governed by passion rather than reason.[1] Reason, for Burke, was 'fallible and feeble' whereas natural instinct was 'unerring and powerful'.[2] His view of government was that it had to be constituted from natural forces beyond human reason and that the legitimacy of government and social hierarchy rested on the fact that 'Our political system is placed in a just correspondence and symmetry with the order of the world'.[3]

Burke's views on reason and government came to dominate the political stage and rational dissenters were forced to rethink their use of reason as a standard for political change. They considered reason to be a higher authority than the Established Church and state, and as providing the proper mechanism for both secular and spiritual progress and it was an appeal to reason that informed their claim for equal rights. Much of their reforming project was directed to the progressive revelation of God through the exercise of reason in uncovering God's will, yet Richard Price's claim in his famous *Discourse on the Love of our Country* that the French Revolution introduced 'The dominion of reason and conscience' rang hollow in the face of the massacres in France.[4] After the September massacres in particular it became progressively harder to use 'reason' as a platform on which to justify social change or promote Unitarianism because in the realms of both politics and religion, the appeal to 'reason' as part of a polemical strategy or a rhetorical device was removed from the armoury of the dissenter. The realities of Robespierre's France cast the vision of a reformed and democratic government only as a possibility for the very long term, rather than for the immediate or medium-term future.

There is an ironic twist in the tale of Joyce's political career after Christmas 1795, the implications of which are frustratingly impossible to resolve yet quite intriguing. Whilst Joyce and the reformers were clearly defeated on the political stage, on a personal level Joyce did not completely lose his battle with Prime Minister Pitt. If part of Pitt's anger was targeted at Joyce – his brother-in-law's secretary – there must have been a very bitter taste left lingering in Pitt's mouth after the Treason Trials. When Joyce left prison he returned to teach the children of Pitt's sister and his male second cousins one of whom would inherit the massive Stanhope estates! Joyce would have educational responsibility for one of the most important aristocratic lineages in the country, which just happened to be Pitt's closest blood ties. No sources survive to indicate either Pitt's or Joyce's sentiments in the matter but it is reasonable to surmise that Pitt would have felt uncomfortable at the thought of his cousins under the charge of the man he had unsuccessfully tried to hang and who clearly held democratic views and aspirations. Joyce's experiences made him something of a temporary celebrity and he might well have recounted his version of

---

1 Claeys, G. (1989), *Thomas Paine: Social and Political Thought*, Unwin Hyman, London, p. 66.

2 Edmund Burke, *Reflections on the Revolution in France*, in L.G. Mitchell, (ed.) (1989),*The Writings and Speeches of Edmund Burke*, Clarendon, Oxford, Vol. 8, p. 84.

3 Ibid.

4 Price, *Discourse*.

events to Pitt's relatives – and this would be a significantly different account from that given by more orthodox sources, and William Pitt in particular.

From the mid 1780s Pitt and Stanhope had had a very sour relationship and in the late 1790s Pitt actively sought to help his cousins escape from Stanhope's household at Chevening. His prosecution of Stanhope's secretary could not escape a certain air of personal grudge and the fact that his prosecution had failed must have left him smarting. Joyce had been in one sense at least a pawn in a game of combatorial chess conducted between two public and very powerful figures related by close aristocratic family ties. Pitt had clearly won the game on the grand scale, but in the affair of Joyce he had lost an important personal skirmish. Joyce was placed in the middle of this family feud but unfortunately there are no substantial clues on which to base an account of his sentiment. It would be a fair surmise however, that when Pitt's name came into conversation, Joyce would have been able to indulge in one of those internal feelings of personal gratification gained from the experience of having cheated death. Whilst Joyce had very little power of any sort, his experience of having dodged the deadly thrusts of a powerful adversary must have left him with a certain personal cachet.

From Political to General Education

The educational writings of John Locke offered a theory and mechanics of the understanding that had 'practically biblical status' for educationalists of the late eighteenth century.[5] It is clear that most dissenters were highly influenced by Locke and the leading Unitarian, Joseph Priestley, combined much of Locke's thought with the associationist psychology of David Hartley to produce a vision of liberal education designed to serve the interests of rational religion and new forms of commerce and industry.[6] Through inculcation of appropriate habits, childhood development could be directed to produce good citizens able to thrive in the new economic conditions.

The ideas of Locke and Hartley presented Joyce with a pedagogical framework with which to form children's morals and practical skills and thereby influence the future development of society. Joyce's educational project never completely lost its radical and dissenting agenda and he used the psychology of Locke and Hartley both as a model for child development and as an explanation for the causes of social injustice. What he viewed as the shortcomings of society he explained, in Lockean terms, as being due to the 'habits and character' formed by current social and political arrangements acting to produce uniformly unthinking men.

> The prescriptions of civil authority universally act as barriers to the improvement of the Arts and which produce a uniformity of habit and character [which] tends to lower the

---

5 Pickering, S.F. (1981), *John Locke and Children's Books in Eighteenth Century England*, University of Tennessee, Knoxville, p. 9.
6 Watts, R. (1983), 'Joseph Priestley and Education', *Enlightenment & Dissent*, 2, pp. 83–100, p. 83 and 100.

man to the level of brutal instinct, rather than raise him higher in the scale of intelligent creation.[7]

Nearly all Joyce's works were educational and, particularly after 1800, concerned with education that extended knowledge to new and expanding audiences that included readers from a variety of social origins. Yet his sentiments of educational gradualism were neither immediately nor directly targeted at the lower orders – who were quite obviously not in a position to buy his books. Joyce's educational gradualism was not proto-socialist. Rather, he adopted a position of intellectual and theological paternalism which supported a vision of general social development pursued by the upper and middle classes that would gradually trickle down and raise the level of understanding of the whole of God's creation. His vision was not shared by more conservative thinkers, who saw any extension of education as a dangerous threat to the social order. Therefore, whilst not directly political in the sense that his distribution of the radical literature of political education had been, Joyce's gradualist educational vision retained the radical political goal of extending reason and learning to all levels of society.

---

[7] Shepherd, W., Carpenter, L. and Joyce, J. (1815), *Systematic Education*, Longmans, London, p. 6.

Chapter 8
Life and Death, 1795 – 1816

Stanhope's Unhappy Household, 1795 – 1800

The deliberate silence surrounding Joyce's life is both loud and profound. The fact that Lord Holland removed large sections of the Stanhope papers and Stanhope's widow ordered that many of her own were to be burnt on her death has meant that very little can be gleaned about the details of Joyce's roles and actions in the Stanhope household.

After the Treason Trials Joyce spent much more of his time out of the metropolis at Stanhope's country residence at Chevening, Kent. Stanhope provided him with a servant and built him a house in the grounds 'not a bow shot from the house' which possessed a library 'five yards square'.[1] He occupied a position of considerable privilege and was invited to share the company of aristocratic visitors to Chevening – a fact that struck Joyce's friend William Shepherd as amusing, as he recorded the spectacle of Joyce 'an acquitted felon' in discussion with the high government official Sir Isaac Heird, Garter King-at-Arms.[2] Francis Webbe, MP for Taunton and Order of the Garter, was at the same meeting and was a lifelong friend.[3] Webbe later accompanied Frances Jackson, Minister to Berlin, to the negotiations of the Peace of Amiens in 1801 and wrote Joyce a lengthy description of the layout and workings of the French National Assembly.[4]

In 1796 Joyce married Elizabeth Harding (1776–1847) whom Shepherd described as 'a handsome woman'.[5] Elizabeth, who was thirteen years younger than Joyce, was niece of the celebrated Captain Fagg, who provided relief at the siege of Gibraltar by audaciously sailing through the Spanish blockade. The Fagg family had formerly been wealthy but had lost the greater part of its fortune in the South Sea Bubble.[6] Elizabeth's own parents were tallow chandlers in London and Joyce may have encountered Elizabeth through his brother Joshua who was also a tallow chandler. Their first child, Hannah, was born in 1797 and with mother and daughter through the dangerous events of childbirth, equipped with a good livelihood and a comfortable position at Chevening and with the social respect gained from having

---

1   Ridyard, H. pp. 65/6.
2   Ibid., p. 68.
3   Shepherd MSS. Vol. 3, No. 165. Hannah compiled the Shepherd Manuscripts and wrote a foreword to a letter from Francis Webbe to Joyce 1 Dec. 1801.
4   Ibid.
5   Shepherd MSS Shepherd to Mrs Shepherd 8 July 1797 Vol. 4, No. 6.
6   Shepherd MSS. Vol. 10, No. 89. Helen Joyce to Hannah Ridyard, Lowestoft 1856.

been in the public eye and being seen to have acted with principle and integrity, it is a reasonable to assume that Joyce began to enjoy his new young family.

Unfortunately the Stanhope household was not a happy one. All Stanhope's children became increasingly disgruntled at Chevening (although there is no indication that this unhappiness was due in any way to Joyce), and all left between 1796 and 1802. Lucy and Grizelda left in 1796, Hester in 1800, Mahon in 1801 and Charles and James in 1802. Stanhope had insisted that all the children were taught at home and refused his male children's requests to be sent to Eton – standard for aristocratic boys – where they would receive the sort of education befitting their social station. This angered the children who later complained of having had their early years wasted.[7]

Joyce himself left in November 1799 for reasons later described by his daughter Hannah as 'motives of high honour', although there is no explicit account.[8] All the children sought the aid and support of their Uncle Pitt and this might be part of the explanation for Joyce's departure. Pitt was particularly active in settling the daughters of his sister – arranging good positions for the husbands of Grizelda and Lucy and he was especially close to Hester, who came to live in his household for several periods in and after 1800 until his death.[9] Lucy, Grizelda and Hester continually and successfully sought Pitt's financial assistance and on Pitt's death they received government pensions – a fact that must have later galled Joyce who had sought to expose such practices as unjust.[10] Pitt also helped to arrange the 'escapes' from Chevening of the three boys. His interference, which Joyce as the children's tutor might have been better positioned to observe than Stanhope himself would have been, might well be the 'motives of high honour' Joyce's daughter alluded to. Pitt had interfered powerfully in Joyce's life in the past and Joyce would have been unlikely to take kindly to his further clandestine manipulations in respect of his charges. It seems likely that the difficulties and unhappiness of the situation in which Joyce was powerless eventually urged his departure.

There is no evidence that the children deflected any of the difficulties they had with their education or the unhappy relations between their father and their uncle, on to Joyce. Indeed there is considerable evidence that there was a strong affection between them as Joyce dedicated a number of his books to Charles and James in which they appear as characters. He maintained his friendship with Hester, whose coming-out party was also the celebration of Joyce's release from the Tower.[11] When Mahon escaped from Chevening in 1801, Joyce lent him 'a substantial sum

---

7 Hughes, J. G. (1960), *Queen of the desert: The Story of Lady Hester Stanhope*, Macmillan, London, p. 18; Ghita Stanhope, p. 239.

8 Shepherd MSS, Vol. 3, No. 179. Letter, Hester Stanhope to Joyce 8 May 180?.

9 Ghita Stanhope, pp. 239–243: Erhman, J. *The Younger Pitt*, p. 545.

10 Ghita Stanhope, 190.

11 Haslip, J. (1934) *Lady Hester Stanhope*, Cobden Sanderson, London, p. 11.

of money' which was never repaid – an oversight for which Hester never forgave her brother.[12]

There is also no evidence to show how the children's mother and step-mother – Louisa Grenville – thought about Joyce. Her relationship with her step children grew increasingly difficult from when she married Stanhope in 1780 and her relationship with her own children, particularly after they left Chevening fared little better. Her marriage was not a very happy affair and Stanhope family tradition has it that it was 'no love match'.[13] Whatever she thought about Joyce she left no record. The same silence comes from Stanhope himself, although he clearly felt to some extent beholden to Joyce, who had suffered the consequence of his and Pitt's mutual antagonism. A year after Joyce had left Stanhope's employment, he wrote to Stanhope expressing his anxiety about losing his sight. In this one surviving record of direct communication between the two, Stanhope assured him that in the worst event he would support him.[14]

After 1795 when Stanhope left the Lords, he threw himself into his scientific work making the main drawing-room at Chevening an experimental laboratory and working on a range of projects including the development of his printing press and the process of stereotyping. He liaised with Robert Fulton in his canal-building projects, and continued his work on the ambi-vessel which was a boat with two bows.[15] There is no record of Joyce being directly involved with any of these projects, but he must have been aware of them and he would later refer to Stanhope's electrical experiments in many of his works.

Stanhope clearly supported Joyce in his political and literary endeavours, although the sense in which Stanhope was Joyce's 'patron', is complex. It is important to distinguish the Hanoverian political notion of patronage, in which royal ministers managed parliament on behalf of the King, from the high cultural or artistic notion of patronage, in which a wealthy supporter sponsors an artist, writer, explorer or architect in the pursuit of their endeavours. This later version of patronage is difficult to fit to Joyce and Stanhope as Joyce wrote abridgements of other writers' texts which became textbooks for students – hardly high culture. Yet both aspects of patronage are present in Joyce's relationship with the aristocratic Stanhope. On the one hand the relationship was one of political patronage: Joyce acted as Stanhope's political agent in the early 1790s, and helped to further Stanhope's political goals of educational gradualism through the later 1790s. As such, Joyce did 'Stanhope's business' in the same way royal ministers did 'The King's business'. On the other hand the relationship was one of artistic patronage in that Joyce was supported to produce works that were a product of Joyce's own concerns and literary skills.

---

12 Shepherd MSS, Vol. 3, No 179. Hester Stanhope to Joyce. Hannah's explanatory note.
13 Ghita Stanhope, p. 186.
14 Shepherd MSS. Vol. 3, No. 293 Stanhope to Joyce Letter 24 Mar. 1801.
15 Ghita Stanhope, pp. 164–186.

1800 – 1808: life as an author and literary sub-contractor

While working for Stanhope, Joyce retained his connection with Essex Street Unitarian Chapel. From 1793 when Theophilus Lindsey retired from the ministry and John Disney took over, until 1804 when Thomas Belsham became Minister, Joyce was 'afternoon preacher' at Essex Street when he would take the less popular afternoon services.[16] Immediately after the Treason Trials he was much sought-after and preached at Hackney and Carter-Lane meetings.[17] In quite a short period however – possibly a mere matter of months – the Unitarian community became apprehensive and embarrassed about Joyce's reputation as an 'acquitted felon' and a pro-French radical. As a result Joyce's public profile became limited to arenas in which his name did not invite negative press. His close friend Theophilus Lindsey tried hard, but failed, to find a ministry for Joyce at Shrewsbury in 1799 due to fears concerning 'the Newgate affair'.[18] Joyce's reputation was sealed – he was now too tainted with radicalism for acceptance as a public leader of the general Unitarian community.

On 11 November 1799 Lindsey wrote to John Rowe the minister at Shrewsbury, informing him that Joyce had rented a house from Mr Travers of Hackney at a 'high rent' and that he had undertaken the education of two of Travers's sons at £50 a year. Lindsey was clearly sorry that he had been unable to obtain a ministry for Joyce but he was sure Joyce would be able to secure 'an honourable subsistence in the great metropolis' and that he would 'attract other boys'.[19] Unable to obtain a full ministerial position until 1815 and without independent means, Joyce's profession as an educator and a tutor was one of the few viable methods open to him of supporting his family.

Joyce's economic status is difficult to estimate although having worked for Stanhope for ten years earning at least 200 guineas a year, he may have been able to accumulate some savings. He must have either had some capital or been able to secure advanced payment for literary commissions because he soon dropped his teaching work. In these new circumstances teaching would have occupied much more of his time and energy than it had done in the aristocratic household of Lord Stanhope and therefore left him with a lot less time in which to write; in 1800 he determined to maintain his family 'from the pen'.[20] For the next fifteen years he was one of relatively few writers who made a living solely from their literary endeavours without the benefit of inherited family money.

---

16 Wilson, W. (1810), *The History and Antiquities of Dissenting Churches and Meeting Houses in London, Westminster and Southwark*, For the Author, Vol. 3, p. 490.

17 Joyce, *Appendix*, p. 24.

18 Manchester, John Rylands Library: Unitarian College MSS, Lindsey to John Rowe, Oct. 5 1799.

19 MCO, *Autograph Letters of Theophilus Lindsey*, Vol. 3 (1785–1800) No. B2.17. Lindsey to Rowe, 11 Nov. 1799.

20 Shepherd MSS. Vol. 10, No. 89. Letter from Helen Joyce to Hannah Ridyard (nee Joyce) Lowerstoft 1856. The letter was largely 'dictated by our mother'.

In January 1801 he moved to 13 Gloucester Place in Camden Town where he remained until 1808. It was here that he became a regular visitor to his near neighbour and fellow radical, the philosopher and, by the time Joyce knew him, thoroughly atheist William Godwin. The two had many things in common. They had been taught by the same tutors – Andrew Kippis and Abraham Rees at Hackney College – they were both heavily influenced by the philosophies of Priestley, Price and Hartley, and they had both aspired to, and failed to find, ministries.[21] Godwin had been present throughout the Treason Trials and was close friends with one of Joyce's fellow accused – the dramatist Thomas Holcroft. He knew many of Joyce's Unitarian and radical friends and, most importantly, they shared the same publishers for many of their works – Joseph Johnson and Richard Phillips. Godwin's minimal diary entries show that between 1799 and 1808 when Joyce moved away to Hackney, they met regularly – sometimes two and three times a week especially when mutual visitors were in town. They dined together, took their families to eat and spend afternoons and evenings together and regularly went together to visit friends and publishers.

It is striking that despite their extensive list of mutual friends, virtually none of the many historians who have trawled the sources relating to Godwin, to the London literary circles surrounding Charles and Mary Lamb and Henry Crabb Robinson and to the highly influential Romantics, and despite considerable publishing and social links, record any mention of Joyce at all. The reason, I believe, is one of literary judgement. Joyce wrote largely non fiction works of science education and he is often referred to in bibliographical notices as a science textbook writer. This is a genre that was and is, simply not recognised as having any literary merit. As a result Joyce the man, Joyce the writer, Joyce the political activist and Joyce the Unitarian has been passed over as uninteresting.

The literary snobbery that has informed many literary judgements is particularly poignant when applied to books aimed at children, over whom the middle and upper classes assumed a sense of moral guardianship. In some circles the popular works Joyce produced were considered a low form of literature and categorised as merely didactic. The disdain that many literary intellectuals felt for instructional works was mainly due to the lack of literary characterisation and the central role that science and factual information played in them. The nominal Unitarian Charles Lamb's famous comment to Samuel Taylor Coleridge criticised the kind of factual and instructional reading represented by Mrs Baulbauld's *Evenings at Home* (1792–6) which Joyce took as his starting point for the *Scientific Dialogues*:

> Science has succeeded to poetry no less in the little walks of children than with men. Is there no possibility of averting this sore evil? Think what you would have been now, if instead of being fed with tales and old wives fables in childhood you had been crammed with geography and natural history?. Damn them – I mean the cursed Baulbauld crew, those Blights and Blasts of all that is human in man and child.[22]

---

21 Marshall, P. (1984), *William Godwin*, Yale University Press, London.

22 Lucas, E. V. (1935), *The Letters of Charles & Mary Lamb*, Vol. 1, p. 326; John Aikin & Anna Letitia Barbauld, *Evenings at Home ; or the Juvenile Budget Opened, Consisting*

Lamb's comment rings with the Romantic sentiment that elevated the imagination as the natural source and means of valuable learning. From such a perspective Joyce's trade in writing instructional books was considered as a low form of literary activity and served to distance him from Unitarians whose social credentials engaged them in the world of polite society.

Following Mary Wollstonecraft's death and through the years 1798 – 1802 Godwin's literary and political reputation had been constantly under attack in the press and his financial situation was very difficult. Yet Godwin, like Joyce, needed to provide for a growing family and turned to writing and producing material for the children's market. Like Joyce, Godwin's reputation as a radical did him no favours when it came to selling books and, like Joyce, he wrote many works under pseudonyms. Godwin's minimal diary entries tell us very little but they do show that in 1804 in particular Joyce and Godwin were exchanging manuscripts and clearly working together on a mutual project. For instance on 23 June the Joyce family called on the Godwins. On 7 July Godwin met Joyce. On 19 and 27 July Godwin went to Joyce's house with manuscripts and advanced him some money and on 19 October Godwin called to collect a manuscript. What the project was it is impossible to determine, but as Joyce was a jobbing writer, it may well have been one of many commissions he was working on at that time.

Throughout the first decade of the nineteenth century Joyce was hard-pressed for money and it was only in the last few years of his life that he began to gain some financial success through book sales and copyright revenue. The years 1800 – 08 were fairly gruelling and he had to take commissioned work from both individual publishers and publisher congers. He had to work extremely hard especially in the years 1806 – 09 when he was engaged in a large number of literary enterprises. A combination of fatigue and 'an attack of the Typhus fever' in 1807 brought ill health from which he 'never fully recovered'.[23]

1808 – 1816

Very little survives to tell us anything about Joyce's life in this period and most of what does comes from the minimal obituary notices following his death. We know he had an operation in 1813 from which he expected 'the very worst issue'.[24] Some reports record that Joyce had six children yet notices of only four have been found and of those four very few details remain: Hannah who became housekeeper to Joyce's close friend William Shepherd, Helen who married a minister from Lowestoft, Charles who lived at 4 Porchester Place, Paddington and William who later started the successful shipbuilding firm of Joyce and Co. of Moorgate Street, London.

---

of a Variety of Miscellaneous Pieces for the Instruction and Amusement of Youth (Johnson, 1792–6).

23 *Imperial Dictionary*, Joyce entry.

24 MCO, Shepherd MSS. Vol. 10, No. 89. Helen to Hannah Joyce; Aspland 'Memoir of Joyce', p. 703.

In 1808 Joyce had moved his family to 4 Holly Terrace, Highgate, a property owned by the family of Sir Francis Burdett. In Highgate – a village that was at that point clearly separated from the central conurbation of the city – Joyce was a lot less likely to interact with other writers and members of the publishing world. His works had achieved a moderate status and he was able to work on projects with a slightly more leisurely pace and with less of a necessity to be visible and operating in the business 'in town'.

For about 18 months in 1814 – 15 Joyce acted as mathematical tutor at Robert Aspland's Unitarian Academy in Hackney, set up 'for popular rather than learned ministers'.[25] According to Aspland, he gave up the post, 'only in consequence of his being engaged in a manner the most flattering to him, to superintend the education of the younger branches of a noble family'.[26] Despite considerable searching, the identity of this 'noble family' has not been found, but the appointment didn't take him away from home so he must have either taught the children at his house or at a place sufficiently nearby for him to return home relatively easily.

He eventually secured a ministry although not at one of the high profile meetings such as Hackney, Essex Street or Salter's Hall, but in the relatively small meeting – the Rosslyn Hill Chapel in Hampstead.[27] Almost nothing is known about Joyce's ministry except that he succeeded Rochemont Barbauld, husband of the children's writer Mrs Barbauld (nee Aikin), and there is some evidence of the Joyce family establishing connections with the group of literary families living in the area, as Joyce's daughter Hannah's correspondence with the writer and playwright Joanna Baillie reveals a substantial friendship.[28]

The year 1816 was a bad one for the Joyces. Both Joyce's mother Hannah and his brother Joshua died only a few months before he did. On the night of Friday 21 June 1816, Joyce returned home, 'complained of a stomach pain and laid down on the sofa and a few minutes later died'.[29] His will, written in 1813 just prior to an operation, mentions some 'Jewels', 'plate' and a quantity of furniture including 'two eighteen inch Globes', some 'mathematical and philosophical instruments', which he directed to be passed on to his descendants, and an unspecified amount of 'money securities' due to him from the 'Equitable Insurance office'.[30] Whatever the extent of Joyce's capital, it was insufficient to provide a significant inheritance and

---

25 Gordan, p. 330.
26 Aspland, 'Memoir of Joyce', p. 703.
27 Shore, H. (1914), *The Meeting House on Red Lion Hill and Rosslyn Chapel, Hampstead*, Priory Press, London, p. 32.
28 Rodgers, B. (1958), *Georgian Chronicles*, Methuen, London, Letter, Susan Aikin to Catherine Aikin (nd), pp. 268/9: MCO Shepherd Papers, Vol. 11, numerous letters between Hannah Joyce and Joanna Baillie.
29 Thomas Jervis, 'Obituary notice of Jeremiah Joyce', *Monthly Repository*, 11, Aug. 1816, p. 434/5.
30 PRO, Ref. Prob 11/1582, signed 26 Aug. 1813 and proved 15 July 1816.

his friend J.T. Rutt lamented to Henry Crabb Robinson that Joyce 'left a large family unprovided for'.[31]

Rutt was visibly shaken when the news of Joyce's death circulated at Robert Aspland's Hackney Meeting on the following Sunday.[32] Writing in June the next year, Rutt traced his thirty-year friendship with Joyce, first meeting him at Hackney College and becoming firm friends with him as a fellow member of the Society for Constitutional Information. Rutt lamented the paucity of biographical notices concerning Joyce and supplied one that recounted Joyce's generosity to the printer Daniel Holt imprisoned in Newgate in 1797 for printing seditious material. Rutt eulogised Joyce's 'consistency of character and conduct as a Christian, laudably engaging in the active duties of a political life'.[33]

Several other members of the Unitarian community wrote notices of Joyce in the *Monthly Repository*. Thomas Jervis, Unitarian minister in Leeds, described Joyce as:

> ..ardent in temper & unsophisticated in principle. He was always solicitous to promote the spread of truth, the love of liberty and the interests of humanity...Distinguished by his attainments in philosophy and general literature, he possessed the happy art of turning his talent to the purposes of general utility.[34]

It fell to Joyce's friend and editor of the *Monthly Repository*, Robert Aspland, to write the substantial memoir that appeared six months after Joyce's death on the front page of the December 1816 issue. Joyce had fulfilled the role of hero for Aspland who, as a boy, had been in the crowds observing Joyce and the state prisoners taking exercise on the Tower ramparts in the summer of 1794. Extolling Joyce's virtues, Aspland recorded Joyce's activities in the Unitarian world and included an account of his notorious involvement in the Treason Trials of 1794. Aspland included a substantial extract from Joyce's own record of his interrogation before the Privy Council which he offered as testimony to the strength and quality of Joyce's character.

> Mr Joyce's conduct before the Privy council was truly admirable: the same unpretending firmness would have characterised him on the scaffold, had Mr. Pitt succeeded in the scheme for his destruction.[35]

Aspland's memoir contains one of the few personal characterisations of Joyce and is worth quoting at length.

> A remarkable plainness of appearance and straightforwardness, and perhaps bluntness of manner, which characterised Mr. Joyce, sometimes led superficial and distant observers to form an erroneous notion of his temper. On a nearer acquaintance they discovered that,

---

31 DWL, Henry Crabb Robinson, *Diaries*, 23 June 1816, Vol. 5, p. 194.
32 Ibid.
33 *Monthly Repository*, Vol. 12, June 1817, p. 357.
34 Thomas Jervis, 'Obituary notice of Jeremiah Joyce'.
35 Aspland, 'Memoir of Joyce', p. 701.

under a somewhat rough exterior there lay all the amiable and virtuous dispositions which qualify a man for friendship and social and domestic happiness. In company Mr. Joyce was unobtrusive and even retiring; yet not so as to abstract himself from his companions, much less so to appear to watch their discourse: His countenance shewed that he took an interest in whatever was the subject of discourse, and he was not backward to take his share in conversation when he could communicate pertinent information, or bear testimony to what he considered to be the truth. The ordinary state of Mr. Joyce's mind was calm and equable; but he was sometimes excited to considerable warmth of feeling, and to a corresponding strength of expression. He displayed his earnestness chiefly when exposing the misrepresentations of sophists and the calumnies of bigots. He was tolerant to all but baseness and hypocrisy.[36]

Aspland acknowledged Joyce's social awkwardness and his sometimes inappropriate and indignant outbursts that contrasted with periods of silence. The 'bluntness of manner' Aspland referred to is explained by the combination of two factors: First, Joyce's lack of social skill in negotiating the refined sentiments of polite and middle class culture from which his own, relatively humble origins, alienated him; and second, from the tradition of candour which Joyce imbibed so heavily through both his dissenting and artisan background and the metropolitan radical circles he moved in as a young man.

It was left to Joyce's friend William Shepherd to write the following lines inscribed on Joyce's headstone standing in Cheshunt Churchyard and printed in the *Monthly Repository*:

> Rev. Jeremiah Joyce: 1816 aged 53 years
> Ye who in solemn contemplation tread
> These precincts sacred to the silent dead
> Pause and with reverence mark the spot where rest
> His cold remains who erst with dauntless breast
> Firm to his countries, and Freedoms cause
> Braved the dread peril of perverted laws
> Though bold, yet gentle, his well cultivated mind
> Glowed with a generous love for humankind
> While friendships, joys expansive and sincere
> The bliss domestic crowned each passing year
> Swift flew the bolt that sped him to the tomb.
> But check the bursting tear that mourns his doom
> The task performed to humble mortals given
> A sudden death's the easiest way to heaven.[37]

---

36 Ibid., p. 703.
37 Cheshunt Churchyard and Monthly Repository, 11, (Oct. 1816), p. 614.

Chapter 9

Joyce in the Unitarian World

Rational Piety

John Seed's picture of Joyce as subject to the vicissitudes of the radical intelligentsia is well observed.[1] In the early part of Joyce's life through the 1780s and early 1790s he was accommodated, even celebrated, within an intellectual climate that permitted links between well-heeled radical intellectuals and aspiring artisans. From the period of the Treason Trials on, however, his notoriety as an 'aquitted felon' touched delicate memories within the middle class Unitarian mindset and invited negative judgements about him. On a more general level, Joyce's eighteenth century intellectual inheritance also began to alienate him from the overall direction of Unitarianism. The years following the French Revolution saw a watershed in British social history and a restructuring of the intellectual climate which, in Unitarian circles, was manifest in the shift from 'the radical and vigorous rationalism of Priestley' to 'the pious utilitarianism of Belsham'.[2] Joyce became to some extent alienated from this progressive movement amongst Unitarians as he retained much of the rational programme of Price and Priestley, and his intellectual disposition was secured steadfastly in an eighteenth century dissenting mindset which demanded political justice and emphasised candour to the point of brutal honesty. As British society responded to the French Revolution and the Napoleonic wars, Joyce's intellectual and theological disposition, which reflected older dissenting traditions, failed to find comfortable lodgings in the emerging version of Unitarianism.

Despite this general historical shift there is nevertheless a strong thread connecting the ideas of Priestley and Belsham and which serves to characterise Joyce's Unitarian style. This is the theme nicely articulated by the historian R.K. Webb in his description of 'rational piety', and was precisely one of the terms used by Robert Aspland, who said of Joyce that 'His character may be summed up in a few words: probity, industry, simplicity, fortitude, benevolence and rational piety'.[3] Joyce lived out the theme of rational piety through his works which were founded on the presupposition of the rationality and intelligibility of God's plan, and the possibility of a reason-based explanation for physical and mental phenomena. At the same time his engagements with the social world were fervently conducted according to the values of Christian

---

[1] John Seed, 'Jeremiah Joyce and the Vicissitudes of the Radical Intelligentsia', *TUHS*, 17, 3 (April 1981), pp 97–108.

[2] Ibid., p. 97.

[3] Webb, 'Rational Piety' in Haakonssen; Aspland, 'Memoir of Joyce', p. 703.

piety. From a Unitarian perspective the combination of rationality and piety in an individual is not a combination of two distinct elements, with rationality leading to a scientific world view and piety leading to Christian morality. Rather, the pursuit and explication of science was considered a pious act, and piety was to be achieved through scientific pursuits. The two elements of rationality and piety were fused together to form both a scientific and a religious engagement with the world.

Rational piety is strongly linked to the educational emphasis in the accolade 'practical preacher', which was the highest praise that could be given to a dissenting minister. Such a minister would be notable for delivering sermons that led the congregation to a wide range of reflections on living a Christian life.[4] Joyce used this accolade to describe the Revd Hugh Worthington whose sermons he praised as 'uniformly practical'.[5] The figure of the practical preacher in Unitarian terms, was created from a blend of pious engagement with God's world, and utility in the service of one's fellow human beings and society as a whole. In the figure of the practical preacher, education provided the link between pious engagement and personal service and was pivotal in the chain of ideas which built the vision of rational dissent. Unable to take a position as a full-time minister, Joyce endeavoured to fulfil the model of rational piety through his work in publishing and Unitarian projects. He attempted to combine rationality as the claimed basis for understanding the world, and piety as the proper form of engagement with life through his role as a science educator.

In Joyce's memoir of Worthington, Joyce saw himself as emulating Worthington in 'guiding the steps of the young into the temple of knowledge' and thought of himself as labouring in the cause of virtue and the promotion of true knowledge. This memoir also contains the following revealing passage in which Joyce is talking about himself as one of Worthington's prodigies:

> If a train of circumstances which, after all, he has no reason to regret or be ashamed of, has deprived him of what he long esteemed, and still regards, as one of the most important and useful stations in life, that of a public teacher of the Christian religion, he cannot reproach himself with any great share of inactivity: if denied the opportunity of labouring in the cause of virtue and the promotion of true knowledge, on the first day of the week, he is teaching by his works, humble as they are, not a few on the other six.[6]

Writing in 1813 after 18 years as a writer, Joyce lamented that he had not obtained a ministership but he clearly saw his Christian ministry as extending beyond the pulpit to his work in the world of education.

---

4   Webb, p. 299.
5   Joyce, J. 'Memoir of Worthington', p. 573.
6   Ibid.

Secretary of the Unitarian Society

Joyce was a tireless worker for the Unitarian Society for the Promotion of Christian Knowledge and Virtue through the Distribution of Books, and he had attended the very first meetings of the Society in 1791. Joyce was on the 1792 committee which met at the shop of the Unitarian publisher Joseph Johnson and which ordered copies of various titles to be revised, corrected and placed on their catalogue.[7] His name disappears from the minimal minutes of the Unitarian Society after 1792 and until April 1802. In that year he became a committee member and took over the office of Secretary from John Kentish. From 1802 the minute book is largely in Joyce's handwriting with brief exceptions corresponding to periods in which he was ill. As the central contact point both for the individual members of the Unitarian Society and for regional Unitarian societies, he had to maintain and manage an extensive network.

Through Joyce the Essex Street Chapel had strong links to the Unitarian Society which was 'committed to vigorous dissemination of Unitarian propaganda' and 'produced a stream of literature to the provinces'.[8] From 1791 to 1804 the Unitarian Society spent £2555 on printing and distributing books.[9] They produced thirteen duodecimo volumes entitled 'Unitarian Tracts' which included works by the leading lights of the Unitarian movement – Joseph Priestley, Theophilus Lindsey, Thomas Belsham, William Frend, and John Disney – and also included writings which Unitarians claimed as consistent with their position – those of Richard Price, Dr. Lardner and Hugh Farmer. The list expanded during the 1790s to embrace books aimed at children and included Mrs. Barbauld's *Hymns for Children* (1st edn, 1781), *Practical Instruction for Youth* [Anon] (1st edn, 1796), and Watts' *Hymns* (1st edn, 1758). The Society minutes record print runs of 3000 of each title. Stocks were first held at the Society's room at no. 89 Chancery lane and then moved to Dean Street in 1803. On 13 May 1802 Joyce was requested to prepare Mason's *Self Knowledge* (1st edn, 1789), for publication and circulation and he reported to the quarterly meeting of the Society on 27 October, held in the New London Tavern, Cheapside, that 2000 had been printed and were to be sold at 1s 3d in boards.[10]

Joyce threw himself into the Society's work. By June that year he had taken an inventory of the stock and at the quarterly meeting was requested to review, with John Kentish, the rules of the Society. Joyce was instrumental in producing the second edition of the Society's *Tracts* (1805), which carry advertisements he signed, and new additions to the catalogue including his own *Analysis of Dr. Paley's Natural*

---

7 Essex St Unitarian Headquarters, Private Archive, Unitarian Society Minute Books, 1792.

8 Ibid., p. 264.

9 Aspland, Robert Brooke (1850), *Memoir of the life, works and Correspondence of Robert Aspland*, Whitfield, London, p. 186.

10 Mason's *Self Knowledge. A Treatise Shewing the Nature and Benefit of that Important Science and the Way to Obtain it* (1st ed., 1745).

Theology (1804).[11] Joyce arranged the sale and distribution of individual copies to members but also bulk sales to the publishers Joseph Johnson and William Vidler, with whom he negotiated levels of commission. In January 1804 the Society awarded Joyce 10 guineas and made him a life member for 'his attention and assiduity in the duties of his office'.[12] Joyce began to receive a small but regular income and at the quarterly meeting of January the following year, he was given a salary of 20 guineas a year backdated to 1804 'for his services'.[13]

Joyce was present at regular monthly meetings at the Dean Street Room with Thomas Belsham and Robert Aspland, who were the new leaders of the Unitarian community. He clearly held the trust of the Society which later allowed him to use the room for teaching some of the students at Aspland's new academy and 'to assist in the instruction of Geometry to young men in his charge' with the full support of the Society in 1813.[14] Joyce resigned the office of Secretary on 29 March 1816 and when his account books were examined the new secretary and Joyce's friend, the Revd Thomas Rees and a committee reported that the accounts were satisfactory and that they could not 'close their report of the examination of Mr. Joyce's account without expressing the high sense they entertain of the value of his long service of this society'.[15]

The Unitarian New Testament

On 11 April 1806 the Unitarian minute books record the setting up of a committee to plan the production of a new version of the New Testament. Joyce was on the committee which included Thomas Belsham, J.T. Rutt and five other Unitarian London ministers. Belsham is reported to have been happy to accept the Archbishop of Armagh's (John Newcome), version was overruled by the committee who insisted on revising it.[16] The five reports of the committee were written up and signed by Joyce and were later published in the *Monthly Repository*.[17]

---

11 The best UK collection of different bindings and editions of these Tracts are to be found in the archives of Manchester College Oxford.

12 Unitarian Society Minute Books 1804. Jan 12.

13 Ibid., 1805. Jan 10. Hugh Farmer, *Essay on Demoniacs of the New Testament* (1st ed., 1775).

14 Unitarian Society Minutes 30 July 1813.

15 Ibid., Feb. 13, 1817. Sp. General Meeting.

16 Gordon, A. (1922), *Addresses Biographical and Historical*, Lindsey Press, London, p. 304.

17 *Monthly Repository*, Jan., Feb., Mar., Dec., 1807 and Feb. 1808. A copy of this new edition held by the DWL has copies of all these reports plus all the copies of the circular letters and the subscription lists to the project, all written and addressed by Joyce and bound at the back – *The New Testament an Improved Version* (London: A Society promoting Christian Knowledge and the practice of virtue, by the distribution of Books, 1808). Cat. No. 2016. D.23.

Since its inception in 1791, the Unitarian Society had intended to publish a new translation of the New Testament in line with the tenets of Unitarian theology and biblical criticism.[18] It had been hoped that the classical scholar Gilbert Wakefield's translation from the Greek would have been available, but due to Wakefield's involvement with a bookseller this became impossible. Consequently the committee decided to use Newcome's English translation as the basis for the new version and 'keep an eye to Mr. Wakefield's Translation'. They determined to omit Newcome's notes in order to keep the new version 'as cheap as possible' and alter the text only where Newcome's judgement was 'misled'. The original plan of how the new version would be constructed is laid out in Joyce's first report circulated to all members of the Unitarian Society:

> In order to facilitate the object of the society, it is proposed to add to the present committee for preparing the improved version, all the Ministers who are members of the Unitarian Society, requesting them to send any remarks or improvements which may occur to them, addressed to the Secretary of the Unitarian Society [Joyce] before Christmas.

The intention was therefore to create a Unitarian version from the views of the Unitarian community at large. This initiative reveals both a democratic concern to include all members but also, at a practical level, a concern to spread the labour and reduce the amount of work required by the London committee. In the event the minute books reveal that only three people did the greatest amount of work – Joyce, Belsham and John Hinckley, about whom very little is known. In the fifth report of the committee of 20 April 1808, after the project was complete and the copy was 'in the printers hands', Joyce reported:

> The committee has to regret, that they have not experienced all the assistance, from persons who are skilled in sacred literature, with which they flattered themselves at the outset of their labours; and which had it been communicated, would have contributed greatly to the improvement of the work.

Joyce was the organising force behind the project. He produced the published reports, circulated them among the Unitarian community and received any written contributions. He also received many of the subscriptions which he forwarded to the Society's treasurer, Ebenezer Johnson. It is unfortunately not possible to ascertain which sections of the text were Joyce's responsibility. Belsham has been credited with 'the admirable introduction and most of the notes', and this is likely given his high standing in the Unitarian community and his reputation as a biblical scholar. However, as a compiler of encyclopaedias and writer of textbooks (discussed in Part Three), Joyce possessed expertise in the compilation of contributions from a range of sources, and given that he was the person to whom such views were directed, it is likely that he had a major hand in constructing the text.

---

18 1st report. 3 Jan 1806. Note 17.

The project was not particularly successful in terms of sales or reprints. It also brought a considerable amount of negative press, and the new version was generally badly received and subsequently used to reproach Unitarians.[19] The Archdeacon of Sarum, Charles Daubeny, was amongst many who objected strongly to the new version and sought to show that 'The Unitarian God of Reason and the Christian God of Revelation cannot both stand on the ground of the same divine word'. Daubeny equated Unitarianism with Mahometism and claimed that Unitarians had 'perverted scripture' which they had 'wrested and tortured for the purpose of making them speak the Unitarian language'.[20]

The project was also unsuccessful as it failed to produce a version that represented Unitarian views. Rather than being a Unitarian version of the New Testament, the end result displayed controversy over biblical interpretation. Figure 6 shows the theological dilemmas over the crucial opening passages of St John's Gospel and presents only a few lines of text and a much longer, dense commentary and interpretation. This pattern continues for the following six pages and the Unitarian version of the passage written by the founder of English Unitarianism, Theophilus Lindsey, appears in the footnotes of the fifth page of the section. Lindsey's alternative version which starts 'In the beginning there was Wisdom, and the Wisdom was with God and God was Wisdom', was a 'sense of the passage approved by Dr. Lardner, Dr Priestley, Mr Wakefield and others'.[21] That the Unitarian interpretation of such an important passage which was sanctioned by the most important Unitarian luminaries, was relegated to the footnotes, shows the nervousness the committee felt in publishing its radical theology.

The issue of whether to provide a properly Unitarian version had been discussed in Unitarian circles and Joyce's third report of the committee of 23 April 1807 reveals how the committee dismissed such a radical project on practical grounds.

> The difficulty and delay attending a completely new version, which some seem to desire, would be very great. Few are qualified, fewer still would have been willing, to undertake the task. And, after all it would have been open to as many cavils, and possibly to as many solid objections as that of the learned prelate.[22]

---

19 Gordon, p. 304.
20 Daubeny, Revd C. (1815), *Some Remarks on the Unitarian Method of Interpreting the Scriptures*, Rivington, London, p. 8.
21 Unitarian *New Testament*, 1808, p. 203.
22 Printed in *Monthly Repository*, Dec. 1807.

THE GOSPEL ACCORDING TO ST. JOHN.

CHAP. I.

THE Word* was in the beginning†, and the Word was 2 with God‡, and the Word was a god§. This *Word* was 3 in the beginning with God ||. All things were done by

---

* *The Word.*] "Jesus is so called because God revealed himself or his word by him." Newcome. The same title is given to Christ, Luke i. 2. For the same reason he is called the Word of life, 1 John i. 1. which passage is so clear and useful a comment upon the proem to the gospel, that it may be proper to cite the whole of it. "That which was *from the beginning*, which we have heard, which we have seen with our eyes, which we have *looked upon*, and our hands have handled of *the Word of life*, for the *Life was manifested*, and we have seen it, and bear witness, and *show* unto you, that eternal *Life* which was *with the Father*, and was manifested unto us, that which we have seen and heard declare we unto you." By a similar metonymy Christ is called the Life, the Light, the Way, the Truth, and the Resurrection. See Cappe's Dissert. vol. i. p. 19.

† *in the beginning.*] Or, from the *first*, i. e. from the commencement of the gospel dispensation, or of the ministry of Christ. This is the usual sense of the word in the writings of this evangelist. John vi. 64, Jesus knew from the beginning, or from the first; ch. xv. 27, ye have been with me from the beginning. See ch. xvi. 14; ii. 24; iii. 11; also 1 John i. 1; ii. 7, 8; 2 John 6, 7. Nor is this sense of the word uncommon in other passages of the New Testament. 2 Thess. ii. 13; Phil. iv. 15; Luke i. 2.

‡ *the Word was with God.*] He withdrew from the world to commune with God, and to receive divine instructions and qualifications previously to his public ministry. As Moses was with God in the mount, Exod. xxxiv. 28, so was Christ in the wilderness, or elsewhere, to be instructed and disciplined for his high and important office. See Cappe, ibid. p. 22.

§ *and the Word was a god.*] "was God," Newcome. Jesus received a commission as a prophet of the Most High, and was invested with extraordinary miraculous powers. But in the Jewish phraseology they were called gods to whom the word of God came, John x. 35. So Moses is declared to be a god to Pharoah. Exod. vii. 1. Some translate the passage, God was the Word. q. d. it was not so properly he that spake to men as God that spake to them by him. Cappe, ibid. See John x. 30, compared with xvii. 8, 11, 16; iii. 34; v. 23; xii. 44. Crellius conjectured that the true reading was Θυ, the Word was God's, q. d. the first teacher of the gospel derived his commission from God. But this conjecture, however plausible, rests upon no authority.

|| *was in the beginning with God.*] Before he entered upon his ministry he was fully instructed, by intercourse with God, in the nature and extent of his commission.

Figure 6: Extract from the Unitarian version of the *New Testament*, 1808.

The difficulty of the task and the considerable theological dilemmas that the committee encountered in producing a version that would effectively represent the theology of the Unitarian community, are expressed in the committee's admission that they should leave Newcombe's version 'even where in their own judgement it might have been altered to advantage, knowing how difficult it is in many cases to give a translation which shall be universally satisfactory'.[23] It would seem that the committee had not envisaged the difficulties of the project and the sensitivity of the issues prior to actually doing the work. As a partial compromise, instead of cutting or substantially changing the translated text the committee employed the unusual technique of italicising sections of the text which they felt 'had doubtful authority'.[24]

A subscription was drawn up, to which 1200 contributions were made mostly from individuals but also from various Unitarian societies. Large contributions were made from the Duke of Grafton, who gave 50 guineas, and the London Unitarian Society which gave £100. John Disney and other wealthy Unitarians gave £10 or £20 but most gave a guinea for which they received either two octavo volumes or four duodecimo volumes. A small pocket edition (18mo) was produced without explanatory notes and sold to members at one guinea for seven copies. As individual subscribers received more than one copy, the intention was, presumably, that the excess copies should be extended to other readers or given as gifts, probably to family members.

The Dissenting Deputies

The production of the new version of the New Testament involved Joyce in an enormous amount of work and brought him into contact with most of the leading Unitarians. He gained a position of sufficient respect amongst the Unitarian community to enable him to summon a special meeting of the Society at the Essex Street Chapel on 30 July 1813 'to discuss the 1813 Act of Relief of persons who impugn the doctrine of the trinity'. The Act was a major landmark in the extension of rights to dissenters and at the meeting tribute was paid to the MP William Smith – a lifelong friend of Stanhope – who had steered the Bill through parliament and was a regular attender at Essex Street Chapel. It was Smith who, as the leader of the Committee of the Protestant dissenting deputies in 1814, achieved full membership of the committee for Essex Street Unitarians. This Committee had formerly only recognised orthodox dissenters as members although it substantially reflected the grievances and demands of Unitarians.[25] It was Smith who inspired *A Sketch of the History and Proceedings of the Deputies appointed to protect the civil rights of Protestant Dissenters* (Samuel Burton, 1813), that in 1811 the committee

---

23 Second edition of the fourth report 29 January 1808. Note 17.
24 Unitarian *New Testament*, p. 2 fn.
25 Davis, R. (1971), *Dissent in Politics* 1780–1830, Epworth, London, p. 199.

commissioned Joyce to compile.[26] Connected to Smith and having steered the new Unitarian version of the New Testament to completion and having established a reputation as a compiler of encyclopaedias, Joyce was an obvious choice and the *Sketch* is typical of Joyce's literary work and style which built a text from a number of sources. Joyce assembled the *Sketch* from the minutes of the Committee, from previous abstracts from the minutes and from previous committee statements, and produced a chronicle of the defence of dissenters over an eighty-year period beginning in 1732. The work is a form of mild dissenting propaganda and served as a practical reminder of the disadvantages under which dissenters lived and of the value of combined action. Yet Joyce is not credited for the work on the title page or throughout the book, and the omission of his name, once again, probably indicates the concern to distance respectable dissenters from political radicalism through the associations of Joyce's past.

Joyce had won the respect of many Unitarians by his efforts to develop Unitarianism by promoting Christian knowledge through gradual extension of understanding resulting from the distribution of books. Joyce's last published sermon in 1816 (discussed below) was dedicated to the Unitarian Society, which he saw as concerned to spread rational religion and develop the condition of mankind. He listed the authors of works that the Society felt illustrated the 'foundation of their holy religion' as 'a Locke, a Hartley, a Paley and a Priestley.'.[27] The list reflects the major co-ordinates of Joyce's Unitarian thinking – a metaphysics of understanding from Locke, a mechanism of learning from Hartley, a natural theology from Paley and scientific experimentalism and biblical criticism from Priestley.

Writing in the *Monthly Repository*

Under the editorship of Robert Aspland, the *Monthly Repository* was a literary and religious periodical that did not pay its contributors.[28] Joyce could not afford the time to write many unpaid contributions, but a significant number of entries did carry Joyce's name. He wrote obituary notices of the radical Unitarian publisher, Joseph Johnson and the transported Thomas Palmer, an extensive memoir of the Arian preacher Hugh Worthington, all the reports of the committee to produce a new version of the New Testament in the section entitled 'Religion, Literary and politico-religious Intelligence', many reports and notices of the meetings and dinners of the Unitarian Society, as well as a substantial 13-essay series on natural theology and several other short notices.

Using the pseudonyms A.B. and A.L. Joyce also contributed a large number of largely biographical notices recording the deaths of, and responding to queries

---

26 Manning, B. (1952), *The Protestant Dissenting Deputies*, Cambridge University Press, p. 14.

27 Joyce, J., *A Discourse*, 1816, For the Author, London, p. 26.

28 Mineka, F. (1944), *The Dissidence of Dissent*, University of North Carolina Press, p. 111 and p. 127.

concerning, various Unitarians and General Baptists, many of whom were members of the thriving General Baptist (at that time largely Unitarian), meetings in Ditchling and Lewes, Sussex, where Joyce had given sermons.[29] Joyce's contributions as A.B. were not solely obituary notices and he made several contributions to the Biblical Criticism section and gave notices of books. One such notice was his account of an anonymous work, entitled 'Liberty and Necessity' and signed 'a Necissitarian Deist', which he attributed to one William Corry.[30] This is one of the few places where Joyce reveals his views on the doctrine of philosophical necessity – a subject of intense debate in the pages of the *Monthly Repository*. Corry had supported the deist Anthony Collins against the criticisms of Samuel Clarke from whom Joyce and many Unitarians claimed much of their theological heritage. Joyce thought that Corry's version of the doctrine of Necessity was 'incompatible with Christianity', 'profane', led to 'mischievous consequences' and denied the possibility of an 'afterlife'. Yet Joyce also thought Corry's book was 'not without cleverness'.[31]

One of the few occasions when Joyce was given a highly visible and respectable place in the Unitarian world was when he contributed a substantial series of essays on natural theology beginning January 1815. The series was aimed at both 'young persons' and 'those further advanced in life who perhaps may from circumstances not necessary to be enumerated, have hitherto paid little or almost no attention to the wisdom and contrivance displayed in the works of the almighty'.[32]

The series opens with an anticipatory defence of natural theology by presenting the argument against natural theology that 'the great disadvantage of the subject is its extreme simplicity and the vast multiplicity of obvious and decisive evidences that may be found for its illustration'. Joyce recognised that both the banal simplicity and ubiquitous application of the design argument might weigh against its acceptance. He mounted a fairly sophisticated defence that avoided taking on the arguments of David Hume directly and was formulated on three grounds. First, that anybody who deploys reason cannot 'possibly doubt that there are abundant marks of design in the universe'; second, that the ancient sceptics 'had nothing to set up against a designing deity but the doctrine of chance and the combination of a chaos of atoms in endless motion' which Joyce debunked as ridiculous and easily refuted by other ancients who 'could appeal to the order and symmetry that pervaded the whole of nature'; and third, by reference to the works of James Beattie former professor of moral philosophy at Aberdeen who developed the argument of the irrationality of the idea of society being 'produced by the accidental blowing of winds and rolling of sands'. Joyce's defence was typical of the position of natural theologians – the sheer weight of evidence of design and the ridiculousness of any contrary view meant that any other explanation ran counter to common sense.

---

29 The source for Joyce's pseudonyms in the *Monthly Repository* is Aspland R. p. 192fn: Joyce gave a Sermon at Ditchling 19 Sept. 1808 – *Monthly Repository*, 3, pp. 651/2.

30 I have been unable to locate this work.

31 *Monthly Repository* 3 (Jan 1808), p. 12.

32 *Monthly Repository* Mar. 1815, p. 35.

Joyce used the literary strategy that he used in many of his writings and counterpoised both the sense of immense and infinite space of the universe, and the minutiae of anatomy as combined evidence of the deity. He constantly combined and merged images of the precision arrangement of planetary orbitals with 'the intelligence and variety and delicacy of animal mechanism'. Tracing natural theology from Cicero and Galen, Joyce outlined the lineage of ideas through 'a Ray, a Derham and a Paley'. The effect of the study of natural theology, he argued, was to produce 'a feeling of pious and almost enthusiastic glory of gratitude towards its author and supporter'. Joyce's Unitarian vision and inculcation of piety was twinned with his educational gradualist goal of the diffusion of knowledge, which presented knowledge within a pedagogic formula:

> ..at the head of each article [the series of essays to follow], to give a brief, but accurate and scientific description of the subject to be discussed. By this method of procedure, we trust, that while we are inculcating the principles of piety, we shall, at the same time be diffusing amongst our youthful readers, a certain portion of natural knowledge with which, in this enlightened period, no person claiming the advantages of education, should be unacquainted.

The series of lectures examined the five senses. When describing the eye, he discusses its anatomy, and the optical mechanisms of vision which he described as designed to suit the physics of optics in different environmental conditions. The opening and closing of the eyelids to permit varying levels of light is 'an admirable provision for those animals, as the cat, squirrel &c that have occasion to waylay their prey both by day and night'. In essay four the emphasis is on how the eye 'surpasses the contrivances of art in the complexity, subtlety, and curiosity of the mechanism', but examines the telescope as one of 'the most perfect productions of human ingenuity' and characterises both the eye and the telescope as 'instruments'. Using a fairly standard suite of rhetorical, persuasive and polemical devices Joyce appealed directly to the testimony of Nature and undermined any alternative explanation. His argument was conducted in the same way that a lawyer might prosecute an imagined atheist.

Essays five and six concern the senses of smell, taste, hearing and feeling. Essays seven, eight and nine were concerned with 'the mechanical arrangement of the human body' with essay eight considering 'the trunk' and essay nine 'the superior and inferior extremities', and dedicated 'to show how the systems of the human body fall into the most compact and convenient form'. In yet another proof of design Joyce compares the human frame with a man-made machine.

> If the animal structure be contemplated in this light, and compared with any other machine in which human art has exerted its utmost skill, it will be evident that intelligence and power have been exerted in its formation surpassing anything to which human wisdom can pretend.

Essay ten considers the 'posture of the human body: the muscles' but essay eleven appears not to have been printed. Essay twelve printed in January 1816, is on 'the Brain and the nerves' and essay thirteen printed in April 1816, is entitled 'Of the face, Complexion and speech. Joyce's text moves very quickly from discussing the minutiae of anatomy, to social and political subjects that he tried to encompass with the same claims of providence and design. For example, in a discussion of different human species, Joyce introduced the subject of slavery which he opposed on the basis of its 'violation of the eternal principles of justice and the sacred rights of humanity', and he saw 'the diversities of the human race as merely varieties of the same species produced by natural causes.' His liberal vision embraced what he saw as 'pliancy of nature' as 'favourable to the increase and extension of mankind and to the cultivation and settlement of the earth and was optimistic in predicting 'feelings of a common nature and a common interest'.

Editing the *Imperial Review*

The short-lived *Imperial Review or London and Dublin Literary Journal* was published by Cadell and Davies in London and a number of Irish publishers in Dublin, Cork and Belfast from January 1804 to December 1805.[33] It was printed by Luke Hansard, the printer of government proceedings, but the editors, throughout all 23 issues signed themselves simply 'the editors'. Confirmation that Joyce was one of these editors comes from two sources: first, a letter from Cadell and Davies to the 'Conductors of the Imperial Review' which was addressed to Joyce's friend and fellow Unitarian William Shepherd in which Joyce is named as one of the editors, and to which Joyce replies; and second, in a letter from the Quaker William Rathbone to Joyce regarding a review of Rathbone's *Narrative of Events in Ireland among the Quakers* (1786) which appears in the *Imperial Review*.[34]

The prospectus in the *Imperial Review*'s first issue of January 1804 outlines the motive for publication:

> The Metropolis of Ireland, a part of the United Kingdom, which has given birth to a fair proportion of literary eminence, is still in want of its "review". The present undertaking, it is hoped, will supply that want, as well as tend to strengthen the literary connection between the Sister Islands.

Part of the connection with Ireland was the proximity of William Shepherd in the port of Liverpool, which was the main conduit of trade and passage between England and Ireland. However, in substance the *Review*'s claimed motivation to strengthen

---

33 Sullivan, A. (1983), *British Literary Magazines: The Romantic Age* 1789–1836 Greenwood, London, pp 189–191; *Imperial Review* English Literary periodicals (Michigan: Ann Arbor, 1972), E.196, reel 1.

34 Shepherd MSS, Vol. 10, No. 19. Bundle of papers including Joyce's response. Letter from Cadell and Davies dated 11 April 1804. University of Liverpool Rathbone Collection. Letterbook, ref. RP II.1.168. Rathbone to Joyce, 20 Jan., 1805.

literary connections wasn't realised since it failed to carry extensive Irish or Irish-related contributions. The main contents were reviews of classical authors, weighty scientific treatises and the works of prominent dissenters placed in subsections on Antiquities, Biography, Chemistry, Medicine and Surgery, Classical Literature and Theology. The works of William Godwin, Thomas Malthus, Joseph Priestley and many more were given lengthy reviews by anonymous reviewers probably including Joyce. The introduction to the first issue claims justification for the 'art of criticism' from 'maxims of antiquity' and also claims that 'the rules of criticism' were deduced 'from the study of Homer and other Greek writers' and serve as 'principles which have been universally received by the enlightened part of the world as the standard of true taste'.

In their letter to the 'Conductors of the Imperial Review' the Publishers Cadell and Davies suggest that they felt themselves in an awkward position as a result of the anonymity of the editors. Spurred by 'many objections to the reviews' and 'the concerns of a very respectable clergyman', they claimed that the review of John Mason Good's *Life of Dr Geddes*, was unfair and mischievous.[35] They urged the editors to make a statement of their general position. Joyce's draft response was to have been published in the *Review* but failed to appear. Here Joyce gave ground to the particular objection concerning the anonymous review of the *Life of Dr Geddes*, conceding that it was 'insufficiently qualified'. He gave less ground on the general point of the political position of the editors and largely avoided the point by trying to offer acceptable personal credentials and a liberal editorial policy. Such claimed credentials, given Joyce's radical past and the Unitarian position of the editors, were clearly contrived to provide a respectable image which, at one level at least, was simply untrue.

> The Conductors of the Imperial Review are, and always have been, friends to the establishment in church and state, yet they do not on that account mean to exclude from their work, liberal discussion on all topics and from persons in all parties.[36]

The penultimate issue in November 1805 carries a curious review of Joyce's *Scientific Dialogues*. This substantial review covers eight and a half pages and contains large extracts from the *Dialogues* but it also contains a three-page list of quite damning and substantial errors. Whilst the reviewer says that the *Dialogues* are 'useful and elegant' he insists the errors need to be corrected before they can be considered 'an agreeable guide to his [Joyce's] young pupils in the paths of natural philosophy'.[37] The review must have been painful to Joyce and as an editor he must have called heavily on his tradition and belief in candour to publish such critical comments as 'the author's attempt to compare momentum with pressure is founded only on erroneous and superficial conceptions'.[38] Joyce's explanations of liquids, suction, the

---

35 MCO, Shepherd MSS, Vol. 10, No. 19. Cadell and Davies to Joyce.
36 Ibid. Draft of position of the *Imperial Review* signed by Joyce note 34.
37 *Imperial Review* 5 (Nov. 1805), pp. 508–516.
38 Ibid.

wedge, aspects of his section on optics and 'the electric fluid' are damningly shown to be erroneous by a reviewer who must have been very familiar with mechanics and natural philosophy.

It is impossible to determine whether such a negative review prompted the early demise of the periodical, but the end of 1805 was a period in which Joyce had an enormous workload as a compiler of encyclopaedias and as a writer for Richard Phillips. The sheer pressure of work and the need to secure sufficient and immediate income no doubt aided the decision to abandon his career as a periodical editor.

Chapter 10

Respectable Sermons

Courage and Union

In general Joyce maintained a very low political profile for the rest of his life. On two occasions, however, he published sermons with political and social implications. On 9 October 1803 Joyce delivered the highly successful sermon, *Courage and Union in a time of National Danger*, to the Essex Street congregation at a time when his own profile at the chapel was relatively high as the minister John Disney was ill and Joyce was fulfilling many of the duties. The sermon, whose publishing details read 'Published at the desire of several persons who heard it', was a patriotic exhortation to join and support the Volunteer system then being promoted by Addington's ministry in response to the threat of invasion from France. Addington had invited the people to join in March 1803 and 414,000 had joined by December 1803. The system proved very popular because it offered men a way of serving the country with relatively little inconvenience and exempted them from the militia or the army of reserve.

The unnamed title-page poem exhibits the patriotic flavours of the sermon.

> A fairer isle than *Britain* never Sun
> Viewed in his wide career!
> ....It is our home –
> Our *native* isle.
> Face then th' *invading* foe:– disdain to fly:–
> Like *Britons* Conquer, or like *Britons* die.

Joyce's advertisement for the sermon calls for unity and national duty.

> To the friends of freedom, then in Britain, the line of duty is clear and easily defined: – the independence of their country must, above all things be vindicated. Parties of every kind must consolidate themselves into a body, and the motto of every man must be MY COUNTRY, MY COUNTRY.

Using Nehemiah 6 Verse 11 'as an example which calls aloud for the imitation of my countrymen at the present crisis', Joyce asserted in his opening comments that that there was 'no excuse but age and absolute inability for not joining the Volunteer system'. He saw the hostilities as a defensive war necessary to stop Napoleon's expansion. His patriotic call to arms, however, was not simply cast in terms of national identity, it was justified on the basis of a superior British constitution which:

..not withstanding all the defects of our constitution, [had] many invaluable privileges transmitted to us by our forefathers, of which they [the French] could form no idea.

The major privilege Joyce was referring to was the right to trial by jury which he felt was the major distinction between the British state and the French nation which 'cannot comprehend the nature of trial by jury, which of itself is a people's chief bulwark against oppression'. Joyce introduced a minor radical edge to the sermon through his combination of the theme of the hard-won rights of juries reflecting his own political history, but the major thrust of the sermon was a patriotic call to Englishmen. The sermon was flatteringly reviewed In the *Gentleman's Magazine*, the *Monthly Review* and in Vidler's *Universal Theological Magazine* for October 1803 in which the reviewer – possibly Vidler – anticipated a catalogue of potential accusations with which it might have been considered possible to charge Joyce – the acquitted felon.

> No unworthy retraction of opinion, no unmanly incongruity of sentiment and conduct, no base compromise of principle, no courtly adulation of persons of high status, no fulsome incense offered at the shrine of power... Its true praise is that it is decided and unequivocal, honest, manly and consistent throughout; the production of a correct understanding, a benevolent temper, and an upright mind.[1]

Such a patriotic exhortation at a time of crisis was within the limits of respectable pulpit oration and was the only type of overtly political sermon acceptable by the rational dissenting community.[2]

Subserviency of Free Enquiry

On Joyce's resignation as Secretary to the Unitarian Society in March 1816, he delivered a sermon at Essex Street Chapel. The sermon was entitled *On the Subserviency of Free Enquiry and Religious Knowledge, among the Lower Classes of Society to the Prosperity and Permanence of the State*. The Sermon came in the year of the first enquiry into the need for education of the poor of the metropolis and was printed following a subscription which paid for 400 copies. Its title-page extract from Mathew (Chapter 11 verse 5), 'the poor shall have the Gospel preached to them', clearly positions the poor as being administered to by enlightened ministers and re-inforces what appears as the main thrust of the Sermon announced in the title – that free enquiry *should* be subservient to the interests of the state.

Joyce's title does not accurately represent the contents of the sermon, which addresses the issue of benevolence to the poor and attempts to justify a quite radical and egalitarian vision of the future development of society. Joyce bemoans the failure

---

1   Review of Joyce's 'Courage and Union', *Universal Theological Magazine*, 9 (Oct. 1803), pp. 214–216.
2   Webb, 'Rational Piety', p. 289.

and inequalities of ancient civilisation in forthright language and with a pronounced sense of injustice in his opening:

> The splendour of those ancient states was the splendour of the few. The wealth upon which they revelled, and by means of which they indulged in every sensual gratification, it cannot be concealed, was obtained by keeping in a state of ignorance, and even by the oppression of unnumbered thousands, whose condition indeed makes little or no show on the page of history, but whose wretchedness was not the less real because it was disregarded by those in the higher classes of society.

Joyce argues that the reason for the downfall of the ancient civilisations 'long since reduced to the depths of hell', was that they were not 'reared on foundations consisting on more lasting materials'. Greece and Rome would not have fallen if

> ..the principles of immutable justice had been better consulted: and the gaudy splendour and artificial distinctions of the few had given place to the real advantages of the whole.

Here both Unitarian and utilitarian lines of argument mingle in Joyce's account which moves forward to argue that 'state policy and general happiness shall be considered as one and the same principle', and 'the duty of extensive benevolence' should be 'enforced'. Joyce's idealised image of society was that all people have 'one common nature', and that society was intended by God to be an harmonious whole whose nature was a 'social compact: that society was intended to render each one serviceable to his fellow creatures; to connect all as members of one great family'.

The concept of benevolence was to some extent secularised through the eighteenth century and became a central feature of Jeremy Bentham's utilitarianism. Benevolence as a Christian virtue had similarities to benevolence as a personal ethic in the utilitarian programme. Within the mutual scientific outlook of both rational dissent and utilitarianism, benevolence provided a subject of mutual concern and interest. There were strong connections between Benthamite utilitarianism and the Unitarian circles surrounding Robert Aspland, whose *Monthly Repository*, in which Joyce wrote, carried an extract from the conclusion of Bentham's *Fragment on Government* as its front-page motto.[3] Joyce's relationship to the utilitarians, who became known as the 'philosophic radicals', is not well documented, although one of the leading members, Francis Place, wrote to Joyce on at least one occasion.[4]

The utilitarian idea of quantitative benefits to the whole and the Unitarian emphasis on piety are combined in Joyce's *Sermon* through his emphasis on benevolence. The benefits of benevolence to the poor would, according to Joyce, have two greater benefits to the whole. First, 'The quantity of suffering and of ignorance in the world would go down' and second, 'In promoting the happiness and the knowledge of our fellow creatures we are cherishing in our minds the tenderest feelings, which are the

---

3 Mineka, *The Dissidence of Dissent*, p. 101/2.
4 Place Papers. Add MSS 27816. Harvester Microfilm reel 115. Copy of the *Narrative*. F. 97 Letter from Place to Joyce, 30 Jan, 1815.

ornaments of the man and the Christian.' Joyce argued that the Unitarian Society's efforts were directed to these benevolent ends which it sought to achieve through the distribution of books to 'inculcate the rational principles of religion, and the necessity of free enquiry on topics essential to the best interests of man', in order to facilitate 'the spread of rational knowledge among the people [which] will be the stability of that people'.

The vision that Joyce promoted accepts the existence of inequalities but aspires to a gradual development which will be produced after a period of gradual Christian and rational education. He did not aspire to a society based on complete equality but sought to reduce the excessive gap between the extremes of the social hierarchy.

> It cannot be doubted, that so long as there exists a difference in the talents, and a distinction in the capacities of individuals, there must be, as a necessary result, an inequality in the condition of mankind. But it is neither natural nor necessary that there should be such enormous disproportions as we know there are in the situations of individuals belonging to almost every civilised society in the world.

In fact the sermon does not directly discuss the relative positions of free enquiry and the 'Prosperity and permanence of the State' which the title suggests. The discussion reflects a concern with inequalities and produces a mechanism – Christian benevolence – with which to address such inequalities. The requirement for a prosperous state is taken as given and the focus is on how to incorporate all the people into such a state of prosperity and material comfort.

These two sermons show that Joyce was concerned to present himself and his Unitarian perspective as respectable, but that he did not lose his radical impulses or vision altogether. The reminder of the hard-won rights of juries in the 1803 sermon, and the rather stronger egalitarian aspiration of the 1816 sermon, suggest that Joyce, rather than rejecting the revolutionary ideas of the 1790s and retreating to a more conservative perspective, learnt the skills of adaptation, accommodation and compromise.

PART 3
Joyce the Science Writer

Chapter 11
Patronage, Education and Writing

Patronage

Traditional accounts of the history of patronage of literary production in the eighteenth century describe an arrangement in which wealthy noblemen supported the endeavours of inspired writers, and suggest that this relationship began to fall away when the truly modern independent writer appeared around 1750 – particularly with the work of Samuel Johnson. On this account patronage had begun to disappear as a serious feature of literary production by the time Joyce was writing – the main determining feature of literary success or failure had become the new and voracious market-place for books. The early twentieth century literary historian A.S. Collins was one of the most significant proponents of this, account arguing that:

> A man who took to his pen for a living in 1780 gave patronage scarcely a thought. It had outgrown its use, which had been an honourable use when a writer could not maintain himself without a patron. When he could not get a public to support him, because the reading public was too small, it was no shame to be dependent on a patron.[1]

Collins's traditional historiography reflects that most precious value of modernity – financial independence. Such independence and the integrity and status that goes with it, has to be achieved through success in the free market rather than kow-towing to the compromising interests of a patron. Collins's image here is a classic example of whig history that reads the past in terms of the values of the present – or at least the values that Collins imbued and expressed. Notwithstanding this whigishness, Collins's argument does have a clear relevance to Joyce, for whom the late eighteenth century shift to the market was a particularly important historical development. As a Protestant dissenter Joyce valued the independence of mind resulting from economic independence above all other social values. For Joyce, his social respectability and his personal integrity had to be sustained through professional and financial independence and therefore as an aspiring author, his position with Stanhope was heavily compromised – a factor which may well have been important in Joyce's decision to leave the comforts of Chevening for the rigours and dangers of life as a jobbing author in London.

Furthermore, Collins's account does reflect the undeniable influence of commercial reality. The power of the market-place was instrumental in transforming

---

1   Collins, A.S. (1928), *The Profession of Letters, 1780–1832*, Routledge, London, p. 115.

the working relationships of authors and was the most important factor in determining both Joyce's working life and the nature of the books he produced. As is the case for most working people, Joyce was always compromised to the sources of his income and there is a strong sense in which the compromises of Stanhope's patronage were replaced by the compromises of the commercial market-place. The causal factors determining what Joyce produced and to whom it was targeted, were always closely linked to the commercial strategies of his publishers. Indeed the fact that Joyce produced popular science and educational books, which were a fairly low form of cultural production and for which the number of purchasers was growing but was still fairly limited, meant that Joyce was intimately dependant upon, and compromised to, his publisher's skill in developing and exploiting relatively small markets.

In recent years however, Collins's account of patronage has come under increasing challenge and scrutiny. Dustin Griffin argues that the 'golden age' of patronage, in which writers enjoyed handsome pensions and were free to develop their literary pursuits, is largely a myth created by later writers who assumed that the life of previous writers must have been better than their own. Griffin claims that the traditional image of literary patronage is both selective and nostalgic and ignores the complex political and social dimensions of the arrangement. He argues that patronage was always a complex relationship involving both an exchange of goods and services and a cultural economics in which what was at stake was the control of high literary culture. Furthermore, Griffin disputes the simplistic account given by Collins, and elaborates a process of contestation in which patrons, booksellers/publishers and authors, struggled for position and authority in the overlapping cultural economies of patronage and the shifting realities of the market-place. He argues that rather than declining, by the end of the eighteenth century the system of patronage remained strong but had evolved new forms in which societies, book clubs and literary circles assumed greater roles in supporting the arts.[2]

For Griffin, patronage is better understood as having a number of modes and as fulfilling different functions, in different ways, in different contexts. Griffin's account provides a more sophisticated and nuanced set of analytic tools that can be deployed to describe some of the complex features of Joyce's working life, many of which cannot be sufficiently explained with the traditional (Collins) model. Indeed, Joyce's working life reflects precisely the complexity and compromises Griffin appeals to. To some extent Stanhope was Joyce's patron in the sense of a nobleman's support, but this was not the only working relationship between the two – Joyce was also Stanhope's secretary and the tutor to his children. Joyce's involvement in the Society for Constitutional Information, which sponsored the distribution of politically radical material, was a form of patronage and he was therefore, in this sense, himself a patron to Tom Paine and his influential *Rights of Man*. Similarly, Joyce's work in producing and distributing tracts for the Unitarian Society was a way of extending and promoting Unitarian culture – one of the main functions of

---

2 Griffin, D. (1996), *Literary Patronage in England, 1650–1800*, Cambridge University Press, pp. 10/11, p. 277.

patronage. Clearly Joyce was at the same, and at different, times, patronee, patron and engaged in group patronage.

One of the most important developments in literary production at the turn of the eighteenth to the nineteenth century, serving to re-align the relationships of patronage in new directions, was the emergence of powerful group of London based publishers with all of whom Joyce had long and largely fruitful relationships with over a twenty year period – Joseph Johnson, Sir Richard Phillips and the firm of Longmans. Joseph Johnson was generous to a number of struggling writers, and therefore partially acted in the traditional sense of patron. Richard Phillips, whilst clearly a clever entrepreneur who speculated on the basis of a commercial estimation of the market, operated a network of writers and compilers to which he assumed the figure of patron. Similarly, in cultivating their own network of authors, the firm of Longmans adopted some of the features of patronage witnessed most notably in the hosting and provision of their famous literary dinner parties. Clearly, one of the functions of this new breed of publishers was to nurture and encourage writers – whom they would then be able to exploit commercially.

Conflicts between personal intellectual integrity and commercial reality often force compromise in the process of literary production. The context in which Joyce worked was the commercial world of book production which could only generate enough wealth to support a limited number of writers. This fact forced Joyce to adapt his Unitarian aspirations to commercial incentives and the study of Joyce's works clearly reveal these two – Unitarian and commercial – factors in sharp relief. The two pressures however, cannot be considered as expressing a consistently oppositional relationship, as Joyce's Unitarian world view was partly built on the values of commercial entrepeneurship.

Joyce was writing at a time when the patterns of social and intellectual life in Britain, were being profoundly shaken by the after effects of French Revolution and the continuing French wars. In this new climate the nature and promise of education – especially education that could conceivably be extended to low social classes – was a hot and potentially volatile issue. After the Revolution the debate over education began to take new directions.[3] In broad terms, on the one hand radical sentiment, witnessed most provocatively in the writings of Thomas Paine, saw education as promising emancipation and social progress. On the other, conservatives looked in horror at the possible consequences of assisting the people against their rulers. It was against this background of sharply opposing sentiments that the educational systems of the first decades of the nineteenth century were formed. In contrast to France where views on education were divided between secular and religious positions, Britain's educational debate centred on the question of whether or not education should be controlled by the Established Church and much of the debate focused on the introduction of new forms of schooling. Dissenters largely supported the Quaker, Joseph Lancaster, whilst the establishment supported the Anglican Andrew Bell, in

---

3   Barnard, H.C. (1969), *Education and the French Revolution*, Cambridge University Press, p. 246.

what was essentially the same monitorial method. The debate in England therefore was not a debate over whether or not education should have a religious dimension, but who should control it.

The arguments for and against the extension of education to the working classes were complex and heartfelt. Many supporters of the Anglican establishment characterised Lancaster's system as subversive to Christianity and as favouring Unitarianism.[4] Radical writers on education however, developed a range of positions. William Godwin for instance, in contrast to Thomas Paine, argued against a national provision on grounds that it would reflect the interest of the national government and was therefore an evil rather than an emancipatory force.[5] Indeed a large section of the politically radical community accepted Godwin's argument against the direction of learning by any authority.[6]

As schooling increased through 1800–1816, educational materials for use in schools became a more and more important source of income for educational publishers. With all his contacts Joyce was well placed to share in the development of such new learning materials. Yet for many radicals and dissenters, home materials and individual learning offered a more attractive solution.[7] As a result, nearly all Joyce's works, either as he created them or as they were subsequently adapted, responded to the commercial pressure to cater for as many markets as possible and design books for the individual learner and for the use of schools. The duality of their target markets inevitably influenced pedagogical design and presentation of ideas. Joyce's works therefore resulted from a compromise between several factors: political debates over education, the commercial imperative to cater for as many different markets as possible, and Joyce's own pedagogical and dissenting concerns.

What is clear is that despite this debate, or possibly because of it, the market for educational books increased. Several additional factors aided the creation of a market for Joyce's works. The introduction of stronger iron presses began to produce a more efficient printing industry. The presentation of science through popular scientific lectures, particularly at the Royal Institution, served to boost the profile of science in the public imagination. Most importantly, the need for literate workers to manage the industrial production and commercial interests of an expanding capitalist society, stimulated the demand for educational materials. Through the first decade of the nineteenth century, with the high cost of paper serving to price books beyond the pockets of most people in a society suffering the privations of a costly war, the market for books was notable for its increase in variety, rather than its volume of

---

4 Adams, F. (1882), *History of the Elementary School Contest in England*, ed. by Asa Briggs (1972), Harvester Press, Brighton, p. 61.

5 Barnard, p. 235.

6 Johnson, R. (1979), 'Really useful knowledge' in Clarke, J., Critcher, C. and Johnson, R. *Working Class Culture: Studies in History and Theory*, Hutchinson, London, pp. 75–102, p. 95.

7 Simon, B. (1960), *Studies in the History of Education*, Lawrence & Wishart, London, pp. 183–189.

sales.[8] The three main publishers with whom Joyce worked – Joseph Johnson, Sir Richard Phillips, and Thomas Longman – were all involved in the exploitation of the educational market, although their motivations and styles were very different. Indeed their various productions shared in the creation of a more diverse and segmented market in which products covered a wider range of subjects and were increasingly priced to suit different pockets. The range of Joyce's titles is as eclectic as it is voluminous and exhibits some of this variety of his production but also reflects an increasing sophistication in the construction of educational products for different ages and types of readers. He produced science texts, school texts, home texts, geographies, encyclopaedias, and books aimed at different age and social groups. He produced an arithmetic, a set of letters, a system of education, guides to microscopes and telescopes and a description of the trades. He worked on an almanac, a history of the admirals and he provided the commentary on a set of pictoral illustrations of Shakespeare. He covered natural philosophy, including hydrostatics, pneumatics, optics, astronomy, electricity and galvanism. He wrote on natural theology, physiology, anatomy, chemistry, botany, zoology and meteorology.

Joyce was writing at a time when many educational authors compiled rather than composed and wrote on very different subjects.[9] Although some of his writings are wholly original, he borrowed, stole, combined, quoted, abbreviated, used and re-used material that he generally referenced but sometimes didn't. In one sense at least Joyce's literary craft is not dissimilar to that of most writers – most do precisely what Joyce did to lesser or greater extent. Nevertheless Joyce's status and identity as an 'author' is problematic especially in a period when the capacity for writers to operate as financially independent agents, was relatively new. Without independent means, many writers were forced to act as literary proletarians in response to cold commercial logic, and therefore, their products expressed the exigencies of the market-place rather than their own literary aspirations. Herein lies yet another reason why Joyce has been passed over unrecognised by so many different types of historians. The romantic discourse of authorship and creativity which infuses most forms of high culture and serves to differentiate 'valuable' literary products that are genuinely artistic from the 'merely' commercial – a category which includes educational works – is a discourse which specifically excluded the kind of works Joyce produced.

The romantic model of creativity and originality is linked to the notion of the ownership of ideas and poses some difficult questions in respect to Joyce's works which, in large measure, contain other writers' ideas. In legal terms the ownership of ideas is maintained through copyright but a legal definition of copyright in which authors owned the ideas that appeared in the pages of their books, only began to emerge from the mid eighteenth century. The series of legal cases through the eighteenth and nineteenth centuries, which serve to refine copyright legislation,

---

8 Plant, M. (1965), *The English Book Trade*, Allen & Unwin, London, p. 445.

9 Whalley, J. (1974), *Cobwebs to Catch flies, illustrated books for the nursery and schoolroom 1700 – 1900*, Elek, London, p. 114.

progressively constructed copyright as a concept over which authors had some control, rather than as a piece of property held by the owners of the physical books.[10] However, for the kind of works Joyce came to produce – abridgements, compilations, children's books, encyclopaedias and miscellaneous educational works, the concepts of originality and ownership and the copyright law relating such concepts to legal statute, was far from clear. The issue of the status of abridgements had appeared in the case of *Gyles v. Wilcox* (1740), in which the issue was whether or not an abridgement was a new work and whether an abridger was an author. Lord Chancellor Harwicke decided that an abridgement was 'a new work, and that an abridger, whose work required invention, learning and judgement, was an author'.[11] However, the *Gyles v. Wilcox* case was insufficient to clearly define legal statute in all related cases, and in the period Joyce was writing, conflict between authorial and commercial interests relating to abridgements, translations, textbooks and other forms of literary production, could not be resolved through appeal to precedent. It is important to recognise that one of the conceptual foundations of Joyce's works lay in the older tradition of copyright as ownership of the copies of the books themselves. Such a view of copyright favoured publishers rather than authors, and secured their exclusive rights to printing books. It also enabled them to commission publishing speculations in which the writer's personal investment would be in terms of organisation, arrangement and construction rather than an inspirational offering of original ideas. As the case of *Gyles v. Wilcox* shows, there was a tradition of abridgement and compilation which, whilst it may not have fulfilled romantic notions of artistic credibility or fitted the highest canons of literary respectability, was a recognised and partly respectable literary profession.

On a wider literary and philosophical stage, the thorny debate over the ownership of ideas and the production of meaning is highly problematic. Joyce's literary craft clearly influenced the meaning in the books he produced. In addition to his own knowledge of subjects, his craft was to select from sources he thought useful or appropriate to create a work in anticipation of the needs of his audiences and in line with the directives of his publishers. In particular he shaped and presented the information in his books and he linked and positioned ideas in response to the impulses which informed his actions. Whilst nearly all those ideas had a prehistory, he was responsible for them as they appeared on the page.

The books that Joyce and his publishers produced were to a significant extent publishing experiments. They were speculations sometimes based on established genres, but also new products with which they tested, probed and exploited new audiences. Such products did not simply exploit the market for educational books; they shared in its creation. The type of educational works that were produced relied heavily on publishers' estimation of the market and the possibilities of a successful commercial venture. Johnson, a Unitarian and close friend of Priestley, was elderly

---

10 Feather, J. (1994), *Publishing, Piracy and Politics: an Historical study of Copyright in Britain*, Mansell, London, p. 95.

11 Rose, M. (1994), *Authors and Owners*, Harvard University Press, p. 51.

by the time Joyce worked with him. The kind of works Joyce published with Johnson had a sophisticated pedagogy and a literary style that his work with other publishers lacked and were clearly weighted towards upper middle-class readers. With Johnson, Joyce produced works that retained elements of an eighteenth century version of liberal education in which aesthetics and literary style held a high profile. Richard Phillips was a contemporary of Joyce, an entrepreneurial businessman unpopular with the literary intelligentsia as a consequence of his business brutality, who speculated upon and marketed a huge range of cheap didactic works, many of which he commissioned Joyce to write. The works Joyce produced with him were constructed on formulas derived from Phillips's commercial skill and understanding of the market. Joyce was commissioned to produce works, many of which came out under pseudonyms and all of which give the impression of being conceived as a potential financial earner by Phillips, and produced by Joyce the literary sub-contractor. Thomas Norton Longman's firm was growing in size and was one of the first major publishing houses operating with a corporate ethos rather than as an independent publisher. Joyce was employed on the major project of *Nicholson's Dictionary* (1807, discussed below), when he received a monthly wage and he went on to establish a half-profits agreement on other works. The works he produced with Longmans had none of the feeling of literary aspiration of those he produced for Johnson, nor any of the feeling of raw entrepreneurial speculation that Phillips's commissions had. Rather, they were more measured productions that approached more established sectors of the market.

The traditional and dominant model of popularisation sees popular works as carrying less intrinsic worth than works which have come to be seen as the products of more original thinkers.[12] Most of Joyce's works were popular formulations of science, were low priced, were educational, were for children, and were compilations. There have therefore been plenty of reasons why Joyce's works have not been taken as a serious source of study by historical and literary researchers. From the perspective of the dominant model of popularisation, Joyce's works represent cheap commercial profiteering that simply stole and rearranged the ideas produced by more original thinkers. Such a line of analysis inevitably foregrounds profit as the exclusive motivation for the type of work Joyce produced. The drive for financial benefit was clearly the major impetus directing publisher speculations. However, the binary opposition of commercial interest versus genuine knowledge production, which is a conceptual opposition informing many canonic literatures, is an oversimplistic dissection of the trade in educational products. The biographies, the motivations and the perspectives of the publishers, authors, printers and booksellers involved, were far more complex that can be sufficiently explained using the commercial/genuine binary. Furthermore, an important piece of empirical evidence urges taking Joyce's works seriously in the study of science publishing in the early nineteenth century – their extraordinary success. Many of Joyce's works were heavily reprinted, updated

---

12 Hilgartner, S. (1990), 'The dominant view of popularisation: conceptual problems, political uses', *Social Studies of Science*, 20, 519–39.

and edited for over a 60-year period; some titles were printed in the hundreds of thousands and also appear in America, the British Colonies and Europe. Whilst the extent to which a book was printed does not simply equate to its influence or even the extent to which it was read, it does indicate that it was bought in large numbers and took a place in the windows and catalogues of booksellers and the shelves of public and private libraries. If individual acts of reading science are considered quantitatively, Joyce's *Scientific Dialogues*, published from 1800 to 1892, was doubtless more widely read than Newton's extremely hard *Principia* over the same period. Through their presentation of science in the public domain, the kind of works that Joyce produced were instrumental both to the public understanding of science and the cultural values attendant upon science in the nineteenth century.

In the following account of Joyce's works I have endeavoured to reflect each production as a unique project except in cases where such projects were obviously related. My motivation for taking this approach, rather than selecting and exploring key themes and aspects of Joyce's works, is that it explains Joyce's working circumstances and production. The most striking feature of his works is their eclecticism. He had to design a range of books and respond to a variety of publishing directives to produce new products in order to exploit the expanding market place for books. The treatment below endeavours, as far as possible, to provide an account of Joyce's literary production from his perspective as a jobbing author facing a series of new commissions. The treatment aspires to reflect both a sense of progress of Joyce's literary endeavours and an impression of his day-to-day working life.

Joyce was largely a commission and project worker. His eclectic projects, over which he had varying degrees of control, were often running at the same time. He worked on single projects with the publishers H.D. Symonds and Sherwood Neely, about whom very little is known, but by far the largest proportion of his works were published by Johnson, Phillips and Longmans for whom Joyce sometimes worked simultaneously. Despite some periods when Joyce was involved in concurrent projects for all three publishers, in large measure his working life progressed through his relationship with Johnson to Phillips to Longmans. Joyce emerges as a protégé of the Unitarian world to some extent nurtured by Joseph Johnson and under the wing of the radical Whig Lord Stanhope. From 1802 he entered the cut-throat world of commercial speculation with Richard Phillips and towards the end of the decade he found a relative safe home in the no less commercial, but considerably less volatile, successful house of Longman.

Chapter 12

A Literary Apprenticeship

The Case of the Scottish Martyrs

Joyce made one more appearance in front of the public in which he was heavily associated with radical politics. This was his publication of the case of the Scottish Martyrs and their hardships suffered in their transportation to Botany Bay whilst Joyce was in the Tower.

Joyce had many connections with the Scottish Martyrs through the Society for Constitutional Information and the London Corresponding Society, which sent delegates to the first and second general conventions of Scottish reformers in Edinburgh in December 1792 and April 1793. These conventions caught the attention of the authorities and resulted in the arrest and prosecution for sedition of the five 'Martyrs'. Through the Unitarian community Joyce had come to know one of the most prominent of the Martyrs – the Unitarian minister Thomas Fyshe Palmer (1747–1802), sentenced to seven years in Botany Bay by Lord Braxfield in 1793. Joyce, Stanhope, Thomas Hardy (the leader of the London Corresponding Society), and many others in the Unitarian community had supported the Martyrs and campaigned for a re-trial, but the *Surprize* transport carrying convicts and settlers, including Palmer and his fellow Martyrs, sailed from Portsmouth on 2 May 1794 – twelve days before Joyce was himself arrested – arriving six months later in Port Jackson. The journey was very eventful. Palmer, along with Thomas Muir and William Skirving was accused of plotting to murder the ship's Captain Campbell, and had become estranged from another of the Martyrs, Maurice Margarot, whom they felt had been instrumental in creating the charges against them. As a result, throughout the greater part of the journey Palmer and Skirving were confined in a very small cabin and deprived of many of their provisions and the comforts they had paid for. Their treatment was considerably less severe than that meted out to non-paying prisoners accused of plotting against the captain, some of whom were flogged, heavily manacled, chained on deck and given a minimum of biscuits and water.[1]

Joyce had become aware of difficulties on board the *Surprize* as early as January 1795 when he saw a letter from Margarot which was sent from Rio de Janeiro when

---

1 This story is retold in a number of sources including Bewley, C. (1981), *Muir of Huntershill*, Oxford University press; Clune F. (1969), *The Scottish Martyrs*, Angus & Robertson, Sydney; and Baker Smith, L. (1964), 'Thomas Fysche Palmer, From Eton to Botany Bay', *TUHS*, 13, 37 – 68.

the *Surprize* docked there.[2] Over the summer of 1795 Joyce received numerous communications from the Martyrs and he did best to communicate such letters to the public without his own name appearing. Muir's letters appeared in the *Morning Chronicle* of July 1795 addressed to an unnamed 'friend in London' (Joyce).[3] The *Telegraph* reproduced one of Skirving's letters alongside an account of the voyage of the *Surprize* entitled 'Botany Bay' based on papers 'in the possession of a gentleman of this city' [Joyce].[4]

Palmer wrote regularly to his friends in the Unitarian community, including Joyce, who supplied him with a jacket and trousers and sent him books.[5] Palmer sent his full account of the journey to surgeon John White, who in December 1794 was returning to England, with instructions to pass it on to Joyce. Palmer's text reached Joyce in late April 1795 and was jointly signed by Palmer, Muir and Skirving. It recounted their mutual grievances, their denial of the charges against them, the reasons they had fallen out with Margarot and included a letter urging Joyce to publish.[6] It was Palmer's account that was to form the basis of the publication organised, edited and introduced by Joyce – the *Narrative of the Sufferings of T.F.Palmer and W.Skirving during a Voyage to New South Wales, 1794, on board the Surprize Transport* (Cambridge: Lunn, Deighton, Nicholson, 1797).

Joyce set about preparing Palmer's 'case' to present to the public from a number of sources: the letters from the Martyrs, the journal of William Skirving recording the events of the voyage, Palmer's own account and over 60 depositions collected by Palmer, Muir and Skirving from witnesses on board. He also added Stanhope's protest over the original convictions to the Lords on 31 January 1794 (recorded in the Journals of the House of Lords), and a copy of the address of the Society for Constitutional Information to the Martyrs as they waited to sail to Botany Bay.

The publishing details of the *Narrative* reveal a complex story which prevented its publication for eighteen months until December 1796. The printing and publication was done in Cambridge – where Palmer had been a fellow at Queens College before leaving to become a Unitarian minister and where he had a lot of support.[7] The University had expelled him from his fellowship following his conviction in 1793 – an act which outraged many Cambridge intellectuals. All three publishers set to publish the *Narrative* – Lunn, Deighton and Nicholson were respectable Cambridge publishers but in publishing Palmer's account they were making available a potentially dangerous political document for what was probably very little commercial benefit

---

2 McLachlan, H. (1920), *The Letters of Theophilus Lindsey*, Longmans, Manchester 1920, Lindsey to John Rowe, (23 Jan. 1795), p. 96.

3 *Morning Chronicle* (29 July 1795), p. 3.

4 *Telegraph* (13 July 1795), p. 3.

5 Shepherd MSS. Vol. 10, No 13, Palmer to Joyce, 5 May 1796.

6 Joyce, J. (1796), *Narrative*, Letter dated 9 Nov. 1794, Palmer, Muir and Skirving to Joyce.

7 McKitterick, D. (1998), *History of Cambridge University Press*, Vol. 2, Cambridge University Press, pp. 246/7; Gascoigne, J. (1989), *Cambridge in the Age of the Enlightenment*, Cambridge University Press, p. 198.

and which potentially violated the Gagging Acts which prevented the publication of radical material. The text which was prepared by one of the accused in the Treason Trials and reported the views of a transported convict convicted of sedition might well have drawn the attention of the authorities. The actions of this trio of publishers are at least partially explained by their position in Cambridge – a university city which had always maintained and guarded its critical distance from the metropolis. Furthermore, Cambridge was an independent centre of printing and publishing in which some publishers resented the shift from the older traditions of Cambridge as a Whig University to Toryism and were keen to present their opposition at e very opportunity.

The front-page publishing details are extensive and exhaustive, giving printer, publisher and bookseller details. This may have been an anticipatory manoeuvre – if the government chose to prosecute, they would have to charge a lot of people.[8] Benjamin Flower is listed as the printer but he was also a publisher and a newspaper editor. His *Cambridge Intelligencer* was 'the last national organ of intellectual Jacobinism' and published critical and condemnatory blasts against Pitt's government.[9] Flower and Joyce were to have a long relationship starting from May 1795 when Flower reprinted Joyce's *Account* of his arrest and imprisonment.

Joyce justifies the *Narrative* in his preface by saying that Palmer and Skirving had sought to clear their names through the English courts but that 'their last resort is by means of the press' and that it was not his business to comment on the facts but to 'transmit the papers to the press'. The sense in which Joyce prepared Palmer's 'case' to be presented to the judiciary of the public is profound. After a 'note to the reader' by Flower, who apologised for the delay in publishing, Joyce's introduction opens by claiming that the Martyrs' original conviction and sentences were 'cruel and unprecedented' and that 'unnumbered thousands sympathise with them'. His introduction carries the flavours of legal discourse as he presented evidence for each step of his account. The severity of the treatment of the Martyrs is emphasised by an extract from Skirving's log recording the flogging of two girls with the purpose of making them own up to the conspiracy. Stanhope's protest and the Society of Constitutional Information's address is used as evidence of the good standing in which the Martyrs were held and of the injustices done to them. The depositions from which Joyce selected six to appear as appendices, were all from reputable travellers on the *Surprize* – settlers, military personnel and the ship's surgeon – and all supported Palmer's account.

To reproduce such a potentially inflammatory text when the war was going badly, when social conditions were harsh due to a series of bad harvests, when anti-

---

8 For further details of the sequence of publication see John Issitt, 'The life and work of Jeremiah Joyce' unpublished doctoral thesis, The Open University, 2000, pp. 109 – 116.

9 Thompson, E.P. (1969), 'Disenchantment or Default' in O'Brien, C. C. & Vanech, W. D, (eds) (1969), *Power and consciousness*, University of London Press, 1969, pp. 149–182 (p.166); Murphy, M.J. (1977), *Cambridge Newspapers and Opinion 1780–1850*, Oleander, Cambridge, p. 42.

Jacobin feeling was dominant and when Pitt's government was pursuing repressive action against reformers, must have caused all those involved some concern. Yet the *Narrative* was reviewed very favourably in the *Monthly Review* for February 1797, although the reviewer chose not mention the cause of the Martyrs or the political issues at stake and focused on the injustice of their treatment on board ship:

> Such inhumanity (according to the representation here given, of the truth of which we have no suspicion), loudly calls for a strict inquiry and exemplary justice.[10]

The story would figure again in Joyce's life. The only survivor of the four Martyrs who managed to get back to England was Maurice Margarot, with whom the others had felt so aggrieved. In Francis Place's papers in the British Library there are accounts compiled mainly from the records of Joyce's friend Thomas Hardy, which detail Margarot's attempts to clear his name in 1810/11 and repudiate Palmer's account. There are several letters between Joyce and Hardy, which show that Joyce gave a guinea to the subscription raised for Margarot, that he was uncomfortable at his involvement but that he defended the truth of Palmer's account.[11]

The *Analysis* Series

Joyce's first non political publication, *An Analysis of Paley's View of the Evidences of Christianity in Three Parts* (1795) was also published by Benjamin Flower. This was an abridgement of William Paley's original *A View of the Evidences of Christianity* published only one year earlier. Paley's *Evidences* argued that it was reasonable to accept revelation as evidence of the existence of God and as confirming evidence for the design of the natural world. Revelation, he argued, gave natural theology greater certainty and added the assurance of a future state after death. The *Evidences* responded directly to the philosopher David Hume's 1748 essay on *Miracles* which argued that miracles were contrary to universal experience and, since universal experience conferred truth, there were no grounds on which to believe them. The line Paley took was that it was more reasonable to believe the biblical testimony of men who suffered persecution and death than to deny the truth of such accounts.[12]

Joyce's *Analysis* is a condensed version of Paley's original and was intended to exploit the Cambridge student market. Joyce went through Paley's original, cut out what he considered extraneous arguments and presented a condensed and much tighter formulation. He faithfully followed Paley's parts, chapters and sections, and generally followed the sequential presentation of the arguments. Figure 7 comes from the opening lines of the two works under the title 'Preliminary Considerations',

---

10 *Monthly Review*, 24 (Feb. 1797), p. 236.

11 British Library, Place Papers, Add. Manuscripts 27816, ff. 80–82, ff. 97, Add. Manuscripts 27818, n98.

12 Clarke, M.L. (1974), *Paley: Evidences for the Man*, SPCK, London, p. 102.

and shows how Joyce's text is shorter, punchier, more direct, and lays out the bones of the argument.

Joyce was probably commissioned by Flower for the work and it is unsurprising that an enterprising publisher in Cambridge would try to exploit the student market by producing a cheap distillation of the hugely successful Paley's *Evidences*, which had quickly become a student book although it is unclear when it became a set text.[13] Yet in politics Joyce and Paley held quite starkly contrasting positions. In 1793, at the same time that Joyce was involved in publishing and distributing Paine's *Rights of Man* which contained a vision of democratic egalitarianism applicable to the whole of society, Paley had published *Reasons for Contentment Addressed to the Labouring Part of the British Public*, which, whilst projecting a potential future of greater ease for everyone, argued that the labourer could be happier than the wealthy man by being free from the 'heavy anxieties of the rich', and warned against disturbing 'our ancient course'.[14]

Given the apparent political distance between Paley and Joyce, it is tempting to see the radical Joyce, having just escaped the charge of treason, as trying to recover a position of social respectability by publishing a work that flattered a liberal but highly reputable establishment cleric. However, political positions did not necessarily follow theological positions with all radicals on one side, and all establishment figures on the other. In sentiment, Unitarians had many sympathies with liberal Anglicanism and their social positions – Joyce was after all working for an aristocrat – were closer to those of establishment ministers than the labouring poor. Shared perspectives in which both Unitarian and Anglican ministers looked down, albeit with the benevolent motivations of paternalism, upon the 'humble cottager' served to resolve contradictory political positions which could be conveniently overlooked in the interests of a bigger theological issue and the shared authority of didactic preaching. In this sense, the co-ordinates of turn-of-the-century thinking were sufficiently elastic to accommodate a writer who had a reputation both as a political radical and as a writer distilling theological argument for use by one of the established universities.

---

13   Fyfe, A. (1997), 'Paley's Natural Theology', *BJHS*, 30, pp. 321–35, p. 324.

14   Paley, W., *Reasons for Contentment Addressed to the Labouring Part of the British Public*, in Paxton (1838), *Works*, Vol. 3, pp. 287 300, p. 290.

Paley's original (1794)	Joyce's *Analysis* (1795)
I deem it unnecessary to prove that mankind stood in need of a revelation, because I have met with no serious person who thinks that even under Christian Revelation, we have too much light, or any degree of assurance which is superfluous. I desire moreover, **that in judging of Christianity**, it may be remembered that **the question lies between this religion and none: for if the Christian religion be not credible, no one, with whom we have to do will support the pretensions of any other**. Suppose then, the world we live in to have had a Creator: suppose it to appear, from the predominant aim and tendency of the provisions and contrivances observable in the universe, that the Deity, when he formed it, **consulted for the happiness of his sensitive creation**: suppose the disposition which dictated this counsel to continue: **suppose a part of creation to have received faculties from their maker**, by which they are **capable of rendering a moral obedience to his will** and of voluntarily pursuing any end for which he designed them; **suppose the Creator** to **intend** for **these** his **rational and accountable agents, a second state of existence, in which their situation will be regulated by their behaviour in the first state**, by which supposition (and by no other) the objection to the divine government in not putting a difference the good and the bad, and the inconsistency of this confusion with the care and benevolence discoverable in the works of the deity, is done away: suppose it to be of the utmost importance to the subjects of this dispensation to know what is intended for them; that is, **suppose the knowledge of it to be** highly **conducive to the happiness of the species**, a purpose which so many provisions of nature are calculated to promote. Suppose, nevertheless, almost the whole race, either by the imperfection of their faculties, the misfortune of their situation, or by the loss of some prior revelation, to want this knowledge, and not to be likely, without the aid of a new revelation, to attain it. **Under these circumstances, is it** improbable that a **revelation should be made**? Is it incredible that God should interpose for such for such a purpose? Suppose him to design for mankind a future state: is it unlikely that he **should acquaint them with it?**	Without attempting to prove the necessity of a revelation it may be observed that in judging of Christianity, the question lies between this religion and none: for if the Christian religion be not credible, no one, with whom we have to do will support the pretensions of any other. Suppose, then, there be a Creator, who in his works, has consulted the happiness of his sensitive creation;- suppose a part of creation to have received faculties capable of rendering a moral obedience to his will;- suppose the Creator intends for these rational agents, a *second* state of existence, in which their situation will be regulated by their behaviour in the *first*;- suppose the knowledge of it be conducive to the happiness of the species; under these circumstances, is it impossible that revelation should be made to acquaint them with it? Notes. Bolded text appears verbatim in Joyce's text. Paleys' original covered 3 pages with 394 words. Joyce's Analysis covered half a page with 133 words.

Figure 7: Extract from 'Preliminary Considerations' (1794) compared with Joyce's *Analysis* (1795) – the opening sections of Paley's *Evidences*.

Joyce's *Analysis* sold at 3s – much cheaper than the 20s for Paley's original – and was a successful commercial speculation, reaching its ninth edition by 1826, although it is not known whether Joyce or his descendants received any subsequent payment.[15] The market for the *Analysis* was not confined to the Cambridge students and it was published in London and Norwich. Apart from the much lower cost, the *Analysis* may well have appealed to those who wanted an abbreviated version for reasons of ease of understanding, for their children or for the purpose of study. Flower advertised the series of *Analyses* as:

> ..useful not only to persons who do not have the leisure to peruse the original, but to those who have perused them as they contain not merely a copious index, but the substance of the different volumes: they have been found particularly serviceable to students in the Universities.[16]

Flower tried to appeal to as wide a market as possible and as a result the *Analysis* had to compete with a flood of cheap religious literature much of which was produced by the evangelical Hannah More and the Clapham sect and was explicitly designed to combat what was seen as the dangerous implications of Paine's *Rights of Man*.[17] Joyce's *Analysis* however, was not the same type of religious propaganda. Joyce's theology held that the individual had to come to a knowledge of God through the use of reason. In a telling letter to Thomas Belsham in 1808, Joyce's faith in reason is reflected in his fundamental premise that:

> Unitarianism is not the doctrine that can make its way, in the same manner that Methodism is gaining ground: the one can only appeal to the reason and the understanding, the other by dealing out damnation to all around, terrifying thousands to profess a faith in what they know not.[18]

Joyce followed the same recipe of extracting important lines of text and presenting a more economic account of the argument in his *Analysis of Adam Smith's Wealth of Nations* (1797), which was a substantially larger task than the *Evidences*. Flower announced publication in the *Cambridge Intelligencer* of 22 July 1797 and advertised it at 5s in boards. Published throughout the nineteenth century, although having a slightly more restricted market than the *Analysis of the Evidences*, its final edition was one updated eighty years later by Wolfson Emerton in 1877 and reprinted as an aid for Oxford students.

Smith's *Wealth of Nations* was attractive to Unitarians because of his image of the 'invisible hand' of God, his scientific approach and his emphasis on individual

---

15 Peddie, R.A. and Waddington, Q. (1914), *English Catalogue of Books*, Publisher's Circular.

16 Flower, B (1808), *A statement of Facts*, B. Flower, Harlow. Advertisement at the end.

17 Altick, R. (1988), *The English Common Reader*, Ohio State University Press, p. 75 for an account of these.

18 DWL, MSS 12.58.20, Letter, Joyce to Belsham, 2 Dec. 1808

enterprise and profit seeking – which were all consistent with Unitarian intellectual and social dispositions. The *Wealth of Nations* was a highly successful work that reflected many of the economic and social prejudices of the emergent bourgeoisie and abridgement of such a successful text offered Flower and Joyce genuine commercial potential.[19] Flower went on to produce a series of abridgements which included another by Joyce – *An Analysis of Paley's Natural Theology* (1804) based on Paley's original of 1802.

An Eminent Literary Character: Publishing with H.D. Symonds

By the beginning of the nineteenth century Shakespeare studies were recognised as part of high culture in Britain.[20] Numerous writers and publishers exploited the market for Shakespeare and produced a wide range of material notably including Charles Lamb's famous *Tales from Shakespeare* (1807). On 3 August 1800 Benjamin Flower's *Cambridge Intelligencer* carried the following advertisement on its front page:

> The Public are respectfully informed that this day was published at 7s 6d each, Number 1 & 2 of highly finished engravings from Shakespeare's Seven Ages of man... Accompanied with description, historical and entertaining, by AN EMMINENT LITERARY CHARACTER.

The work was published in four monthly numbers, each consisting of two large engraved plates drawn by Thomas Stothard and engraved by William Bromley, and four pages of letter press. The work was published by H.D. Symonds and sold by Flower and two up-market London booksellers – Richardson in the Royal Exchange and Debrett in Piccadilly. The 'Emminent Literary Character' was Jeremiah Joyce.

Stothard took many of his subjects from Shakespeare and many of his Shakespeare drawings were reproduced in different forms.[21] The Seven Ages of Man from Jaques's speech in *As You Like it*, provided a series of studies and engravings had been published and engraved separately by Bromley in 1799. The details of the project to incorporate Joyce's text with Stothard's drawings have not been discovered. It is clear that having just left Stanhope and in need of income, Joyce found that some of his contacts were clearly disposed to both help and use him. The relatively small world of London publishing at the turn of the century may well have brought Joyce into contact with Stothard, whose close friend, William Blake, used to frequent Joseph Johnson's shop, also much frequented by Joyce. The publisher

---

19 Campbell, T.D. (1971), *Adam Smith's Science of Morals*, Allen & Unwin, London, p. 15.

20 Daiches, D. (1974), 'Presenting Shakespeare', in Briggs, A. (ed.) *Essays in the history of Publishing*, Longmans, London, pp. 90/91.

21 Coxhead, A.C. (1906), *Thomas Stothard*, A.H. Bullen, London, p. 94.

Symonds is likely to have had sympathies with Joyce as he had published several political tracts for which he had gone to prison for 'some months'.[22]

Bound together, the plates and text constitute a large coffee-table type book designed for middle and upper class audiences. Joyce's text is littered with quotations from the famous literary figures of Dryden, Spencer, Milton, Ovid and Cicero. However, his ardent scientific tendencies inform his attempts to describe Shakespeare's sevenfold division of the life of man. Of the first 'age', Joyce says:

> It is probable, however, that the pain felt by infants recently born, and which is expressed by their cries, or as Shakespeare describes it, "by their mewling in the nurses arms", is only a corporeal sensation, similar to that experienced by other animals. Mental sensation, is supposed, by most writers on the subject, to commence no sooner than at the end of five or six weeks; for smiles and tears which are the indication of it, and which depend on the action of the mind, are, according to M. Buffon, never seen in children till they are about forty days old: the former originate from the sight and recollection of a known and desirable object; the latter are the consequences of some disagreeable agitation, composed of sympathy and anxiety for one's own welfare.

Joyce cited Buffon as the major authority on human development throughout and Buffon's *Histoire Naturelle* (1749), provided him with sources for many of his other literary endeavours. The *Histoire*'s second and third volumes included a natural historical description of the life of man from infancy to old age, and Joyce's project combined the developmental sequence of Shakespeare's Seven Ages with the developmental sequence laid out by Buffon.

Whenever the extract from Jaques's speech alluded to a physical feature, Joyce took the opportunity to provide a physical and mildly scientific explanation. Joyce describes the infant's 'puking' as being due to nature, which has 'provided against any inconvenience which might otherwise arise from the stomach being overcharged with milk, by making the infant throw up the superfluous quantity'. In similarly natural historical tones, Joyce's exegesis of Shakespeare's third age 'And then, the lover; Sighing like a furnace, with a woeful ballad made to his mistress's eyebrow', focuses on the eyebrow as 'an essential part of beauty', and gives a number of poetical extracts from Horace and Spencer which demonstrate how the anatomical features of the eyebrow, the eyelid and hair, are important in forming beautiful women.

Joyce was not successful at blending high literature and natural history and he produced an awkward text. To readers familiar with Shakespeare and seeking sophisticated stimulation, Joyce's naturalistic and mechanical language describing the sixth age (old age) may well have jarred their sensibilities:

> At this age man's outward form contracts, and every movement of the limbs is performed with difficulty and languor. The circulation of the fluids becomes sluggish and interrupted; perspiration is diminished; the nutritious juices are less abundant, and being rejected by the parts already too dense, they can communicate no fresh supplies.

---

22 Rees, T. (1974), *Reminiscences of Literary London from 1779 to 1853*, Garland, London, p. 63.

Whilst Joyce drew on Buffon as a source for natural historical information with which to generate a scientific account of the development of the physical and thinking faculties of mankind, he considered Buffon's claim that 'the first fifteen years of our existence can be regarded as nothing' as 'exaggerated'. He focused on the importance of the early years, claiming that 'the desire and passions, which exist in the youthful breast are as many checks and disappointments as can be conceived to militate against the pursuits and projects of riper years'. No doubt under the influence of Rousseau's idea that society corrupted the individual, Joyce argued that society deprived children of their natural sense of independence and that their play was disturbed by the requirement for gravity extorted through 'the effect of fear'.

Joyce's conceptual linkage between notions of the relative independence of the human spirit in children and the appropriate pedagogy with which to approach children, is also displayed in his arguments against rote learning. Joyce's explanation of Stothard's depiction of Shakespeare's schoolboy 'creeping like a snail unwilling to go to school' was that the boy's sense of independence was shortly to receive unnatural subjugation. Such subjugation included, Joyce argued, the mistaken methodology of rote-learning, 'which can convey to him no pleasurable idea, and which he would resist if he enjoyed the smallest share of independence'.

In contrast, and using the example of the self education of Queen Elizabeth, Joyce promoted learning by regular and practical engagement with the subject:

> It may, however be doubted whether this method for learning [rote learning], though so long established in our schools, be the best that can be adapted for the purpose. Queen Elizabeth, whose attainments in classical literature were of the first rate, is said never to have taken a grammar into her hand, unless for the sake of declining nouns and verbs, but by translating something every day from Latin and Greek..

John Locke's natural history of the mind, Buffon's *Histoire Naturelle* and Rousseau's concept of the state of nature were influential in fashioning eighteenth century images of humanity.[23] In his natural historical account of Shakespeare's seven ages, Joyce drew on all three sources. The image of human development that Joyce promoted was, however, also one which reflected the position and struggle of rational dissent. For Joyce, human beings are essentially autonomous and independent, yet created on the basis of a rational plan. Their full potential could only be realised by a liberal education and conducive social circumstances.

This was Joyce's only significant attempt at high literature. If he hoped that it would lead to literary honours, he was mistaken. There is no evidence that sales were particularly high or that there were any further editions. Only four copies of the bound work are currently in public or university libraries. As with many of his works, he was not credited by name due to the reputation he had gained from the 1794 Treason Trials and which encouraged the publishers to conceal the fact of his authorship. This is also one of the few texts in which Joyce made no direct mention

---

23 Wood, P. B. (1996), 'The Science of man' in Jardine, N., Secord, J.A. and Spray, E. C. (eds.) *Cultures of Natural History*, Cambridge University Press, pp. 197–210, p. 197.

or allusion to God. Whether the subject matter, the publisher, Stothard or his own understanding of the nature of the project debarred him from mentioning divine providence, without the consistent underpinning of natural theology, his text lacks both clarity of ideas and strength of argument.

Figure 8: Illustration from *Shakespeare's Seven Ages of Man Illustrated* (H.D. Symonds, 1800) Drawn by Thomas Stothard and engraved by William Bromley 1799.

Chapter 13

Learning to Present Science: Publishing with Joseph Johnson

Enfield's *Institutes*

Joyce's contact with Unitarian and radical Joseph Johnson began in the early 1780s when he attended Lindsey's Essex Street Unitarian Chapel, which Johnson had partly sponsored. Johnson, like Joyce, had been a member of the Society for Constitutional Information and was the most obvious first publisher for Joyce.

William Enfield (1741–97) had published *The Institutes of Natural Philosophy Theoretical and Experimental* (1785) through Johnson. Enfield's writings had proven lucrative for Johnson and there had been a long and friendly relationship between the two men and there is some evidence that Johnson sought to help Enfield's widow after Enfield's death by re-issuing some of his works in 1799.[1] This may have been the initial motive to commission Joyce to update the *Institutes* for a new edition. Joyce increased the length of the work by one third, added substantial sections, introduced many new scientific developments and entered a new 24 page section entitled 'Of the Factitious Airs and the First Principles of Chemistry'. Johnson was the most prolific publisher on the subject of factitious airs and the addition of such a section, reflecting the work of Thomas Beddoes and Humphry Davy in the Bristol Pneumatic Institution, may have been Johnson's rather than Joyce's idea.

This new edition was to be the first in a long line of Joyce's works that did not carry his name – as either editor or author. The advertisement for the revised and updated 1799 version is signed 'the editor' and the evidence that it was Joyce comes from two sources. First, Robert Aspland's list of Joyce's publications;[2] second, there is a curious work signed by Joyce and credited to him by the Dr Williams Library, to whom it was donated, entitled *A Short Introduction to Magnetism, Electricity and the First Principles of Chemistry*, whose publishing details are only 'London 1799', but which contains exactly the same sections on Magnetism, Electricity and Chemistry as those which appear in the 1799 edition of Enfield's *Institutes*. Joyce donated a copy of the sheets of these sections in which he made his most significant changes to the *Institutes* for use in Dr Williams's Library which then had them bound.

---

1 Tyson, G.P. (1979), *Joseph Johnson: A liberal publisher*, University of Iowa Press, p. 153.
2 Aspland, 'Memoir of Joyce', p. 704.

One of the most important features of Joyce's update of Enfield is the way which chemistry is dealt. This was a period in which French chemistry – particularly that of Lavoisier – was being negotiated, resisted and absorbed by the chemical research community in Britain. This was the period of the 'chemical revolution' in which Lavoisier's chemistry, which held oxygen and hydrogen as the components of water and types of air as discrete types of gases separated by heat, gained ground over Priestley's theory of phlogiston. In fact Joyce's new chemistry section did not survive long and it was removed from the later 1820 American editions as 'it was found defective' and 'not used in seminaries', no doubt partly due to its adherence to the, by then outdated phlogiston theory.[3] Nevertheless this chemistry section exhibits how two competing scientific theories – Priestley's and Lavoisier's – were presented to young scholars.

In discussing 'inflammable air', which Joyce notes is called 'hydrogenous gas' by the 'French Chemists', Joyce records two explanations for the production of 'inflammable air' from the decomposition of water as it is either passed through an extremely hot metal tube or thrown onto iron 'strongly heated'. Joyce writes:

> It should be noted that the two parties into which chemists are divided do not agree on their theories on these facts: the one, with Dr. Priestley at their head, contends that the air comes from the metal; the other [French Chemists], that it is really a constituent part of the water.

The reader is invited into the controversy rather than being excluded from it and Joyce, ostensibly at least, adopts a neutral position over which is the most persuasive explanation. Similarly, the contrasting ideas of Lavoisier and Priestley are handled together in the section entitled 'Of Dephlogisticated or Vital Air'.

> This air is called, in the nomenclature of Lavoisier, oxygene, or oxigenous gas. It was first discovered by Dr. Priestley on the first of August, 1774 and called by him dephlogisticated air.

In general, however, Joyce relies more on French chemistry throughout and adopts the nomenclature of oxygene and hydrogene, although he introduces Priestley, the senior statesman of the Unitarian movement, where possible always casting him as the world's leading chemical discoverer. Indeed the *Institutes* was dedicated to Priestley with whom Enfield had a long but sometimes difficult relationship due their disagreements about the status of chemistry.[4] Enfield had not included a separate section of his original work. Joyce's addition of a chemical section in his new edition may have addressed what was likely to have been seen by the Unitarian community as a shortcoming at the same time as presenting discoveries made in the sixteen years since the *Institutes* was first published. As well as excluding chemistry, it did

---

3   *Institutes* (1824), Cummings, Hilliard & Co., Boston, p. ix, fn.
4   Schofield, R. (1997) *The Enlightenment of Joseph Priestley*, Pennsylvania State University Press, p. 223.

not contain the new discoveries by Herschel in astronomy, much of Priestley's work, the lesser known work by Delaval on the theory of colour, Cavallo on magnetism and electricity and Blair on achromatic lenses, all of which Joyce included.

Enfield's original is laid out under the system of definitions, propositions, scholia, corollaries and experiments – consistent with Newton's presentation in the *Principia*. Joyce kept this format but was not constrained by it where he felt the need to make changes. Throughout the 1799 edition Joyce presented more tables of information, added more description and more experimental data. For instance, in both the original and the 1799 edition, proposition five of the first section on matter and its properties begins:

> The attribution of cohesion takes place between two solid bodies of the same kind, and the more perfect the contact the greater attraction.

The original then gives a list of demonstrating experiments including:

> 4. Two plates of lead with equal plane surfaces, heated in boiling water, and immediately put together with tallow on their surfaces, will cohere so forcibly as to require a great weight to separate them.

Whereas Joyce has substituted this one sentence with:

> M. Mussenbrock found that the adhesion of polished planes, about two inches in diameter, heated in boiling water, and smeared with grease, required the following weights to separate them.

Then he added a table indicating the weight required to force the two planes apart in the cases of a range of different materials and two temperatures of grease:

	Cold grease	**Hot grease**
Planes of Glass	130 lbs	300 lbs
Brass	150	800
Copper	200	850
Marble	225	600
Silver	150	250
Iron	300	950

Joyce did not select work or findings simply on the grounds that they were contemporary and in this case used the work of Mussenbrock from the 1730s to provide more precise information. In general however, contemporary discoveries were added throughout. To the original section on pneumatics describing the syphon, the syringe, the common pump, the forcing pump, the condenser and the air pump, Joyce added sections on the barometer, the thermometer, the hygrometer, the steam engine and the hydrometer. The section on electricity is heavily updated and contains many more detailed experiments including those of Cavallo and several by Earl

Stanhope. Similarly the section on magnetism is developed considerably and the original's opening definition:

> That mineral substance which is called the loadstone, or Magnet, has the property of attracting iron, and no other body whatever unless it has a mixture of iron.

becomes split into two definitions:

> Definition 1. The Earth contains a mineral substance which attracts iron, steel and all ferruginous substance: this is called a natural magnet.
> Definition 2. The same substance has the power to communicate its properties to all ferruginous bodies: these bodies after having acquired the magnetical properties, are called artificial magnets.

Joyce's modernisation attempted to provide more detailed presentation of scientific knowledge, an account of recent discoveries and more precise and explicit definitions of scientific terms. He tried to explain scientific claims and phenomena and put the subject under discussion into plain language and he tried to give tangible illustrations of phenomena that appeal, where possible, to the likely experience of the reader. In a discussion about the emission of heat when a substance passes from a fluid to an 'aeriform' state, Joyce explains the phenomena in terms of human perspiration:

> Hence perspiration produces a certain degree of cold. Workmen employed on glasshouses, foundries, &c, live in a medium much hotter than their own bodies, the natural temperature of which is equalised by perspiration. Hence all fevers end in perspiration, thereby carrying off the matter of heat.

Through Joyce's update of the *Institutes* and his efforts to modernise, to find interesting ways of engaging his reader and to use accessible language, he developed the skills he would use through the following years.

Scientific Dialogues

Joyce's most famous and successful work is the *Scientific Dialogues Intended for the Instruction and Entertainment of Young People: in which the first Principles of Natural and Experimental Philosophy are fully explained* (Johnson, 1800–03) published until 1892. The *Dialogues* continued the lineage of commercial science books aimed at children that began with John Newbery's *The Newtonian System of Philosophy* (1761). In the popular form of conversations using elements of dramatic and fictional narrative they, presented scientific knowledge in a discourse of entertainment.[5]

---

5 Secord, J. (1981), 'Newton in the Nursery: Tom Telescope and the philosophy of Tops and Balls, 1761–1838' *Hist. Sci.* 23, pp. 127 – 151, p. 129.

The *Scientific Dialogues* maintained their commercial success through the nineteenth century and were edited and updated by 'a gentleman of high scientific reputation' (1821), by Olinthus Gregory (1829), by William Pinnock (1846), by J.W. Griffith (1846), by C.V. Walker (1846), by J.H. Pepper (1861) and by J.A. Smith (1868). The first two volumes on Mechanics and Astronomy were quickly translated into French by Theodore Pierre Bertin and entitled *Le Neuton de la Jeunesse* (1804–5) and all six volumes were translated into French, German and Welsh. They were used as a school book prize for the Calcutta School Book Society (1818) and the Ashburton School book prize scheme (1853); they were heavily published in the American market, became part of the well known Bohn's Scientific Library and moved from being titled *Scientific Dialogues* to *Joyce's Scientific Dialogues*.

The *Dialogues* were enjoyed by the young John Stuart Mill, John Ruskin, and the educationalist Joseph Payne, but were rejected by both the social reformer James Mill and the high church Bishop Heber.[6] The extent of their success in the nineteenth century is revealed by the novelist Wilkie Collins who used Joyce's *Scientific Dialogues* as part of a plot in his novel *No Name* (1862). Wilkie has his con-man Captain Wragge, who is trying to bamboozle a lady devoted to science, develop a cunning plot with his accomplice Magdelen to obtain her affections with 'ready-made science':

> Mind one thing! I have been at Joyce's Scientific Dialogues all the morning: and I am quite serious in meaning to give Mrs. Lecount the full benefit of my studies...Small talk won't succeed with that woman; compliments won't succeed – ready made science may recall the deceased professor, and ready-made science may do. We must establish a code of signals to let you know what I am about. Observe this camp stool. When I shift from my left hand to my right, I am talking Joyce. When I shift it from my right hand to my left, I am talking Wragge.[7]

The six volumes of the *Dialogues* and *The Companion to the Scientific Dialogues* (1807) – a series of questions designed to test students on the contents of the *Dialogues* – were appropriated by new and different reading audiences through the nineteenth century. Initially the individual volumes of the *Dialogues* were sold at 2s 6d each and were therefore quite low-priced books.[8] Nevertheless, for a slim educational book which was one of a series costing 15s in total, the price was not insignificant and restricted sales to the middle classes. Over the course of the nineteenth century its price fell significantly to 2s 6d for all volumes in one making it available to a much wider audience. As part of the expanding market for educational literature,

---

6 John Stuart Mill *Autobiography*, in Laskii, H J. (1924) (ed.), Oxford University Press, p. 14; John Ruskin, (1949), *Praeterita*, Rupert Hart–Davis, London, p. 42; Aldrich, R. (1995), *Schools and Society in Victorian Britain: Joseph Payne and the New World of Education*, Garland, London, p. 201; *The life of Reginald Heber* (1830), Vol. 1, Murray, London, p. 365.

7 Wilkie Collins (1966), *No Name*, Blond, London, p. 283.

8 Eliot, S. (1995) 'Some Trends in British Book Production', in Jordan, J. O. and Patten, R. L, *Literature in the Marketplace*, Cambridge University Press, pp. 19–43, p. 39.

their audience moved from the mainly middle and upper class audiences of 'young people of ten or eleven years of age' targeted in the preface to the original and whose parents were the most likely to purchase the works, to an audience which included older age groups and readers from lower social classes.

What was innovative about the *Dialogues* was that they were produced as six slim and relatively affordable pocket-size (duodecimo), volumes on different scientific subjects. Volume 1 covered mechanics, volume 2 astronomy, volume 3 hydrostatics, volume 4 pneumatics, volume 5 optics and volume 6 magnetism, electricity and galvanism. Many other contemporary works on elementary science covering the same range of subjects were either quarto or octavo, were less portable and did not fit in a child's hands so easily. Considered as a marketing strategy, a series of cheaper volumes offered the dual benefit of increasing sales and turnover, at the same time as enabling the publisher to test the water – if the first volumes were not profitable the project could be abandoned without further cost.[9]

Joyce's opening paragraph presents the *Dialogues* as appropriate material for children after having read the children's book *Evenings at Home* (1792–6), written by Joyce's fellow Unitarians John Aikin and his sister Anna Laetitia Barbauld, with whom Joyce had much contact. *Evenings at Home* was designed to be both entertaining and instructive and consisted of 96 'evenings' which were a selection of dialogues and entertaining stories with practical and moral lessons.[10] The *Scientific Dialogues* was also designed to be read at home, and the upper class setting implied through the voices of a tutor and two pupils confers social authority on the narrative. The pupils names are Charles and James which were the names of Stanhope's two youngest boys, and the second volume of the *Dialogues* is dedicated to Charles who died in the Peninsular campaign. The setting of the *Dialogues* is therefore Joyce's own history – as tutor to an aristocrat's children – and much of the appeal of the *Dialogues* rests on this aristocratic setting. The setting and similarly the characters, are not developed significantly however, but merely act as vehicles for didactic instruction.

The *Dialogues* are not unusual in their choice of subjects and their sections on Mechanics, Astronomy, Hydrostatics, Pneumatics, Optics, Magnetism, Electricity and Galvanism – were the staple of many of the lectures on, introductions to, and institutes of, natural philosophy at the time Joyce was writing. In particular, Joyce clearly modelled the *Dialogues* on William Nicholson's *Introduction to Natural Philosophy* (Johnson, 1782) from which he took the sequence of his subjects and many substantial ideas and examples. His first substantial section follows the presentational sequence of discussing the properties of matter, considering the divisibility of matter and then theories of attraction (gravity). Nicholson had introduced the notion of the infinitely small as a way of considering infinite divisibility and Joyce similarly

---

9   Plant, p. 232.

10 Fyfe, A. (1999), 'How the Squirrel became a Squgg: The Long History of a Children's Book', *Paradigm*, 27, pp. 26–37.

seized on the opportunity to use the imaginative potential of the issue of the infinite divisibility of matter but developed it considerably. The Nicholson reads:

> The animalculae observed in the milt of a cod-fish are so small, that many thousands of them might stand on the point of a needle.

Joyce develops and crafts this image to appeal to a child's imagination whilst invoking the authority of scientists and directing the analogy to a specific end.

> Tutor: Again, it is said by those who have used the most powerful microscopes, and whose accuracy can be relied on, that there are more animals in the milt of a single cod fish, than there are men on the whole earth, and that a single grain of sand is larger that four million of these animals. Now, if it be admitted that these little animals are possessed of organised parts, such as a heart, stomach, muscles, veins, arteires, &c., and that they are possessed of a system of circulating fluids, similar to those found in larger animals, we seem to approach to an idea of the infinite divisibility of matter.

The *Dialogues* express some of the tension between the educational ideas of Rousseau and those of Locke – a tension that defined much of the educational debate in this period at least amongst liberal intellectuals and was essentially a debate about the balance between freedom (Rousseau) and control (Locke) in education and child rearing. Joyce doesn't solve these tensions but his work is an interesting formulation of the compromise between the two positions. In his preface Joyce claimed that 'he is solely indebted for the idea of writing on the subject of Natural Philosophy for the use of children', to the authors of *Practical Education* – Richard Lovell Edgeworth and his daughter Maria. In *Practical Education* Rousseau's notions of the sanctity of the natural virtue and purity of the child, had been rejected in favour of the pedagogical formulations of Locke, Hartley and Priestley and the inculcation of appropriate 'habits'. However, the Edgeworths' sensitivity towards the correct management of external pressures on the child, their concern to avoid corruption of the child, and their focus on the child's 'feeling' in a process of learning in which children have to learn for themselves by direct experience rather than through abstracted discussion, carried distinctly Rousseauean flavours. One of the Edgeworths' most important contributions to educational thinking was their focus on the developmental sequence of children's learning. They focused on play as a way of learning and a means of capturing a child's interest. For instance, for the elementary teaching of chemistry, they recommended that 'chemical toys' be purchased from a 'rational toy shop' in order to develop 'rational recreations'.[11] This concern to engage the child in a process of learning by doing and feeling, is a process that Joyce adopted throughout his educational writings and is exhibited in many of the experiments demonstrated in the *Scientific Dialogues*. That the process should also be constructed as rational and that the objects of play be similarly considered as rational, is consistent with

---

11 Richard Lovell Edgeworth and Maria Edgeworth, *Practical Education* 2 vols (1st edn., Johnson, 1798). Reprinted in facsimile (1974) Garland, New York, Vol. 1, p. 25/6.

Dialogues in Chemistry

On 25 March 1807 Joyce dedicated his *Dialogues in Chemistry intended for the Instruction and Entertainment of Young People In Which The First Principles Of That Science Are Fully Explained. To Which are added Questions And Other Exercises For The Examination Of Pupils* (1807), to the 'learned and eloquent' Sir Humphry Davy. These *Dialogues* were intended as an 'easy and familiar' introduction to Davy's lectures at the Royal Institution.

Davy's lectures were to establish chemistry as a component of polite education. and the popularity of chemistry engendered a considerable market for a variety of merchandise sold to amateur chemical experimentalists.[12] Joyce's *Dialogues in Chemistry* was one of a plethora of chemistry manuals and textbooks aimed at middle class children that also appeared. Jane Marcet's hugely successful elementary *Conversations on Chemistry* designed as a popular exposition of Davy's lectures, was published in the same year (1806), and Samuel Parkes' *Chemical Catechism* (1802) was already firmly established. For older readers, William Nicholson's translations of Chaptal and Fourcroy popularised French chemistry and had been available through the 1790s, and the Scottish writer and chemistry lecturer, Thomas Thomson, published his influential *A System of Chemistry* in 1802. Joyce's fellow Unitarian, the Manchester physician and chemist William Henry, had published his *Epitome of Chemistry* (1801, 2nd ed.), and Joyce positioned his *Dialogues in Chemistry* in relation to such substantial works by advertising them as 'easy and complete introductions to the more elaborate works of Henry, Thomson and others'.

The drama of metropolitan scientific performances at the Royal Institution, combined with the aristocratic setting of the *Dialogues* and the relative novelty of chemical knowledge deliberately formulated for children, built an appealing commercial product. Joyce's presentational and narrative formula was the same as he had used in the *Scientific Dialogues*, in which the voices of Charles and James were contrived to provide a platform for the didactic lessons of the tutor. By 1807 the *Scientific Dialogues* were into their third edition and from a publishing perspective, it was a reasonable speculation to extend the elementary dialogue to capture some of the market for chemistry. 'Dialogues in', like 'conversations on', or 'catechisms', were recognisable brands of elementary texts designed to appeal to potential purchasers.

In the same year that Joyce published *Dialogues in Chemistry* (1807), Humphry Davy announced his discovery of the elements sodium and potassium using his voltaic

---

12 Golinski, J. (1992), *Science as Public Culture*, Cambridge University Press, p. 241; Dolan, B. (2000), 'The Language of Experiment in Chemical Textbooks', in Lundgren, A and Bensaude-Vincent, B. (eds.) *Communicating Chemistry: Textbooks and Their Audiences 1789–1939*, Watson Publishing International, Canton, MA, pp. 141–164.

pile. Joyce included this new discovery in his first edition and heavily emphasised the sense of progress in chemical knowledge. In the opening conversation Joyce presented Thomson's table of simple substances which lists potass and soda as simple, but then immediately introduced Davy's discovery and offers a new list which shows that potass and soda can be decomposed to even simpler substances (potassium and sodium) through removal of oxygen. This was very up-to-date knowledge and Joyce was able to utilise both the exciting discoveries and the authority of Davy as part of the appeal of his text. The use of both Thomson and Davy as authorities on chemistry, despite them presenting different tables of simple substances, was consistent with the accepted practices of textbook authorship in which writers were not expected to support particular versions of contested issues: they were expected to appear as humble compilers of ideas and discoveries.[13] However, Joyce's opening dedication to Davy suggests that he was prepared to support Davy's controversial adoption of the French chemistry of Lavoisier at the expense of the British chemists. The line between the conventions of textbook authorship and enthusiasm for particular scientific views, was easily transgressed and Joyce's choice of what to present as old and what to present as new, whilst justified by the premise of progress, also suggests his preference for French chemistry.

Dialogues on the Microscope

In 1812 Joseph Johnson's successor, Rowland Hunter, published Joyce's *Dialogues on the Microscope intended for the Instruction and Entertainment of Young Persons, Desirous of investigating the minuter parts of creation*. These two small 12 mo volumes continue the dialogue series using the narrative formula of father and his two sons, Charles and James. In contrast to both the *Scientific Dialogues* and *Dialogues in Chemistry*, which only sparingly mention a deity at critical points, the *Dialogues on the Microscope* relentlessly deployed natural theology. Joyce's advertisement is typical in its use of the design argument which appears on nearly every page, and asserts that the microscope

> has opened to our view those hidden recesses of nature, which are at once calculated to excite the attention and reward the industry of persons desirous of inquiring into the works of the almighty, which are the true sources of real knowledge, and are calculated to afford the human intellect abundance of interesting employment.

Joyce made liberal and direct use of Paley's *Natural Theology* (1802), throughout and in his advertisement he also acknowledged his sources as Hooke, Baker, Adams and 'the costly, but interesting volumes of Dr. Shaw'. Joyce argued that the microscope offered a means of observing the works of creation beyond those open to the wise Solomon, and showed that what might 'appear as deformities [such as mould and mildew], actually contained, as it were, whole forests of trees and plants'.

---

13 Golinski, p. 257.

The microscope offered a means of 'investigating the nature, habits and economy, of millions of beings actually existing, and enjoying the happiness in the earth'.

The text covers the use of the microscope to observe creation, the history of the microscope, the mechanics of human vision and the optical principles on which the microscope works. It contains sections on individual microscopes – Withering's microscope, Wilson's pocket microscope and Ellis's single and aquatic microscope. Joyce covered the anatomy of leaves, bones and hair and discusses 'the circulation of the blood' and 'vegetable physiology'. He dwelt on the 'analogy between plants and animals' and had a lengthy section which argued that plants were 'capable of perception and enjoyment' on the grounds that some plants (Joyce uses the examples of the honeysuckle and the water lily), respond to stimuli.

In the first decades of the nineteenth century the doctrine of spontaneous generation was gaining ground despite opposition from many British scientists.[14] For a Unitarian, like Joyce, the doctrine was anathema primarily because it endowed nature with the power of creation and removed the intelligent hand of God; it was therefore an atheistic doctrine. Possibly responding to Erasmus Darwin's famous poem *Zoonomia*, whose particulate theory of evolution was primarily influenced by Buffon, Joyce presented and then dismissed Buffon's theory of organic particles in a telling passage. In discussing 'animalcules', Joyce has Charles set up the controversy:

> **Charles:** Have not some philosophers denied the existence of these animalcules?
> **Father:** They have: Buffon and others have concluded that they are substances not really endowed with life, but that they are something proper to compose a living animal, and these philosophers distinguish them by the name of "organic particles:" and they include in this description almost every animal to be discovered by the naked eye, and even some of those whose motions are evidently perceptible to the naked eye. Buffon observes, that almost all microscopic animals are of the same nature with the moving bodies in infusions of animal and vegetable substances. The eels in paste, &c., are all of the same nature and derived from the same origin.

---

14 Farley, J. (1974), *The Spontaneous Generation Controversy: From Descartes to Oparin*, Johns Hopkins University Press, p. 45.

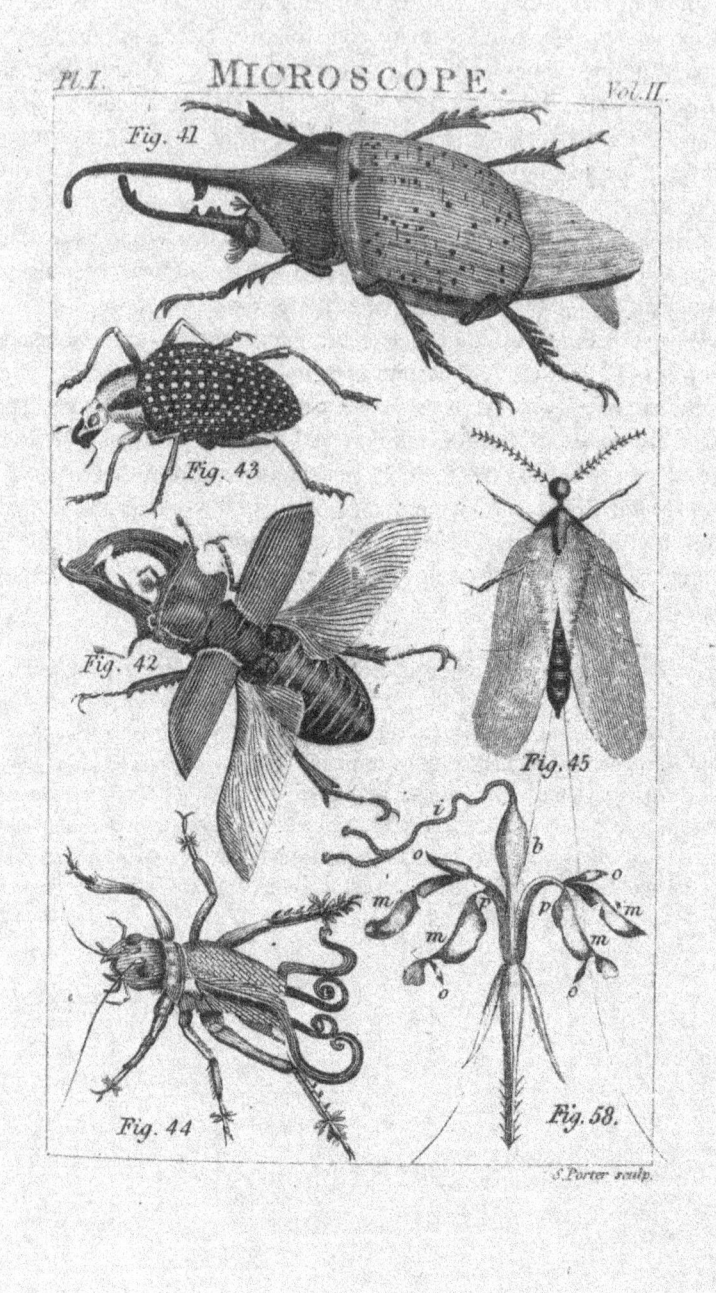

Figure 9: Illustration from Joyce's *Dialogues on the Microscope*, 1812, published by Johnson.

James: How is this opinion refuted?
Father: Most satisfactorily by the experiments of Baker, Ellis, Muller and others. Mr. Baker, for instance has by means of the solar microscope, so magnified eels found in paste, that they appeared each an inch and a half in diameter: they swam up and down very briskly, and even the motion of their intestines was visible. While they were immersed in water, they appeared easy and contented; but when the fluid had nearly evaporated, the little eels died, in apparent agonies, with open mouths as if gasping for that element which was essential for their existence. Which is a clear proof, that they were living animals embued with similar wants and similar feelings to animals of a much larger kind.

James's question assumes the existence of the refutation Joyce proceeds to give and acts as a mechanism through which Joyce can direct his appeal to the design of nature. For Joyce, the Creator has both created the creatures of the world and provided for their vital needs. The image Joyce presents is one of the microscopic world being constructed with the same design and constraints as the visible world in which the hand of God is more clearly seen.

The *Dialogues on the Microscope* had a different commercial and educational appeal from Joyce's other dialogues. Six of the ten plates included were attractive botanical and insect illustrations and part of the target market was the very popular market for illustrated natural history books. Various types of microscope were also illustrated and the book acted as a practical manual for the use of microscopes that might have been given as gifts to children of the wealthy classes. In this project Joyce used his success with the genre of the dialogue and built a natural theology text that possessed substantial commercial appeal, although only one edition of the work was printed, suggesting that it was not particularly successful.

Letters On Natural And Experimental Philosophy

Joyce's *Letters On Natural And Experimental Philosophy Addressed To A Youth Settling In The Metropolis* (1810) was also co-published in a second edition by Johnson's successor Rowland Hunter (1821), and the firm of Baldwin, Cradock and Joy, suggesting that the title was considered to have sufficient commercial potential for both parties.

In Joyce's advertisement to the first edition he said that he had been persuaded to produce the work by his friend 'the late excellent Mr Johnson' despite his initial 'hesitation'. His hesitation, he said, was due to his not wishing to repeat the contents of the *Scientific Dialogues* and *Dialogues in Chemistry*. However, this book was aimed at an older audience than the *Scientific Dialogues* and Johnson may have been speculating on a potential new market. The 'Youths settling in the metropolis' mentioned in the title might have included apprentices from the age of twelve, as well as wealthier young men of up to 21, but Joyce probably had the middle classes in mind as his opening remarks claim that the book is aimed at a youth who 'has lately emerged from a school and who was likely to attend 'the lectures delivered at the Royal'.

The literary contrivance of 'Letters' for the purpose of instruction of young men leaving home and liable to 'the seductions of the world' was well established. Philip Dormer Stanhope, 4th Earl of Chesterfield's, *Letters to his Son* (1744) had achieved by 1810, a publication history of over 60 years and had been adapted, selected from and developed into systems of education by a large number of authors and publishers. Joyce's *Letters On Natural And Experimental Philosophy* contains a series of letters under the headings Mechanics, Hydrostatics, Hydraulics, Pneumatics, Acoustics, Optics, Astronomy, Electricity, Galvanism and Magnetism. His first edition also included letters on Chemistry, Anatomy, Physiology and Botany, but these were 'purposely omitted as not properly belonging to a treatise of this kind' from the second edition in 1821.

Joyce was skilful in using the contrivance of 'Letters' and he composed his introductory letter by deploying several voices. He opens by using his own voice to directly address the youthful reader. He then used an extract from a letter of an imaginary father of the reader, which requested Joyce to 'secure the integrity and virtue of his son' and provide 'full employment for his mind through interesting him in philosophic pursuits and scientific research'. The voice of the father was made to argue that 'Divested of the form of dialogues, they [the *Letters*] will have the advantage of a certain degree of novelty, while at the same time, they will necessarily bring to his recollection all the leading facts contained in the *Scientific Dialogues*. With the project justified by the request of a concerned father, Joyce claimed that he would not 'indulge in any visionary theories' and promised to 'confine myself to principles that are either demonstrable in themselves, or which, having stood the test of examination, are admitted as true'.

The *Letters* was formulated as a self study text with self assessment questions related to each set of letters which were designed to enable the reader 'to examine yourself as to what you have learned from the perusal'. It was the first work published under Joyce's own name to contain an index and to invite the reader to look up particular subjects on the basis of their own interests. Joyce used colourful stories and images to illustrate his points and often developed his account with a sense of fun. In the hydrostatics section he has Archimedes running naked through the streets shouting "Eureka, Eureka". When he discussed Lunardi's first British balloon flight and the descent of Garnerin using a parachute, he rhetorically asked 'how is it possible that a person descending from so great a height should be preserved by a parachute from being dashed to pieces?', before explaining the physical principles of air resistance.

The literary style of the *Letters* is much more discursive than the simpler didactic style of the dialogues and Joyce's own voice has more literary flourish and personal tones. Many of the same images and analogies that appear in the *Scientific Dialogues* were used in the *Letters*. But the *Letters* assumes an older audience and the direct address to the reader with expressions like 'I shall prove to you that it [the world] has two motions', assumes the reader has more power of discernment and judgement. The steps in reasoning are made transparent in the train of ideas and the reader is given many more signals which indicate why the issues are addressed as they are. The introductory letter makes this clear:

> Having explained to you my plan, and laid before you the topics which I mean particularly to engage your attention, I shall, my friend, without further preface, begin with the subject of mechanics. This science which is intimately connected with the arts of life, leads us to enquire into the forces by which bodies, whether animate or inanimate, may be made to act upon one another, and likewise into the means by which these may be increased, so as to overcome such as are more powerful. As introductory to "mechanics" you must be informed of the nature and properties of matter.

Joyce was clearly alive to the role of experimentation in the verification of scientific discoveries and he handled claims made on the basis of experiments with considerable sensitivity. Concerning William Herschel and William Hyde Wollaston's discoveries of 'invisible rays' at the extreme ends of the prismatic spectrum revealed through temperature increases and decreases at positions just beyond the spectrum's visible limits, Joyce judged that 'these experiments though extremely difficult to make, have been repeated and amply verified'. However, the claims based on experiments made by the Marquis Ridolfi and Professor Playfair, concerning the supposed magnetic properties of violet rays, engendered 'great doubts' concerning 'the justness of these experiments which seem, at least, to stand in need of further trial'. Given Joyce's advertisement claim that only established discoveries would be presented, the inclusion of discoveries about which there were 'great doubts', is inconsistent. The decision over what, and what not, to include, could not be made simply on the basis of secure and repeated experimental testing. Contemporary ideas, especially if they were a little fantastical and originating from reputable sources, had to be entertained whilst preserving a healthy degree of scepticism.

In his letters on botany Joyce advocated 'the system of Linnaeus for determining species' and 'the system of Jussieu for determining genus and family'. Joyce thought Jussieu 'a good writer' and his preference for Jussieu's system of determining family and genus based on overall affinities, rather than the simpler and artificial sexual system of Linnaeus, reflected his acceptance of the common idea of a natural series in which the order of the natural world could be shown as a progression from the simple to the complex, in a single chain.[15] The strength of the sexual system of Linnaeus lay in its practical utility, but its failure lay both in grouping together species which were widely disparate in their general characteristics, and in being unable to create natural groupings on the basis of the self evident similarity in the general appearance of many plants.[16] Joyce was clearly aware of the debate concerning natural or artificial systems of classification and the shortcomings of each but he chose not to re-inforce the divisive features of the debate and he promoted a combination of Linnaean and

---

15 Stafleu, F.L. (1971), *Linnaeus and the Linnaeans*, International Association for Plant Taxonomy, Utrecht, p. 328.
16 Oldroyd, D. R. (1980), *Darwinian Impacts*, OU Press, Milton Keynes, p. 19.

Jussian ideas in an progressive vision based on the criterion of utility in the pursuit of scientific knowledge.

> [By] associating these two great authors, we render them truly serviceable to each other, and to the science, whereas by placing them in opposition, as some have indiscreetly done, we only make stumbling blocks of all their defects; for there must be defects in all attempts of the human intellect to keep pace with the infinite wisdom and variety displayed in the works of God.

For Joyce, human society could, indeed necessarily would given God's divine plan, progress and develop. Yet there is no evidence of proto-evolutionary thought in Joyce's writings. Indeed his theological disposition led him to emphasise static and fixed order at all times. He was clearly aware of the existence of acquired and adaptive habits in both animals and plants, but his religious views curtailed any thoughts that challenged the fixity of species. Whilst the efficacy and dominance of the Linnaean system was beginning to weaken by the time Joyce was writing, the theoretical shifts introduced in the field of biology by Lamarck and Cuvier, through the inclusion of a temporal axis along which the natural world developed, are not reflected in his textbooks.

As in all Joyce's texts the design argument is fundamental throughout especially in consideration of astronomy and celestial mechanics. His intention was to pursuade the reader to witness God's handiwork by tracing, scientifically, the fine details of the mechanics of God's design. He illustrated the theory of gravitation in which 'all bodies are drawn to a central point in the earth' and 'the feet of different people on the globe are nearly opposite to one another', and then goes on to explain how 'the deluge, mentioned in the bible has been accounted for'. If the 'point to which bodies naturally tend' were 'shifted ever so little, it would cause immediate overflowing of the lowlands'. By moving the central point 'only two or three miles' it would be sufficient to 'lay the tops of the highest hills under water'. The obvious implication is that this was how God caused the deluge – by shifting the centre of gravity of the earth a minute amount. Joyce's use of science is primarily a reflection of his concern to promote his readers to a religious engagement with the world.

Catechism of Nature for the Use of Children

The Dutch professor of philosophy Johannes Florentius Martinet's *Katechismus der Natuur* (1779), was translated by John Hall in 1790 and became a highly successful title on Johnson's list. The ninth edition, published in 1812, was 'corrected and much enlarged' by Joyce, and the work quickly became known as Joyce's *Catechism of Nature*, reaching its nineteenth edition in 1850.

Natural and revealed religion and the form and substance of scientific knowledge are intimately interwoven in this text directed at children. Joyce's editorial intrusions and significant additions to Martinet's original reflect both his pedagogical style and the appearance of relatively new scientific knowledge considered appropriate for children. The *Catechism of Nature* was a natural theology text which used the religious symbolism of the catechism but instead of catechising through the authority of the church, the *Catechism of Nature* claimed the authority of the natural world. The book of nature, rather than the Bible, was positioned as the source of wonder, learning and witness to God's creation. Martinet's use of 'catechism' in the title, was clearly a religious usage indicating instruction in the knowledge of God. However, the suggestion of a simple doctrinal delivery of information, as in a religious catechism, was inconsistent with the interrogatory educational technology the book actually contained. Martinet organised the work as a series of dialogues and instead of employing the voice of authority to interrogate the student, he used the voice of the anonymous pupil, invested with an endless curiosity, to inform a stream of questions directed to the tutor. The pupil was made to actively interrogate the tutor, whose answers appealed to the natural world and served to reveal the divine hand. The positioning of the voice of the pupil as actively demanding answers to his own questions, was a contrivance consistent with the perspective of Puritanism and many forms of religious dissent, which sought a knowledge of, and relationship with God based on individual acceptance and recognition.

Martinet's original was separated into parts under sub-titles, on, for instance, birds, plants and water. Joyce cleverly changed the organisational structure of the work from separated sets of dialogues under sub-titles, to a continual unnamed but numbered, series of dialogues, but he retained the sense of organisation under topics by moving sub-titles to running headers. This enabled him to add and interject dialogues within a consistently numbered format and avoided the constraints of Martinet's original subdivisions, by then 33 years old.

Joyce also imposed his Unitarian perspective. When the pupil asked whether the stars were created 'only for our use', Joyce followed Martinet's original response that 'it is unreasonable to suppose so on account of their vast distance', but added that the stars were 'probably created for the benefit of other rational creatures'. In the opening dialogue Joyce kept the basic programme of observation and witness to God's natural world set in the context of useful learning and the republic of knowledge.

> Pup. What may I expect from contemplating the works of nature?
> Tut. Both pleasure and profit. As God has formed the eye to behold the beauties of nature, it must be both an agreeable, and useful employment.
> Pup. Is this not confined to the learned?
> Tut. By no means: the peasant as well as the philosopher may partake of this pleasure. A moderate share of knowledge is sufficient. The creation is open to the view of all: it only requires observation.

But Joyce adds to the requirement for observation, the need for 'reflection' on creation. By 'reflection' Joyce intends the pupil to think scientifically. This link between reflection and scientific thinking is neatly made by Joyce in the new dialogues he added on the Linnaean and Wernerian classification systems. Joyce's 25 page addition is introduced in Dialogue 20, 'The Linnaean System'.

> Pup. You said you would give us an account of the Linnaean system of Natural History.
>
> Tut. I did: because I am desirous that you should not only be impressed with the wonders of the natural world as exhibited in the various facts which I have related, but that you should now begin to reflect upon them in a scientific manner, and according to a certain mode of classification.

Joyce does not expand what he meant by 'scientific manner' here, although his text presented it as something different from observation and something that children can learn. Given Joyce's intellectual and theological inheritance, it is reasonable to conclude that Joyce's usage of 'scientific manner' signified the Unitarian requirements for reason in the pursuit of knowledge and called on the grander themes of the Enlightenment which promoted scientific enquiry through a balance of observation and reasoning.

That Joyce should choose to enter Linnaean and Wernerian classification systems in 1812 is not particularly surprising given the dominance both of Linnaean ideas in Britain since the mid eighteenth century, and of Wernerian classification of rocks through the later part of the eighteenth and early nineteenth centuries.[17] Linnaeus's static system of classes, orders and genera offered a way of displaying both the order and the finesse of God's handiwork and appealed to the Unitarian mindset. Werner's ideas in historical geology, however, wandered close to Buffon's introduction of time in theories of biological development which Joyce opposed. The implication of evolution, in contrast to fixed creation, was inherent in the idea of the geological periodisation of rocks. Analysis of the composition of rocks outlined in Werner's *Kurze Klassifikation* (1787), was paralleled in Buffon's *Epoques de la Nature* (1778), which claimed the existence of pre-human periods of earth history. However, as in other places in Joyce's writings where he only selected the ideas of Buffon which he found useful, he selected Werner's mineral classifications system without concern for other aspects of Werner's writings which ran counter to his own vision. Furthermore, mineralogy was beginning to gain a higher profile as it became part of the official curriculum of the universities of Oxford and Cambridge in the second decade of the nineteenth century. Joyce's concern with mineral classification may also have followed the lead of Humphry Davy whose interests in mineralogy were reflected in his Royal Institution lectures and tours to collect specimens.[18]

Joyce introduced the three divisions of the Linnaean system – the animal, vegetable and mineral kingdoms, but the bulk of his 25 page addition is devoted to Zoology. He first introduced the class of Mammalia and described the resemblance that quadrupeds, whales and humans have in giving birth to live offspring which then

---

17 Stafleu, p. 211; Ospovat, A.M. (1969), 'Reflections of A.G. Werner's "Kurze Klassifikation", in C.J, Schneer, (ed.) *Towards a history of Geology*, MIT Press, Cambridge, Mass, pp. 242–256, p. 242.

18 Hartley, Sir H. (1971), *Humphry Davy*, S.R. Publishers Wakefield, p. 44.

suckle. Joyce drew the attention of the pupil to an implication of this classification through the comment that 'it is rather mortifying to have man classed with apes'. He does not develop the point and whilst he has the tutor acknowledge the disturbing implications, he supports the classification in the tutor's response – 'Nevertheless, the resemblance is very striking: in the eye-lashes, hands, feet, fingers, toes, nails, and other parts of the body.'

Joyce then goes on to describe the orders and genera of the 6 classes Mammalia, Birds, Amphibia, Fishes, Insects and Worms and their defining characteristics within the Linnaean system. In the final dialogue – 'The Linnaean system concluded, and the Wernerian system of mineralogy' – Joyce displays Linnaean taxonomy in an interesting comparison between the vegetable world and the human world as example of the class Mammalia:

Vegetables resemble	Man in general
Classes of	Nations of men
Orders of	Tribes or divisions of nations
Genera	Families that compose the tribes
Species	Individuals of which Families consist
Varieties	Individuals under different appearances

Joyce had an eye for novel facts, intriguing observations and sensational stories which he thought would maintain the interest of his audience and secure his pedagogical goals. To compare the organisation of the human world with the organisation of the vegetable world may well have provided an attractive idea to a child, but it also emphasised humanity as part of God's creation. Joyce's concern was constantly to re-inforce the design of God's entire creation and to engage the reader with a sense of wonder at the order consequent upon God's rational plan. The order conferred by the system of classification worked to this end. Joyce presents the Linnaean division of 24 classes of vegetables dependent on the arrangement of parts of the flower in a table containing a neat and clear set of classifications, thereby emphasising the sense of order of God's creation of nature.

Chapter 14

Publishing with Sir Richard Phillips

Joyce's contact with Richard Phillips (1767–1840) probably began through their mutual membership of the Society for Constitutional Information. Both were active members and received and distributed radical tracts.[1] Like Joyce, Phillips suffered a term of imprisonment which was related to the publication of seditious literature and served eighteen months in Leicester gaol for selling *The Rights of Man* in 1793. In the late 1790s and through the first five years of the nineteenth century, Phillips attracted the support of the Unitarian community whose luminaries Joseph Priestley, Joseph Johnson and John Aiken supported his *Monthly Magazine* (1796–1824), which was a major organ of radical criticism. But as Phillips extended his publishing empire and became a Sheriff of London (1807), his reputation fell sharply in literary and liberal circles. Support from the Unitarians was greatly diminished and he lost the friendly rivalry with Joseph Johnson and John Aiken who had edited the *Monthly Magazine* for six years, left in an acrimonious dispute in 1806. Phillips employed many literary figures in his various projects under very harsh financial terms. William Blake, Samuel Taylor Coleridge, Robert Southey, Leigh Hunt and the children's author Dr Wolcot were among the many authors who came to despise him.[2] Wolcot said of him, 'The scoundrel shall never have another line of mine... he would suck the knowledge out of authors skulls and fling the carcasses on the dunghill afterwards'.[3]

There is no evidence to suggest that Joyce had a particularly unhappy relationship with Phillips. Their mutual imprisonment, history of radical activities and lower class origins, may have secured an agreeable working relationship that began on a cash commission basis from 1802 when he wrote the meteorological reports for the *Monthly Magazine*. Much of Phillips's operation concerned with children's books was conducted through Benjamin Tabart's Juvenile Library, which acted as a fashionable metropolitan outlet for many of his educational works.[4] Many of Joyce's titles were sold at Tabart's shop. Several were commissioned by Phillips and published under pseudonyms that functioned as trade or brand names.

---

1 PRO, T.S. 11/962. SCI meeting 29th June 1792.
2 Issitt, J (1998), 'Introducing Sir Richard Phillips', *Paradigm*, 1, 26, pp. 25–29.
3 Dr Wolcot quoted in Redding, C. (1858), *Fifty Years Recollections*, Charles Skeet, London, Vol. ii, p. 259.
4 Moon, M. (1990), *Benjamin Tabart's Juvenile Library*, St Paul's Bibliographies, Winchester, p. 3.

The texts considered below have all been identified as Joyce's works and were on Tabart's lists. Evidence that these titles were composed by Joyce comes from a number of sources. The most important are Robert Aspland's memoir of Joyce, which gives a comprehensive list of Joyce's works, but which has some errors in dating, and the partial memory of Joyce's wife Elizabeth as recorded by Joyce's daughter in a letter to her sister.[5] Supplementary evidence is gleaned from the recollections of Joyce's contemporaries, close study of bibliographical information, advertisements, prefaces and title pages.

Figure 10: A view of Tabart's shop from a plate appearing in *Visits to a Juvenile Library* by Eliza Fenwick, Vol. 1, published by Phillips, 1805.

In the following description of Joyce's titles, Joyce has been identified as author where two sources confirm his authorship and where any available supplementary evidence is consistent. However, it has not always been possible to determine whether Joyce was sole author. Given the concern to keep costs down, it is possible that Phillips acquired an existing, partial or unfinished text which he commissioned Joyce to complete. It is also, in most cases, difficult to determine whether and to what extent projects were collaborative. There is no evidence that Joyce did work with other authors while he worked on Phillips commissions, but given Phillips's large network of authors, the possibility cannot be entirely dismissed.

---

5 Aspland, 'Memoir of Joyce'; MCO, Shepherd MSS. Vol. 10, No. 89. Letter from Helen Joyce to Hannah Ridyard (nee Joyce) Lowerstoft 1856.

Phillips's financial success in publishing educational works was largely due to his production of a range of related products. He would commission an author to write a 'grammar', which attracted low production costs as it consisted mainly of a list of significant facts on a particular subject and could therefore be sold relatively cheaply. Then he would commission a larger text which was written in a more literary style, was considerably more expensive and was a more discursive and entertaining treatment of the facts contained in the grammar. Then he would sell easily and cheaply produced copybooks relating to the texts which were quarto notebooks containing questions with space for students to fill in the answers. The final feature of this educational package was a series of 'Keys' containing solutions and answers to the questions given in the texts, maps, and register books for the tutor to record the progress of students.[6]

Phillips clearly was a brutal businessman, but that should not detract attention from his role in promoting science and education. A.S. Collins, writing about Phillips in the 1920s, acknowledged that although many contemporaries looked upon him as a charlatan, Phillips had 'set out to give popular instruction to the people' and places Phillips as a major figure in the emancipation of the working classes.[7]

Goldsmith's Geographies

Some of Phillips's trade names were the names of living authors while others appear to be wholly fictitious. Joyce wrote *Geography Illustrated on a Popular Plan* (1803) and *An Easy Grammar of General Geography* (1803), under the fictitious name of Reverend J. Goldsmith. Both titles were extremely successful and remained in print until 1868.[8] Longmans later bought the stock and many shares in the copyright of Phillips titles in 1812, and the Longmans archives show that Goldsmith's Geographies were extremely lucrative. Longmans had yearly print runs of between 10,000 and 20,000 of the *Grammar*, and between 500 and 1000 for *Geography Illustrated on a Popular Plan*, in the period 1813 to the mid 1850s.[9]

Goldsmith's Geographies were the first examples of Geographies to be produced as a series and designed to be used as complementary texts.[10] The *Grammar* gave an outline of facts and *Geography Illustrated on a Popular Plan* was a reader. These Geographies reflect the transition in geography textbooks from a collection of isolated details and heterogeneous material to an articulated body of knowledge and

---

6 Sir Richard Phillips (1820), *Illustrations of the Interrogative System*, Phillips, London, p. 2.

7 Collins, p. 114.

8 Issitt, J. (2000), 'The Natural History of a Textbook', *Publishing History*, 47, pp. 5–30.

9 Longman MSS, Phillips purchase Ledgers MS/1393/1/54, 2 vols.

10 Allford, G.R. (1964), 'The development of Geography Textbooks used In England before 1902', unpublished M.A. thesis, University of Leeds, p. 132.

principles.[11] Earlier Geographies centred exclusively on man and man's activities, whereas Goldsmith's used a more extended set of categories including national boundaries, air and soil.

The vogue for educational systems is represented in Goldsmith's Geographies and the *Grammar* was sold as a

> complete synopsis of geography, as he [the author] knows has long been wanted by tutors; and which, united to the popular and fascinating continents of his larger work, will, he believes, form the completist system of geography for the use of schools, which has ever appeared.

The *Grammar* retailed at 2s 6d bound and was largely a list of facts in numbered paragraphs which the pupil was expected to commit to memory at a rate of 'one, two or three per day'. However, Joyce deployed a more sophisticated pedagogy that he ran parallel to the general methodology of rote learning. The preface claimed that the first steps in learning about the construction and use of maps is to 'lay before them [the pupils] a plan or map of the district in which they reside' which can be 'compared with his actual knowledge of the neighbourhood'. In this manner the pupil will be able to 'easily extend his ideas to the objects of general maps'. The method of finding the latitude or longitude of places using a globe was first described under a 'rule' and then a series of 'examples for practice' was given. Therefore, while offering a list of facts to be passively memorised at one level, the *Grammar* also engaged the child in a process of active learning.

Joyce's educational techniques were more constrained by the rote learning formula and number format of the cheaply produced *Grammar*, than they were in the larger and more expensive *Geography Illustrated on a Popular Plan*, which retailed at 15s. One of the opening plates of the larger volume was a fold out exercise which combined estimated population figures and land areas. The impression of the immensity of sea compared with the relatively small land area was conveyed by the comparison between the earth's surface as a one foot diameter circle, and the smaller circles representing the land area of different countries. Pupils were required to pay close attention to these relative sizes and had to draw the circles, thereby gaining a sense of comparative land and sea areas, of the comparative sizes of different countries and comparative population figures, which did not correlate with the relative size of the country. The exercise was novel and effective, and encouraged the pupil to explore geographical facts within geographical relationships.

The *Grammar* contained several engraved maps which also appeared in *Geography Illustrated on a Popular Plan* together with 60 elaborate engravings. These engravings were a major selling feature of the book and contained highly stereotypical images of different nationalities ranging from a Hindoo woman about to burn herself, a Swiss christening and a Chinese waterboatman depicted as rowing with one foot, managing the sail with one hand whilst holding the oar with the other and smoking a pipe. The text was culled from a wide range of travel writings

---

11 Nietz, J. A. (1961), *Old textbooks*, University of Pittsburgh Press, p. 208.

which are given in the preface and are listed as 'authorities relative to the several countries on which the facts and anecdotes are inserted'. In fact over half of the text is built from direct quotations from the listed sources. The craft of compilation was especially suited to Geographies as there were so many popular travel writings in print and a series of extracts arranged by country offered a fairly low cost convenient compilation.

In his preface Joyce divided geography into two categories: first, the divisions of the globe and the relative positions of place which he considered as 'mechanical' and second, the productions and curiosities of countries, and manners and customs of inhabitants which he denoted as 'the mental department'. The first, Joyce argued, could only be taught by 'mechanical means' by which he meant the use of globes and the copying of maps, whilst the second required reading and the appropriate engagement with useful ideas. For Joyce both components were required in learning geography:

> But while the pupil is proceeding with the mechanical part of Geography, the mental department should by no means be neglected. It would be frivolous to become acquainted with the size and relative situations of countries, if no useful ideas were annexed to them, and if their inhabitants, climates, productions,, and curiosities were unknown. In order to furnish complete and ample information relative to these important and highly interesting particulars, the copious accounts of the manners, customs and curiosities of nations have been compiled, and they contain every remarkable and entertaining fact...

Joyce's ascription of 'frivolity' to geographical knowledge which did not also have an aspect of utility, and his insistence on the combination of factual knowledge with useful knowledge, marks the general shift from an eighteenth century expectation of education as entertaining, to a nineteenth century expectation of education as useful. On the one hand Joyce hoped that *Geography Illustrated on a Popular Plan* could be read with 'eagerness and delight' and on the other that geography should be the 'most engaging' and 'useful' pursuit for 'both sexes'. Goldsmith's Geographies embody elements of both the older tradition of polite education in which geographical knowledge was part of an accomplished liberal education, and the early nineteenth century concern for systematic learning.

Figure 11. 'Economy of Time and Labour exemplified in a Chinese Waterman', from *Geography Illustrated on a Popular Plan*, published by Phillips in 1803.

The Book of Trades

The established tradition of books depicting the trades stretches back at least to Jost Amman and Hans Sachs's 1568 *Book of Trades* and Johann Amos Comenius's influential and constantly reprinted 1654 *Orbis Pictus*, which concentrated on arts and crafts and provided a lucrative income for a number of publishers for many years. Joyce's *The Book of Trades or Library of Useful Arts* (London: Tabart, 1804) is situated in this tradition which continued as a financially viable publishing venture throughout the nineteenth century. Joyce's version, which is a series of descriptions of the trades with illustrative plates, was the first to combine the elements of entertainment and instruction to produce a book that was specifically aimed at children.[12]

The Book of Trades has a complex bibliographical history over the period 1804 – 1808. It was published both as a single volume, and as three separate volumes. It carried Benjamin Tabart's and Phillips's names singly and combined on different printings. It has plates that are dated differently in different editions, and it was increased in size by a third between the first (1804), and third (1806) major editions. As the first edition was so successful, Tabart and Phillips probably experimented with different formats in order to maximise sales: some of the changes in illustrative plates may well have been due to the necessity of replacing those too worn. Aspland's

---

12 Stockham, P. (1976), *Early American Crafts & trades*, Dover, New York, introduction, p. vi. This is a facsimile reprint of the 1806 edition of Joyce's *Book of Trades*.

memoir dates *The Book of Trades* as Joyce's in 1806, which was the year in which it was considerably enlarged, but Aspland's dating is inconsistent and his list attributes the whole work to Joyce, as does Joyce's wife Elizabeth. That the first trade described in the 1804 edition is that of Woolcomber – Joyce's father's trade – also suggests that Joyce was the original compiler/author in 1804.

The Book of Trades provides a rich source for social history and change. Progressive editions were updated to include some of the machine and factory based processes of expanding industrialisation and the 1806 edition included consideration of some relatively modern inventions. Richard Arkwright's spinning jenny is recorded as 'very successful' for spinning cotton, but judged not 'yet able to afford worsted yarn so cheap as that which can be spun by hand'. The text is littered with interesting facts, for instance, 25 workmen are involved in the production of a single pin and a fourteen year old lad is able to point 16,000 pins in an hour. Nearly all the descriptions refer to London and prices and practices refer to those found in London, with occasional contrasts with those 'in the country'. The commercial success and the employment created by industry is constantly emphasized and the reader learns of the tin plate factories of 'James and Taylors in Tottenham-Court-Road, and Howards in Old Street', which 'seldom employ less that one hundred or a hundred and fifty men each'.

In general though, the trades are described in terms of individual enterprise and even where the text and plates describe a small factory setting, the emphasis is on the finished product as the result of the individual artisan's work. Joyce's description of the trade of woolcombing is noticeably more detailed than other entries. The plate (given as Figure 4) has a small bird cage in the top left hand corner which is not referred to in the text and may be a recollection of Joyce's childhood in his father's shop. The accompanying text describes the different types of wool and the processes required to prepare it for spinning – which is the next trade that is described. The plate shows two ballads that are hung on the wall of which Joyce says 'there are several in every wool-comber's shop'. Such ballads may well have been sung in the shop and their presence is an unusual detail which again may reflect Joyce's personal experience.

Joyce includes some interesting details of the working practices and organisation of Woolcombers:

> The Journeymen work by the piece, and will earn from sixteen shillings to twenty per week. Like people in many other trades, they often make holidays in the early part of the week. They come on a Monday morning, and, having lighted the fire in the comb-pot, will frequently go away, and perhaps return no more till Wednesday or even Thursday. The men in this trade have a curious custom: when out of work, they set out in search of a master, with a sort of certificate from their last place: this they call going on the tramp; and at every shop where they call, and can get no employment, they receive one penny, which is given from a common stock raised by the men of that shop.

Some of the details in the passage may well have come from Joyce's childhood experiences. The practice of 'holidays' at the beginning of the week, leaving only three or four days for productive work might have come from his father's frustration with his journeymen workers who, had a reputation for insubordination.[13] The practices of tramping and support for out of work journeymen is not recorded elsewhere in the book, and suggests that Joyce witnessed journeymen arriving at his father's shop and was impressed by the practice of giving financial support to out of work fellow tradesmen.

Joyce's seven-year apprenticeship and experiences as a journeyman painter of glass rendered him well placed to describe the building trades. His description of the tools and practices of the bricklayer, carpenter, plumber and stonemason is precise and include considerable detail about the way, and how much, the workers were paid. His description of how pot-metal glass was made comes under the section Glass-Blower and is detailed with scientific precision.

> Glass is sometimes coloured by mixing with it, while in the fluid state, various metallic oxydes. It is coloured blue, by the oxyde of cobalt; red, by the oxyde of gold; green, by the oxyde of copper or iron; yellow, by the oxyde of silver or antimony; and violet by the oxyde of manganese.

The sense of Joyce's enthusiasm for glass is reflected in his introduction to this section in which he claims that there is 'scarcely any manufacture of more real utility than that of glass'. The mix of utility, technical language and genuine enthusiasm produces an interesting text which might well beguile a young reader.

> Though Glass, when cold, is brittle, it is one of the most ductile bodies known. When liquid, if a thread of melted glass be drawn out and fastened to a reel, the whole of the glass may be spun off; and by cutting the threads of a certain length, there is obtained a sort of feather of glass. A thread of glass may be drawn or spun so fine as to be scarcely visible to the naked eye. Glass is very elastic and sonorous. Fluric acid dissolves it, and the alkalis act upon it.

There is a hint of Joyce's dissenting status in his comment in the section on Carpet-Weavers that an Orphan Working School had been set up in 'the city road', to weave carpets from strips of cloth 'through the liberality and public spirit of the dissenters in and near the metropolis'. Joyce uses romantic images of honourable and individual trades, but also generates a sense of social responsibility and paternal guidance. He counselled against young women becoming dressmakers as 'the mere work-women do not make gains adequate to their labour: they are frequently obliged to set up to very late hours, and the recompense for the extra work is not adequate to the time spent'.

The book was well received by the staunchly conservative Mrs Sarah Trimmer, who reviewed it in her influential *Guardian of Education* (1805). While she thought the sections on female trades 'frivolous', she whole-heartedly recommended the book:

---

13 Thompson, *Making of the English Working Class*, p. 311.

This is a very amusing and instructive work from which the general idea of a number of useful arts carried on in this and other kingdoms, may be gained. Subjects of this kind are very proper for young minds to be occupied with in their hours of amusement, when they are not proposed in too scientific a way; an objection which cannot be made to any that are introduced in these volumes.[14]

Had Mrs Trimmer known that the *Book of Trades* actually came from the erstwhile radical Joyce, she might well not have given it such a favourable review.

The *Wonders of the Microscope* and the *Wonders of the Telescope*

Both *Wonders of the Microscope or An Explanation of the Wisdom of the Creator in Objects Comparatively Minute, Adapted to the Understanding of the Young* (1805) and *Wonders of the Telescope or Display of the Starry Heavens Calculated to Promote and Simplify the Study of Astronomy* (1805), were published by Tabart and Phillips but have no stated author. There is firm, although complex, evidence that the works were actually constructed by Joyce. Elizabeth Joyce listed two works together – 'the History of the Microscope and the History of the Telescope' as Joyce's, but no such 'history of' titles exist; Elizabeth may have been confused and was referring to the *Wonders*. Aspland only lists a new edition of the *Wonders of the Telescope* as Joyce's in 1814, yet comparison of the 1814 edition and the original reveals no differences in text, size or content. Both books were sold as having the same author in their advertisements. Furthermore, many of the same analogies, explanatory devices and patterns of argument that appear elsewhere in Joyce's works, appear in the *Wonders*.

Following the twin themes of instruction and entertainment that infuse all Joyce's works for children, Joyce claimed in his introduction that the microscope 'opens to the young and the curious an inexhaustible source of information and pleasure'. Yet he does not plunge straight into the revelations of the microscope, he starts by leading the reader through the scientific knowledge necessary to understand how microscopes work. The introduction is largely devoted to the anatomy and function of the eye and closely resembles the expanded treatment of the same subject in Joyce's series of lectures on natural theology that appeared ten years later in the *Monthly Magazine* in 1815. The first chapter is concerned with the three different types of microscopes – single, compound and solar, with the greatest amount of space given to the compound microscope, which is given in a figure and heavily referred to in the text. The optics of the microscope are described and the relationships between focal distance and lens diameter are discussed using numerical figures to work out magnifying power. Joyce also included a short – one page – list of 'technical terms' at the end of the book which gave definitions of 'animicules, concave, convex, cuticle, focus and lens'. His purpose was, therefore, not simply to display the wonders of

---

14 Sarah Trimmer (1805), *Guardian of Education*, Vol. iv, p. 304.

creation as revealed by the microscope, but also to support children in the actual use of them by providing a practical manual.

Joyce adapted existing sources and welded them into this new publishing speculation. The *Wonders of the Microscope* drew heavily on Robert Hooke's *Micrographia* (1665) and Joyce clearly had a copy of the *Micrographia* in front of him as he worked. The impressive and immense fold-out illustrations of fleas, lice, mites, magnified snowflakes and the point of a needle, which are the features of the *Wonders of the Microscope* that first strike the reader, were simply copied from Hooke. Much of the text was also copied, but a large amount was abbreviated and modified. Joyce chose passages from the *Micrographia* that held interesting stories which he could use to build his own narrative. For instance, he chose an incident in which Hooke observed a mite that sucked blood from his hand, and he added a humanising element to the description. According to Hooke, two mites were kept 'in a box for two or three dayes, so that for all they had nothing to feed on'.[15] Joyce's version is 'Dr Hooke...Kept several in a box for two or three days, by which time they became extremely hungry'. He also updated the language and where Hooke had described the flow of blood into the mite through 'very swift systole and diastole', Joyce used 'alternate dilation and contraction'.[16]

Joyce occasionally used humour as an educational and literary device throughout his works. He chose to record the story of Anthony van Leeuwenhoek, who attempted to estimate the reproductive rates of lice by placing two female lice 'into a black stocking, which he wore night and day', concluding that 'in about eight weeks a louse might see five thousand of its descendants'. Joyce also used the opportunity to instruct the youthful reader in personal cleanliness saying that matter from the 'teeth of those who are inattentive to cleanliness, ...affords another sort of animicules in the form of eels'. He goes on to advise clean linen, gloves and handkerchiefs in order to avoid 'the disorder called the itch' which is the result of 'very nimble' animicules living in clothing.

He concluded the chapter on mites with a vivid image of the world beyond unaided vision.

> Thus an infinite number of animalcules are perpetually floating in the air we breathe, sporting in the fluids we drink, or adhering to the several objects we see and handle.

Joyce's graphic imagery may – like most of his text – have been culled from existing sources, but his relaxed and at times flamboyant prose style in the *Wonders of the Microscope* suggests that his literary confidence was strong in this project – probably because it offered him an opportunity to fulfil the role of preacher. The *Wonders of the Microscope* can be considered as a form of popular preaching of the design argument. The standard arguments – order and harmony in the universe as evidence of design, supported by the claim of the poverty of human artifice as compared

---

15 Robert Hooke, *Micrographia* (1665), facsimile reprint in Gunther, R.T. (1938), Vol. 13 of the Early Science in Oxford, Series, Printed for the subscribers, Oxford, pp. 213/4.

16 *Micrographia*, p. 212; *Wonders of the Microscope*, p. 37.

with God's far superior handywork – are all presented. Joyce makes wonder the central device for what is effectively an extended sermon constructed within the commercial parameters of a publishing speculation. He trades off the religious sense of wonder which he uses in a number of linked rhetorical ploys to develop lines of argument which repeatedly bring the reader to confront the beneficent design of God. For instance, in Joyce's exhortation to wonder at the marvels of God's creation, he presses the sense of suspended belief engendered by wonder, in an appeal to the ability of the imagination to probe beyond the level of physical resolution of the microscope, and deploy a 'mental microscope'.

> What wonders would we see if we could continually improve those glasses, which are invented for the assistance of our sight. Imagination may, in some measure, supply the defect of our eyes, and make it serve as a mental microscope to represent in each atom thousands of new and invisible worlds.

Here Joyce invites the reader to contemplate worlds beyond the limits of human vision. He used the revelatory power of the microscope, in conjunction with the revelatory power of the imagination, to promote sentiments of wonder. But there is no evidence that Joyce's use of the image of atoms as worlds was simply a fantastical literary flourish and that he didn't actually believe there were worlds beyond the resolution of the microscope. The sermonising continues and drives towards a moral lesson:

> He provides with the same kind and parental care for the wants of the insect that crawls in the dust, as for the whale, which appears as a huge mountain in the mighty seas. In this may we, may the young in particular, imitate the example of the Deity, by shewing kindness and humanity to every living creature, since, as they are worthy of His care, they ought not be ill-treated by us.

Much of the religious discourse of the *Wonders* is non-controversially treated here and would have been acceptable to most parents of potential readers. Ideas of a beneficent and omnipotent deity, the limitations of human knowledge, and the requirement for emulation of God's benign generosity were fairly safe territory and considered standard ground on which to build a text for children. Microscopes were increasingly becoming a fashionable gift for the children of the wealthy and middle classes and a text which both provided a manual to guide their use and sanctioned their revelations within established religious sentiment presented a good commercial opportunity.

The *Wonders of the Microscope* was sold at 3s 6d in boards but the *Wonders of the Telescope* sold at 5s in boards or 6s fully bound. The difference in price may be partly explained by the differences in size and cost. Whilst the *Wonders of the Microscope* has bigger illustrations, these could simply be copied, along with much of the text from Hooke's *Micrographia*. The *Wonders of the Telescope* required more work, and fourteen elaborate new plates were commissioned. The *Wonders of the Telescope*'s opening advertisement links it to the *Wonders of the Microscope* and claims that in contradistinction to the study of objects 'comparatively minute', it 'affords us a glimpse of infinite space and the myriads of worlds and systems of worlds'. Both the microscope and the telescope are 'calculated to excite in us sentiments of awe for the creator', and the religious motivations behind both works were utterly consistent in attempting to make readers 'wiser and better'. Justified by religious and moral probity, the further credentials of the work designed to entice potential buyers, were threefold. Firstly, the book was easy to read and not infused with too much 'technical language'. Secondly, unlike other books on astronomy, it had sufficient 'illustrative plates'. Thirdly, it presented knowledge that was normally only found in the 'voluminous transactions of learned societies or in large and expensive works'.

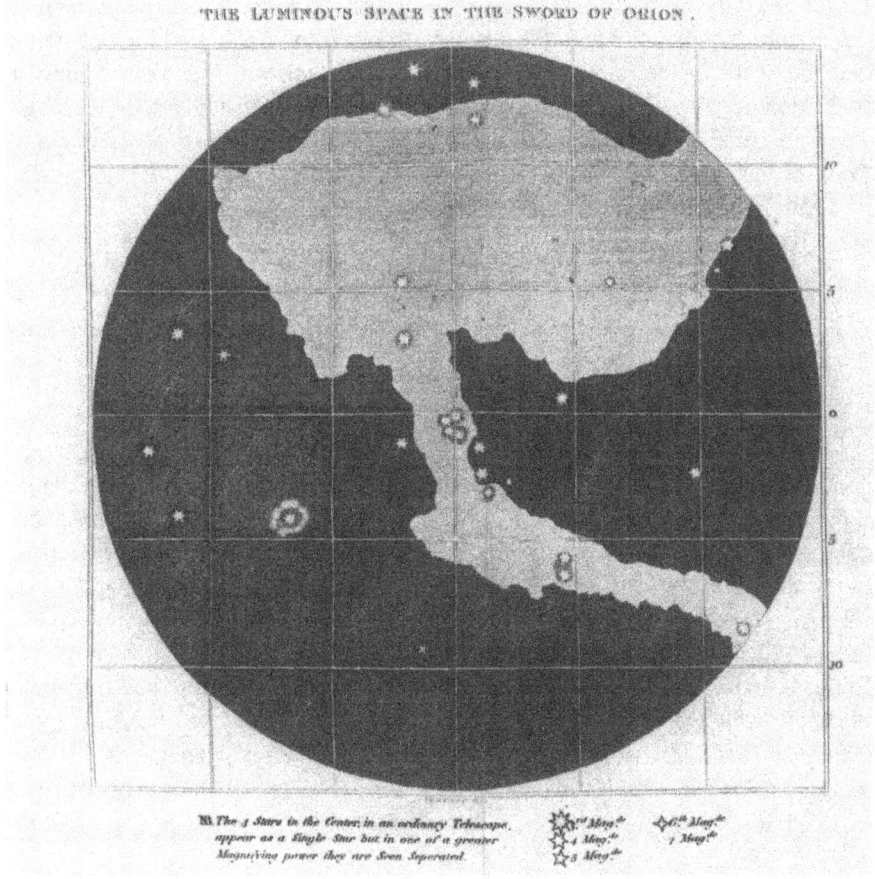

Figure 12: 'The Luminous space in the sword of Orion', from *Wonders of the Telescope*, published by Phillips in 1805.

The literary style of the *Wonders of the Telescope* was a little different from that of the *Wonders of the Microscope*, which was a fairly traditional formulation of natural theology concerned with the immediate and objects of terrestrial world. The celestial realm is more removed from immediate human observation and necessitated a different type of narrative. Where the *Wonders of the Microscope* was a manual for the reader to witness the wonders of God, *Wonders of the Telescope* was more of a theatrical lecture. The fourteen plates were not simply educational devices; they were a literal attempt to do what the title advertised – provide 'A Display of the Starry Heavens'. The plates represented what was seen through the aperture of the telescope. Many of them were superimposed with a grid and the relative luminosity of the stars established by size. The reader, like an attender at a scientific lecture or a pulpit sermon, was invited to witness God's heavens and wonder at His creation.

The *Wonders of the Telescope* opens with the argument for the earth being a globe rather than flat and uses the standard argument of the masts of a ship being seen first or last as they appear or disappear over the horizon. Then there follows a description of the solar system, which includes the most poetic and literary passage in Joyce's entire writings. The passage is littered with poetical extracts from Pope, Barbauld and Young, but the text which is not ascribed to anybody else is unusually colourful:

> The lawn is refreshed by the coolness of the night, and the light of the morning displays its increasing verdure. The flowers that enamel its surface glitter in the sunbeams, and, like the most brilliant stones, reflect a thousand mingled colours to the eye. The cheerful birds unite in choirs, and hail, in concert, the parent of life: not one is silent; all join, each in his different way to shout their Maker's praise.

The following chapters consider the sun and then each of the planets. A chapter entitled 'A walk on a starry night' is really a lesson on how to identify the points of the compass, the poles, the zenith and important constellations. This is the same material covered in the astronomy book of the *Scientific Dialogues*, but reworked into a more literary text. Then comes a chapter entitled 'of the constellations or imaginary divisions of the stars'. This has descriptions of the constellations but does not explain their 'imaginary' nature or give any derivations for their names. The book closes with a chapter on the different types of reflecting and refracting telescopes which includes a large pullout illustration of Herschel's telescope, and a chapter on 'the magnifying power of telescopes'. These final chapters explore the optics of the telescope and provide the same kind of technical knowledge that was provided in the first chapters of the *Wonders of the Microscope*.

A System Of Practical Arithmetic *and* A Key

A System Of Practical Arithmetic Applicable to the Present State of Trade, and Money Transactions, Illustrated by Numerous Examples Under Each rule; For the Use of Schools (1808) and *A Key to Joyce's Arithmetic Containing Solutions and*

Answers (1808) were the only titles Phillips published under Joyce's own name. Joyce received only £105 for the perpetual copyright of the System and 50 guineas for the Key, which represented only a tiny fraction of the long term profits.17 The System and Key were very successful for Phillips and also for Longmans who bought one third of the copyright in 1812 and secured the whole copyright in 1828, going on to publish them until 1868 and regularly printing 2000 copies per year.[18]

The *System* may have been modelled on the mathematician Charles Hutton's highly successful *The Schoolmaster's Guide, or a compleat System of Practical Arithmetic* (1764), which was a standard school textbook used throughout Hutton's life.[19] Following the general format of Hutton's book, Joyce's *System* opens with sections on elementary arithmetic and then moves to consider practical examples. It uses the traditional pedagogic style for mathematics textbooks of an introductory definition, followed by a rule, then worked examples followed by problems set for the student. However, the *System* introduces several new features. Where Hutton's book contains the answers to problems set, Joyce's has a separate *Key* with the answers. This may have been motivated in part by the spread of Lancaster and Bell's monitorial method which provided a low cost education for the lower classes. Where pupil monitors were used, provision of a separate book of answers removed the responsibility for examining the workings of each example, both from the teacher, whose time could also 'be employed to better purposes', and the monitor, whose mathematical competence may itself have been limited. Joyce also justified separating the answers from the questions on pedagogical grounds, arguing from his own experience that 'Preceptors in general, prefer the plan of omitting the answers to the examples they have given their pupils for exercise; it being found conducive to the habits of attention and accuracy'.

Joyce introduced logarithms, arguing in the preface to the 1816 edition that 'it appeared high time to introduce this capital discovery into the ordinary processes of arithmetic, and no longer leave its advantages to those only who have the leisure to cultivate the higher branches of mathematics'. He designed the *System* to act as an introduction for those 'who wish to proceed in that science', but also for the 'thousands who never trouble themselves to learn beyond the elements of Arithmetic'. Over half of the book is divided into sections devoted to 'the application of the several rules to transactions of real business'. The main target audience for the *System* was schools whose pupils might go into commerce and who needed arithmetic for practical purposes. It provided for those 'who seek only for that knowledge which is in some way applicable'. Phillips and Joyce extended their net for potential purchasers to include non-school audiences, and the *System* was also directed at 'Persons who have neglected or forgotten what they what they learned in early life' and who, by purchase of the *System* and *Key*, could 'render themselves completely masters of

---

17 Longman MSS, 1393 24/140.
18 Longman MSS, 1393 24/53; Phillips Purchase Ledgers.
19 Howson, G. (1982), *A history of mathematics education in England*, Cambridge University Press, p. 62.

every part of the science connected with the usual concerns of life'. In the chapter entitled 'reduction', which described methods of conversions, subsections are devoted to the goldsmith, grocer, apothecary and wool weights, cloth, land, cubic, wine, ale, corn, coal measures and 'commercial numbers or articles sold by the tale'. The second half of the book is devoted to particular operations of the commercial world and is divided into chapters, normally only four or five pages long, on interest, commission and brokerage, insurance, profit and loss, partnership, expectations of life and exchange rates. The practices of 'tare and tret', in which wholesalers gave allowances in selling goods by weight, is given a chapter. There is a section on geography with questions designed to work out positions of latitude and longitude in order to trace the passage of shipping. Joyce had to find examples and questions for both the elementary arithmetic sections and the practical sections. Such questions provide additional sources of information about Joyce's work. For instance, the questions given in the section 'commercial numbers' use examples from printing and publishing and relate to his latest compilation – *Dr Gregory's Dictionary of Arts and sciences* (considered below).

Part of the attraction of the *System* and *Key* was that they aided teachers in their classroom practice. The *Key*, while containing the answers to the questions set in the *System*, also included 'Questions for examination' relating to sections of pages or chapters of the *System*, which teachers could use. For instance, the first question of the *Key* 'what do you mean by arithmetic?', anticipates a version of the first definition given in the *System*: 'Arithmetic is the science which explains the various methods of computing numbers.' The *Key* also offered an appendix, a mechanism for learning mental arithmetic which might be used by the autodidact as well as in the classroom. The attractiveness of learning mental arithmetic was presented as giving a superior edge to 'a man of business'.

> In markets and fairs a ready calculator whose constant and never-failing resource is his own mind, will find himself in a superior situation to him who can calculate only by means of his pen.

The *System* and *Key*, then, had been carefully planned. The aids to the teacher in the *Key* also anticipated the needs of the autodidact and included sets of instructions which could be used in both classroom and individual situations. Such sets of instructions supplemented the *System* and encouraged the learner to use mathematics. For instance, referring to the specific pages in the chapter 'reduction' concerned with apothecaries' weights, Joyce gave a set of instructions which encouraged the learner to actively engage with the subject:

> Repeat the apothecaries weight Table
> Write on your slate the characters made use of in this table
> Do apothecaries buy and sell this weight?

The *System* and the *Key* had to compete with a large number of other elementary mathematics texts produced for schools, for engineers and for mariners, and was cleverly designed to appeal to particular sectors of the market. It was for relatively low class schools and was designed to suit the needs of children likely to go into the commercial world at a low level. It was fairly cheap – being sold at 3s – and therefore might also be within the price range of young men just starting in a merchants' office or counting house. It was also a cleverly worked out and practical course in elementary mathematics education built on a solid and innovatory pedagogic design that was likely to appeal to a range of learners. The *System* and *Key* were successful for Phillips and also for Longmans, who went on to publish them until 1865.[20]

Blair's *Grammar*

An Easy Grammar of Natural and Experimental Philosophy for the Use of Schools by Revd David Blair (1807) was a pocket-size volume that retailed at 3s bound and is attributed to Joyce by both Aspland and Elizabeth Joyce. Like Goldsmith, Blair was a fictitious trade name used by Phillips to build a large number of related educational texts. The authors of two texts given the Blair pseudonym have been identified. The highly successful *Blair's Class Book* (1806) was written by Elizabeth Fenwick,[21] and the *Easy Grammar* by Joyce. The benefits to Phillips of using Blair's name were that it conferred the authority of a churchman, it could be used to further Phillips's publishing speculations in whatever way he chose, and, most importantly, avoided having to pay an author for the copyright – Phillips merely commissioned writers like Joyce. The preface, signed 'David Blair, Islington, 1807', is an elaborate charade which has a very different literary style from the rest of the text and was probably written by Phillips himself. It is a little ambiguous in his acknowledgement that that work was 'compiled', but nowhere does it refer to any other writer or source.

Samuel Catlow, who was also one of Phillips's network of writers may well have understood Phillips's operation when he flatteringly reviewed many of Joyce's titles and others actually written by him but published under pseudonyms. He may well have been being deliberately ironic when he reviewed the *Scientific Dialogues* and mentioned *Blair's Grammar*

> of his [Joyce's] Scientific Dialogues we can speak with unqualified approbation, and recommend them to be read as a pleasing companion to Blair's Grammar of Natural Philosophy.[22]

These two books deal with the same subjects in a very similar order and use many of the same examples and illustrations. In the task of preparing the *Easy Grammar*, Joyce could simply reach to his own shelves and use his own *Dialogues* as the source. It is not possible to specify how long it took Joyce to complete the task, but having

---

20 Longman MSS, Phillips Purchase Ledgers.
21 Moon, p. 3.
22 Samuel Catlow's revision of Joshua Collins's (1818) *A guide in the selection and use of elementary School–Books*, T. Hamilton, London, p. 84.

a source he knew well and a format that he had already worked with probably meant that this was not the hardest or longest commission he ever undertook.

Phillips developed a series of Easy Grammars and the format of *An Easy Grammar of Natural Philosophy* is exactly the same as Goldsmith's *Easy Grammar of Geography* (1803), compiled by Joyce, which by 1807 had become a highly successful educational format. Phillips's Grammars became a recognisable brand and their presentational style was standardised. Once the brand was established it was fairly simple for Phillips to use the same recipe again. He could commission an author, get some illustrative plates made and either use a pseudonym or use the name of a recognised author to produce a further extension to his range of schoolbooks.

The preface to the *Easy Grammar* claimed that the definitions which open each subsection had been 'written with a studied brevity in order that they be learnt by rote'. Such definitions are statements which have been formed as answers to questions. For instance in the opening section: the definition: The inherent properties of matter are solidity, divisibility, mobility and inertness', is the answer to the question placed at the end of the section 'what are the properties of matter?' However, once again, Joyce's pedagogical design is more sophisticated than simply rote learning and the preface emphasises that children can only really learn if they submit definitions to memory as well as working – and work is italicised throughout the preface to emphasis its importance – through examples.

> He who only reads about a science can be nothing more than a smatterer, while he who commits its terms and elementary principles to memory and applies them by his own act to the various combinations of the science, soon becomes a master of it.

Each definition is followed by brief illustrations and experiments constrained to three or four line paragraphs which supplied instances in which the student could apply the definitions. In most sections a corollary traced the implications of the experiments to supply a logical deduction of the original definition. Such corollaries were designed to be interesting to the reader in that they might state something deduced from the definition and proven by the experiments, at the same time as making a counter-intuitive claim.

> Corrollary. Therefore water, air and all other fluids, are in a certain space equally solid with the hardest body.

Thus Joyce crafted packages of scientific knowledge into bite-size chunks that took the reader through experiments and trains of logical thinking to interesting conclusions. This was not boring or unsophisticated teaching, but a carefully constructed educational technique.

Gregory's *Dictionary*

In the early nineteenth century encyclopaedia publishing was booming.[23] The spur to Phillips's involvement was a project begun in 1802 by the theologian and mathematician Olinthus Gregory and the physician John Mason Good, to produce a Universal Dictionary. In recalling the inception of the project, Olinthus Gregory commented:

> ...shortly afterwards a speculating bookseller [Phillips] who had ascertained that this Universal Dictionary was in preparation, with a view to anticipate us both in object and name, commenced the publication of a new Cyclopedia of which Dr. [George] Gregory was announced as editor, while in fact, the late Mr Jeremiah Joyce was the principal, if not the only, person engaged in the work.[24]

George Gregory DD, a prolific writer on a range of subjects including natural philosophy, settled in London in 1782 and was the evening preacher at the Foundling Hospital. He was presented to the living of West Ham in 1802, becoming a Prebendary of St Paul's and chaplain to the Bishop of Llandaff in 1806. In the same year Phillips fell out with John Aiken, the then editor of Phillips's *Monthly Magazine* and replaced him with Gregory. To the public Gregory could be presented as a man of letters possessing a sound pedigree in theology, natural philosophy and education – a liberal minded churchman in whose hands knowledge was both sanctified and suitably edited in the interests of truth and duty. For the expensive enterprise of the *Dictionary of Arts and Sciences*, Phillips would have been unlikely to risk the negative associations of radicalism and Unitarianism linked with Joyce. Gregory, on the other hand, could be marketed as a legitimate author and overseer of a large corpus of knowledge for public consumption.

Joyce started work on the project around the middle of 1805 and took roughly eighteen months to produce the two large and heavily illustrated quarto volumes published in February 1807 and sold at 115s. The advertisement for volume one describes the work and promises three benefits to the potential owner. Firstly, that it was a compendium of all human knowledge – 'practical rather than speculative'; secondly that it is a convenient portable size (a curious claim as it is very thick and heavy!!); and thirdly that it was 'Printed to correspond with the Quarto edition of Dr Johnson's Dictionary; and that the possessor of both works will have in 4 quarto volumes, and at moderate expense, all the literary aid which the English student or reader can possibly require'. There was a new edition of *Dr Johnson's Dictionary* in 1807 published by Joseph Johnson and a large conger. *Gregory's Dictionary* is

---

23 Collinson, R. (1966), *Encyclopaedias: Their History Throughout the ages*, Hafner, New York, p. 174.

24 Gregory, O. (1828), *Memoirs of the life writings and character, literary and professional, and religious, of the late John Mason Good, M.D*, Henry Fisher, London, p. 88.

strikingly similar in physical size and appearance, suggesting that Phillips had coordinated production with Johnson over points of design and layout.

Joyce had been writing entries for *Rees's Cyclopedia* produced by Longmans from 1802, and had therefore acquired first-hand experience of a large enterprise. However, this was the first time he was responsible for the compilation of such a large work, which resulted in a densely packed two volume quarto with small type in three columns per page, with 960 pages in volume one and 928 pages in volume two. This was a significant task which had a deleterious effect on Joyce's health.[25] Joyce had to work quickly to build a compilation from a wide range of sources. Quite what proportion of the text Joyce wrote himself is unclear, but he would have had to prepare the various contributions in alphabetical order and write many of the smaller entries himself, no doubt using a wide range of sources. Gregory's preface acknowledged Joyce as assistant and also as being in charge of a particular subject area:

> To his industrious and truly able coadjutor, the Rev. Mr. Joyce, he is indebted for much general assistance, and for the exclusive superintendence of all the mathematical and astronomical articles.

It is not clear what 'exclusive superintendance' means, but there are extensive entries for the various subdivisions of mathematics. The entry on astronomy is also substantial, comprising 40 columns with seven tables and three full page plates covering the history of astronomy as well as contemporary astronomical knowledge.

In the lineage of encyclopaedic dictionaries there is a transition from an alphabetically arranged but systematic treatment of topics in the eighteenth century, to nineteenth century reference works in which connected sub-topics were classified more strictly under their alphabetical listing.[26] At the back of each volume of *Gregory's Dictionary* there is an 'Index to the treatises'. This was a thematic index giving a list of the sequential subsections of a particular topic. Thus under Geometry there are the subsections 'Algebra and Geometry, Definition of Geometry, Explanation of Terms, Problems in Geometry and Usefulness of Geometry' listed on sequential pages. The index is only partial however: some topics actually treated, for instance the large section on comparative anatomy, do not appear anywhere in the index. The index was therefore a partial attempt to accommodate the impulse for systematic organisation wherein a topic could be comprehensively treated and its extent fully circumscribed. But the reader could not rely on the index alone and had to check the alphabetical position of the entry sought. As a result the thematic index unwittingly added a level of complexity to the internal topography of the work as it could not be wholly relied on by a reader trying to navigate its pages.

One of the most interesting features of Joyce's role in *Gregory's Dictionary* is that immediately following the production of the eventual volumes, Joyce became

---

25 Waller, *Imperial Dictionary*, Joyce entry.
26 McArthur, T. (1986), *Worlds of reference*, Cambridge University Press, pp. 110–133

employed by Longmans on behalf a large conger, as managing editor to produce *The British Encyclopaedia or Dictionary of Arts and Sciences* (1809) known as *Nicholson's Encyclopedia* (discussed below). The two works are recorded as being 'framed in opposition' and 'bitter rivals' to one another.[27] Yet through the period of production of *Nicholson's Encyclopedia*, Joyce was still publishing with and taking commissions from Richard Phillips. Furthermore, more than half the text of *Gregory's Dictionary* appears verbatim in *Nicholson's Encyclopedia*, strongly suggesting that Joyce was able to take the manuscript of one and use it as the basis for the other, and that this was in fact an agreement made in the full knowledge of all the publishers involved.

Both Phillips and Longmans produced relatively cheap reference works. The enormous number and size of the volumes of the *Encyclopedia Britannica* and *Rees's Cyclopedia* rendered them beyond the purchasing power of anybody other than wealthy individuals or societies. But there was clearly a growing lower middle class market that might be able to afford 5 or 6 guineas for a family reference work and it was to this market that Phillips and Longmans appealed. In order to do so however, they needed an experienced compiler who could organise the works at a low cost. Phillips was the sole publisher of *Gregory's Dictionary* which would have cost a large amount to prepare thorough payment of Joyce, Gregory and other writers, the costs of the plates and the eventual production of 6000 copies of the work each containing 2000 sheets. It is possible that the manuscript of *Gregory's Dictionary* may have been sold to Longman as a way of recovering some of these costs. Furthermore, Joyce, who knew the manuscript well, was well placed to take charge of the Longman project.

---

27 Walsh, J.P. (1964), *General Encyclopedias in Print*, Reference Book Research Service, Newark USA, p. 40; DNB, William Nicholson entry.

Chapter 15

Publishing with the House of Longmans

Nicholson's Encyclopaedia

Thomas Norton Longman developed the firm of Longmans from a booksellers' shop to a complex organisation with several departments.[1] Longman was well disposed to Unitarians: his first partner, Owen Rees, was a Unitarian. The first project in which Joyce had any direct contact with Longmans was Abraham Rees's *Cyclopedia*. This was an enormous project published between 1802 and 1819 in parts or half issues representing 39 quarto volumes and six volumes of illustrations. Aspland claimed that Joyce made 'large contributions' to the work and Rees, who had been one of Joyce's teachers at Hackney. Rees acknowledged Joyce's contribution of 'a variety of miscellaneous articles', although it has not been possible to identify which these were.[2] Joyce may have attended the winter 'Soirees' held by Longmans, which collected nearly all the contributors to the new *Cyclopedia* which was a major literary enterprise considered subversive in some circles.[3] The *Cyclopedia* and its collection of writers drew the fire of the *Anti-Jacobin Review* which saw its members engaged in 'a new vehicle of infidelity' – yet another Jacobin plot along the lines perpetrated by the French intellectuals who compiled the *Encyclopedie* and who, the *Anti-Jacobin* claimed, were instrumental in producing the French Revolution.[4]

Despite such rabid attacks from the *Anti-Jacobin* who continued to berate producers of educational works and accuse Unitarians of promoting the cause of the French Revolution, the market for educational books continued to grow. Longmans clearly had a positive view of Joyce and his work and were keen to use him as an editor and trade off the success of his *Scientific Dialogues*. The remaining Longman archives record Joyce's activities in three projects, the first of which was *Nicholson's Encyclopaedia*, for which Joyce was paid a monthly wage.

The British Encyclopaedia or Dictionary of Arts and Sciences (1809) is a six volume octavo in two columns per page published by a huge conger whose principal organiser was Longmans and included Joseph Johnson and Richard Phillips. There were 28 subscribers to the project although only 23 names appear on the title page – the other five contributors were private sponsors. In total there were 128 shares

---

1 Wallis, P. (1974), *At the Sign of the Ship 1724–1974*, Longman, Essex, p. 15.
2 Rees's *Cyclopedia*, preface to the 1819 edition, p. iv.
3 Rees, T. pp. 50/5; Woolrich, A.P. (1998), 'John Farey, Jr, technical author and draughtsman: his contribution to Rees's Cyclopedia, *Industrial Archaeology Review*, 20, 49–67, p. 59.
4 *Anti–Jacobin Review* (June 1812) Review of *Rees's Cyclopedia*, pp 178–190 (p.182).

valued at £77, 10s each, of which Longmans held 40, representing an impressive total investment of £9920.[5] The work was initially sold in twelve parts and John Aiken's monthly periodical *Athenaeum*, published by Longmans, advertised part one in the March 1808 at 10s-6d sewn, promising eleven further monthly issues.[6] It was always the intention to sell the *British Encyclopedia* as a complete set, and in March 1809 the *Athenaeum* again advertised the work but this time as six volumes in boards at 6 guineas.[7] There was one print run of 6000 complete sets but no further English editions although, there were three American editions to 1821. If all sets were sold at 126s – six guineas – then the total capital recovery would have been 36,000 guineas – offering a handsome return on the £9,920 initial investment. For this project, Joyce would have been a very attractive option. Not only did he have considerable compiling experience and a substantial network of contributory authors, but most importantly, he came armed with a lot of completed text. The Longmans project could be sold to the investors as part complete, and with Longman's own store of published works on hand to use as sources, it promised a speedy return on investment.

In Nicholson's section of the preface devoted to acknowledging the writers, the following appears:

> The mathematical articles, including the mixed subjects of Astronomy, Optics, Phonics, Statics and many others were drawn up by a popular author who is well known for his writings on these subjects.

As the 'popular author' was well known, the reason for not including his name alongside the other names that are mentioned, is left mysterious. The decision to omit Joyce's name when it was common knowledge in literary circles that Joyce was the real editor may have been forced through concern that Joyce's name would offend either the investors or the potential purchasers.

William Nicholson is referred to as a chemist and inventor.[8] In his early life he had visited the East Indies, and on his return became the commercial agent for Josiah Wedgwood and started a school of mathematics in 1776/7. His first publication was the two volume *Introduction to Natural Philosophy* (1781) which Joyce had used as a template for his *Scientific Dialogues*. Nicholson went on to publish widely in mathematics and other subjects, and to translate several French works in chemistry. He appears to have operated with a number of publishers and had a network of authors producing commissioned work for different projects. He had a prestigious yet safe reputation associated with foreign travel, scholarly activity and a sense of commercial and civic endeavour. He therefore had a more socially acceptable pedigree than did Joyce and his selection as the principal for the Longmans project

---

5   Longmas MSS. Records of the *British Encyclopedia* are in Divide (D1) and Expense Ledgers (A1 & A2) and the Impression Book.

6   *Atheneum*, Mar., 1808.

7   *Atheneum*, Mar., 1809.

8   DNB, Nicholson entry.

made sound business sense. The Longman records show that Nicholson was involved in the project although he received no regular payments but was paid for individual contributions.

Nicholson's Encyclopedia was completed within only eighteen months and Joyce began the project immediately after finishing *Gregory's Dictionary*, therefore spending a solid 30 months compiling encyclopaedic dictionaries. Joyce made a fairly good living from the project. He received £50 per month for his editorial and compiling duties from February 1808 until January 1809, but also received additional amounts for his articles (one payment in January 1808 of £251 4s 2d), indicating that, for Longmans, he had two distinct roles – that of editor/compiler and that of writer. The picture given by the accounts is that Joyce was effectively the editor of the whole project and that he parcelled out work to various people – notably his two Unitarian friends Lant Carpenter and William Shepherd.

Joyce had only two to three months to prepare each issue. This was a demanding task given a work of such size encouraging him to cut and paste as much text from *Gregory's Dictionary* for direct entry to *Nicholson's Encyclopaedia* as possible. The first alphabetical numbers were printed first and volume 1 had a large first print run of 6500, with volume 2 at 6250 and volume 3 at 6100. The slightly higher print-run figures of the early volumes due to review copies sent out for advertising purposes. Joyce developed a robust and workman-like attitude to the task which he described to William Shepherd saying that 'tomorrow I will look after Aristotle', and telling of how he offered 'grammar to [John] Corrie' who refused, and how he then offered it to Lant Carpenter who accepted it.[9]

Joyce began *Nicholson's Encyclopaedia* straight after completing *Gregory's Dictionary* and he clearly set about the task with a concern to avoid the problems caused by the part-thematic and part-alphabetical organisation he had just encountered. He organised *Nicholson's Encyclopaedia* strictly alphabetically and did not have the pages numbered – relying exclusively on the reader's ability to navigate by the alphabet. The benefits of using an invariant series are threefold. Firstly, such a system resolved many of the dilemmas of compilation; secondly, it was an easier and more consistent system for compositors and the technologies of book production; and thirdly, it provided a more consistent internal geography of the work and therefore facilitated easy use by the reader.

As editor, Joyce had to make many decisions over whether to divide or unite subtopics. For instance the large entry on 'Filtration' of which the text is 90 per cent the same in both works, is presented as one entry in *Nicholson's Encyclopaedia* whereas in *Gregory's Dictionary* it appears in three entries – under Filter, Filtering and Filtration within the treatise on Chemistry. Joyce's editorial work reflects the process of designing and shaping a new product from an older one. He lengthened some entries – the entry on comparative anatomy for instance is almost three times longer in *Nicholson's Encyclopaedia*. He reduced other entries for instance the entry on trigonometry is shorter and a lot of the detail and working out of examples has

---

9 Shepherd MSS, Vol. 8, No 89, Joyce to Shepherd 1808.

been removed. In such a general reference work, hard mathematics may not have been considered appropriate on grounds that it might frighten non-mathematicians.

Because so much of the same material is used in both texts, study of these two works exposes some interesting and subtle transitions in the presentation of science. In general, *Gregory's Dictionary* is weighted to presenting science as novel and entertaining, with its workings accessible to the educated general reader and dressed in the elaborate trappings of eighteenth century polite culture. By contrast *Nicholson's Encyclopaedia* anticipates a more eclectic readership. The separately published Prospectus for *Nicholson's Encyclopaedia* claimed that 'Our method will be popular without departing from strictness and precision'.[10] By 'popular' the publishers were cultivating several advertising lines designed to appeal to the market for educational reference works: popular in the sense that many would be likely to desire the work; popular in the sense of being easy to read; and popular in the sense of not being intended simply for elite social groups. Joyce's editorial pen, constrained within the commercial directives of a large publishing speculation, was forced to develop a new product from something that appealed to an older set of values.

Familiar Introduction to the Arts and Sciences for the Use of Schools

Joyce received 50 per cent of all profits relating to the *Familiar Introduction* (1810).[11] The half-profits system, rather than outright sale of copyright or fixed fee commission, began to be popular from the early nineteenth century, especially by authors who had a reasonable expectation of reprints.[12] The agreement however, did not provide very large sums and his first profits were not registered until 1813 when he received a mere £13 14s 4d. He received a further £36 in 1814 on sales from the first print run of 2000 copies in 1810. The second print run of 2000 in 1814 sold out after Joyce's death in 1816 and the royalties presumably went to his wife.

The *Familiar Introduction* sold at 6s in boards. It is a compendium of numbered statement to be learned by rote. The *Monthly Review* recommended 'the volume to parents and instructors as containing much useful matter in a cheap and convenient form', commenting that:

> The plan is very comprehensive especially when compared to the size of the volume: since in the compass of between 3 and 400 small pages, we have the principles of 30 different arts and sciences.[13]

The range of subjects represented in the *Familiar Introduction* reveals Joyce's educational perspective and represents what he thought an appropriate curriculum. The work opens with sections on Grammar and Logic and moves through Geography,

---

10 Prospectus for *Nicholson's Encyclopedia* in BL Tracts, 816.L.47 pp 7–10, p. 9.
11 Longman MSS, MS1396, D1, p. 174.
12 Feather, R. (1988), *A History of British Publishing*, Croom Helm, London, p. 170.
13 *Monthly Review*, Nov. 1811, pp. 318 – 320.

Chronology, Artificial Memory, Mythology, History, the subdivisions of mathematics and natural philosophy and ending with Chemistry, Mineralogy, Botany and Natural History. Each section is divided into lessons which comprise between seven and eighteen numbered statements, some with illustrative examples. Each lesson ends with a set of questions equivalent to the number of statements and designed to elicit a repetition of the original statement. The work was designed as both a home reference work and a basis for classroom teaching: it was not designed to be a course which students would necessarily read from front to back.

The format of numbered statements and questions is consistent throughout but Joyce used different educational devices with respect to particular subject areas. The different techniques reflect different sets of pedagogical assumptions about both the subject matter and the appropriate educational technique necessary to teach that area. To complement the Geography section he added exercises in which the student was required to trace a route. In the various mathematics sections he gave worked examples, and in the science sections he provided experiments as proofs of the numbered statements and, where necessary, further explanations. Thus whilst the format of the text is consistent, the knowledge in each subject has a different set of epistemological features in which different pedagogical styles were deployed. In the traditional area of Grammar, whilst illustrative examples are given, there is no other educational device other than rote learning: The student is required simply to memorise

> An intransitive verb is one in which the action does not pass over to, nor affect any other person or thing: as, I am loved, I run, I walk, &c.

In the Geography section one question required a rote response to 'How is the level of a continent obtained?' but also requires the student to:

> Trace with a pencil the level of the old continent according to exercise 1. Point out the principal chains of mountains according to exercise 2'...

In the natural history section under the lesson on Mammalia, after a statement '11. The felis, or cat genus, has retractile claws and easily climbs trees', an illustration of a lion is given with a description of the Lion which includes:

> It is afraid of flame; is restrained by dogs; easily tamed when young: it roars horribly; sleeps in the sun; eats every third day; and its flesh is eaten by the Americans.

To which the related question is '11. How is the cat genus distinguished? What is said of the lion and the tiger? The standard rote answer is required, but the student also has to report some fantastical descriptions which are 'said' to describe the lion and which therefore rest on the observations of travellers. Thus Joyce used rote learning as the basic pedagogical formula, as a textual strategy and as a consistent format with which to build an educational compendium, but he also managed to inject different qualities relating to the different subject areas. The different subjects have different characteristics: grammar as rule governed, geography as requiring the ability to use maps, mathematics as very hard, science as revealing nature's secrets and natural history as exhibiting fantastical features of the natural world.

By 1810 Joyce had written on most of the areas covered and he was able to adapt his own material to suit this new project. It is very likely that Joyce had compiled material on Grammar, Logic and Rhetoric whilst working for Richard Phillips and published under one of the many pseudonyms Phillips used. However, the *Familiar Introduction* contains the first proven examples of Joyce's work on these subjects. The lengthy section on Logic is a demanding section, especially for students who did not possess the advantage of schooling in the classics. It used Lockean categories to present a metaphysics of learning as well as a rudimentary introduction to philosophy. The following extracts are from lesson 1:

1. There are two modes of perception, viz. sensation and reflection.
4. A sensation is the impression made upon the mind by an object actually present; an idea is a revived impression in the absence of an object.
5. Ideas are either simple or complex.

Lesson 2 further developed the nature of ideas; Lesson 3 described the relations between ideas and words; Lesson 5 introduced definitions; Lesson 5, on Judgement, testimony and propositions, included definitions of consciousness and intuition:

4. Consciousness is the mind's perception of its own existence
6. Intuition is the instant perception of the relation between two ideas; as, "the whole is greater than any of its parts, and equal to all its parts.

Lesson 6, 'Of Reasoning', introduced different forms of syllogistic reasoning, induction and analogy; Lesson 7 gave different types of argumentation; and lesson 8 gave definitions of 'Sophisms' in which Joyce revealed his Unitarian colours in:

2. "A mistake of the question;" that is, when a proposition is proved which has no necessary connection with the question: this is called "ignorantio elenchi:" as if unbelievers argue that Christianity is not true, because "transubstantiation is incredible:" here is a mistake of the question by taking a corruption of Christianity for Christianity itself.

In a fairly low cost general knowledge compendium aimed at the rising market for school textbooks, he could have left such philosophical material out. His Unitarian vision however, required that students understand the operations of reason in order to have a fuller understanding of the works of God and therefore a more truly religious relationship with Him. For Joyce, understanding the operations of the rational mind was an essential part of education. The work was packed with facts and information designed to form the basis of a liberal education. It is a simple and clear formulation that nevertheless manages to signal different textures to the subjects it presents. It was a very successful publication over the long term and was part of the highly popular Bohn's Scientific Library in 1852 from which it was reprinted as late as 1871. Its claim of being a 'Familiar Introduction' is well deserved and its success lay both in its utility and its unassuming simplicity in presenting the basic features of a wide range of subjects with clarity and brevity.

Kendall's *Pocket Encyclopedia*

Edward Augustus Kendall wrote a number of successful children's books. His *Pocket Encyclopedia or a Dictionary of Arts, Sciences and Polite Literature. Compiled from the Best Authorities* was originally published by William Peacock and a conger in 1802, and was produced in six volumes in three different and small sizes – 24mo, 18mo and 12mo – retailing at 18s.[14] Longmans, on the behalf of a conger which included most of the publishers involved in the original, commissioned Joyce to compile a new edition which was issued under the same title and sold as 'corrected and enlarged' in 1811. The new edition changed considerably in format – from six slim volumes to four thicker 12 mo volumes, and retailed at the increased price of £1 4s.[15]

Its pocket-size and mixture of entertaining and educational contents were clearly designed to attract well-off purchasers and parents. Joyce's preface states that the work was increased in size by one third and offered

> A multitude of facts which will instantly delight and surprise the Youthful reader! and in no instance has anything been inserted that can offend the delicacy of the purest mind.

The promise of safe entertainment presented within the limitations and constraints of polite literature, was a major selling point of the work. A potential purchaser might read Joyce's preface and then scan the pages to encounter some of the impressive and sometimes fantastical illustrations. All of the original illustrations and entries concerned with Natural History were retained in the 1811 edition. Figure 13 is the illustration of a supposed 'Orang Outang' with very human-like features, re-published by J. Harris, a member of the congers financing both 1802 and 1811 editions. The related entry uses a mild but measured sense of excitement and danger in describing the supposed activities of the Orang Outang which was known to

> ..carry off women to its wretched habitation, watching them with extraordinary vigilance, as scarcely to admit the possibility of their escape.

Joyce was clearly given licence to make considerable changes and whilst the title retained the sense of social respectability invested in the term 'Polite Literature', his preface states that:

> The former edition was composed chiefly with a view to Polite Literature and the Arts; in the present is combined a vast quantity of materials connected with the sciences so denominated.

---

14 Peddie, *English Catalogue of Books*. Under Miscellaneous. Mar. 1802.
15 *London Catalogue of Books* (1822), W. Bent, London.

The fact that Joyce replaced most of the 'polite' content of the work, relating to social deportment and refined literature, with scientific subjects which included explanations, experiments and worked examples, may reflect the changes in publishers' estimations of the potential market. As a publishing project, the *Pocket Encyclopaedia* retained its commercial potential, but the market was shifting and diversifying. Through the early nineteenth century the potential purchasers of relatively high cost books began to include increasing numbers of the aspiring middle classes, who might be persuaded into a purchase more by the educational benefits and contents of the work, than its pure entertainment value and polite credentials. The *Pocket Encyclopaedia*'s celebration of polite culture, which continued to be used as a marketing device conferring aesthetic authority whilst reflecting the values of the upper echelons of the social hierarchy to which many of the middle classes aspired, but from which they were largely excluded. This change does not represent a major or sudden shift in the sentiments of the book-buying public, but it does reflect the increasing accommodation of concerns for utility and education in the strategies of the publishers involved.

Joyce's preface addressed the work as a 'compilation' and he used his own material as sources. The entries on Electricity, Chemistry, Botany and others, are adaptations from his other works. The mathematical entries use many of the same examples he used in his *System Of Practical Arithmetic* (1808), and the entries for Hydrostatics and Pneumatics are re-workings from the *Scientific Dialogues* (1800–03). In addition to the discourses of entertainment, education and science, the text is also littered with moral messages and sermonising. For instance, the entry on atheism contains a relentless argument that the position of atheism is untenable. After lengthy proofs of the existence of God, the argument that the idea of a creator is 'taught and not natural', is presented as utterly ridiculous on grounds that the truth of revelation had been 'established beyond a possibility of a doubt'.tInterestingly, Joyce entered entries for all the dissenting denominations including one lengthy entry for Unitarianism which is defined as 'humanitarian', and includes a selected list of important doctrines. The three doctrines given are:

1. Unity of God, perfect in every way,
2. His placability to repent sinners without any atonement.
3. Certainty of a life of retribution after death.

Figure 13: Orang Outang. Illustration and entry from Kendall's *Pocket Encyclopaedia*. Vol. 4, published by Longmans 1811.

No explicit mention is made of the most objectionable doctrine of Unitarianism to the orthodox church – the human, rather than divine, origin and status of Christ. In a book designed for a middle-class readership and justified, ostensibly, by the respectable values of polite culture, Joyce quite cleverly presented Unitarianism to young readers, many of whose parents might have found his position unacceptable.

Systematic Education

Systematic education or elementary instruction in the various departments of literature and science with practical rules for studying each branch of useful knowledge (1815) comprises two large octavo volumes of 520 pages each. The work has three Unitarians authors – William Shepherd, Jeremiah Joyce and Lant Carpenter but the Longmans archives show that whilst the trio had a half-profits agreement with Longmans, Joyce received 27/80, Shepherd 5/80 and Carpenter 8/80, reflecting their respective shares in the work and their entitlement to resulting profits. Lant Carpenter wrote the substantial sections on mental and moral philosophy.[16] Given that Shepherd's published works were literary and that there is no evidence of his writing in natural science, he probably wrote the sections on belles lettres and other literary subjects, including prose and poetry composition. Joyce was the largest and organising contributor and his 27/80 share represents the remaining two thirds of the work covering history, geography, chronology, the divisions of mathematics, natural history and natural philosophy. Shortly before Joyce died on 16 June 1816, he received the sum of £184 5s 8d as his share of profits, and a further sum of £100 was paid to his estate in December that year. The first print run of 1500 was nearly sold out by the end of 1816 and, had Joyce lived, he would have received a yearly sum of about £200 in royalties for the following years as *Systematic Education* was regularly reprinted, reaching its third edition in 1822.[17]

Longmans sold most copies wholesale at 22s 6d but sold some at a retail price of one and a half guineas.[18] This was a substantial amount and beyond most pockets, but the work was partly contrived as a leaving home present for readers between 16 and 25 and designed to ensure such readers were not distracted by undesirable pastimes. Concerned parents, whilst not being able to equip their children with expensive encyclopaedias, may have invested one and half guineas in an attempt to ensure their sons filled their spare time usefully. As with most of Joyce's texts, the target audience was built from a number of constituencies. *Systematic Education*'s advertisement claims that it was also designed to be a textbook in 'those schools where instruction comprehends other objects besides the classics', meaning dissenting academies rather than public (fee-paying and generally Anglican) schools. Volume one opens with an 'Essay on Practical Education', which attacks the education received at public schools and the two English universities. This attack on establishment education is

---

16 DNB, Lant Carpenter entry.
17 Longmans MSS, ms1393, D1.
18 Ibid.

pronounced and the essay describes the public schools as fostering 'meanness and hypocrisy', as teaching 'every thing except what will be useful to them in their future destination', and 'puerile rhetoric, intricate logic and a barborous jargon dignified by the name of school divinity'. Traditional and established schools were not the only object of criticism. The reader is also warned against 'the knavery of quacks and charlatans' in the growing field of education, arguing that bad teachers should be charged with 'intellectual murder'. The essay was also radical, although consistent with the general Unitarian perspective, in supporting equal education for women.

In *Systematic Education* the link between the dissenting concern with freedom of enquiry and the focus on science is profound and clearly stated in the preface.

> It is the business of education not to cramp, but to guide the intellect. Its province extends to the inculcation of those principles upon which the structure of science is to be built. To the attainment of truth, freedom of enquiry is vital. A man may as well attempt to penetrate the mazes of an entangled wood in fetters, as to investigate the vast variety of intellectual subjects with a mind trammelled by the imperative decisions of human institutions.

This quotation reflects the dissenting view of the oppressive nature of learning under the aegis of the Established Church and expresses the radical tradition in education. Francis Bacon and, similarly, Thomas Paine, had argued that science should form the basis of true education which would therefore lead to enlightenment and understanding.[19] The most famous Unitarian, Joseph Priestley, was highly critical of Establishment curricula and had pioneered a system of education which been influential on Joyce's own experience at Hackney.[20] Priestley had promoted imaginative study of non-traditional subjects, including history and chemistry, which appeared in *Systematic Education*. From the Unitarian perspective it was the individual, endowed with rational faculties, who needed to witness God's rational world in order to develop a better relationship and understanding of Him. Freedom of enquiry could not be restrained by any institution, however well intentioned, and *Systematic Education* was designed as a system of home learning for the individual.

The format of *Systematic Education* was simple. In all the different sections the subject was introduced and some historical background given. Relevant definitions were covered, then the subject was treated in considerable depth. Each subject was concluded with a section on relevant titles that the authors thought would lead the student further in the study of the subject. Here Joyce took the opportunity to advertise his own works including his *Dialogues on the Microscope* in the microscopy section, his *Analysis* of Adam Smith in the political economy section, and the *Scientific Dialogues* throughout the natural philosophy sections. He also made extensive

---

19 Simon, B. (1972) (ed.), *The Radical Tradition in Education In Britain*, Lawrence and Wishart, London, Simon's introduction p. 12.

20 Watts, R. (1998), 'Some Radical educational networks of the late eighteenth century and their influence' *History of Education*, 27, 1, pp. 1–14, p.5.

reference to articles in *Nicholson's Encyclopaedia* which he puffed as 'finding a very deserving place in the student library'.

Much of Joyce's material was reworked versions of previous productions. The Chronology section follows the same plan he used in *Familiar Introduction*, from which he also used the material from his Artificial Memory section renamed as 'Memoria Technica'. The natural philosophy sections are presented in the same order and with very similar explanations, illustrations and experiments to those that appeared in the *Scientific Dialogues* by then fifteen years old. The Political Economy section is based on Adam Smith's *Wealth of Nations* – a work with which Joyce was very familiar and for which Joyce could use his own *Analysis* and simply sharpen the prose to fit this particular project. In the same Political Economy section Joyce introduced the ideas of Thomas Malthus from his *Essay on the principle of population* (1798), saying 'He [Malthus] has endeavoured to shew that population invariably increases where the means of subsistence increases, unless prevented by some very powerful and obvious checks', going on to explain the Malthusian notion of geometrical population increases against arithmetical increases in the means of subsistence. The inclusion of Malthus is interesting as Malthusian ideas were essentially pessimistic and they challenged the optimistic vision of the radical social theorists who assumed an equation between increases in population and increases in prosperity. In *Systematic Education* the treatment of Malthusian ideas is non-committal in the way Joyce's treatment of Smith's ideas were, but their inclusion at all indicates that Joyce thought them to some extent useful.

The penultimate sections of the book are concerned with the 'Structure and Functions of Man'. Much of this text appeared in a different guise in Joyce's unfinished series of lectures on natural theology that appeared in the *Monthly Repository* at the same time that *Systematic Education* was published. Joyce's prose style and his skill in presenting scientific knowledge were at their height at this point, as the example below, describing the process of respiration, shows.

> In the act of inspiration a quantity of atmospheric air is received into the lungs and retained there for a short time, when expired it is found to be altered in its composition: it has lost part of its oxygen and it now contains a quantity of carbonic acid. These changes are inseparably connected with the conversion of the venous into the arterial blood; for in passing through the lungs, it decomposes the air, imbibing the oxygen, and throwing off the azotic gas.

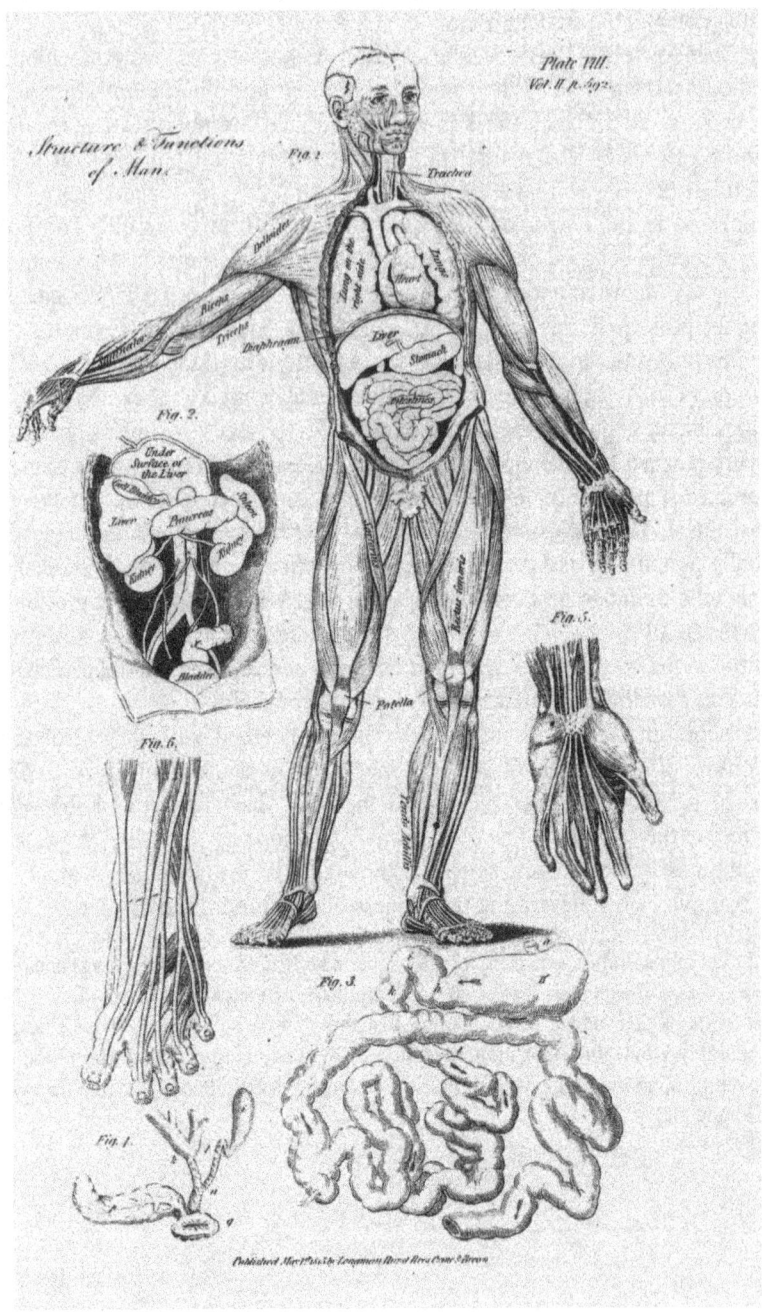

Figure 14: 'Structure and Functions of Man', from *Systematic Education*. Published by Longmans in 1815.

This is a clear, lucid and uncomplicated account of a complex process. Through twenty years of writing expositions of science, Joyce developed the craft of textbook writing and the art of presenting the complex, simply. *Systematic Education* ends with 'A letter from a father to his son on the evidences of the truth of the Christian religion'. Joyce had used this literary device in his own *Letters on Natural Philosophy* and it was a further attempt to keep the book's youthful readers away from the snares and pleasure of society. This was a strictly Unitarian account that described the corruption of Christianity by the Established Church and argued for a Christianity based on a claim for reason and truth. Science was woven into the overall religious purpose of increasing the knowledge of God and readers are sermonised to fulfil their duties to their fellow men.

> Strictly connected with a knowledge of our duty to God, is an acquaintance with our duty to our fellow men and to ourselves. All other studies ought, as it were, to centre in this and are valuable in proportion as they enlighten our understanding, so as to enable us to see what conduct becomes us as rational creatures, or as they tend to meliorate our hearts, and elevate us beyond the sway of baser affections.

Chapter 16

Publishing with Sherwood Neely and C.J. Barrington

Time's Telescope

Very little is known about the firm of Sherwood Neely except that it had a shop in Paternoster Row. *Time's Telescope for 1814; or a Complete Guide to the Almanac: Containing an Explanation of Saints' Days and Holidays* is an interesting annual anthology. Each month contained sections devoted to a 'Naturalist Diary', 'Meteorological Remarks' explanatory notices of 'Saint's Days and Holidays', and the largest sections were devoted to 'Astronomical Occurrences'. This was the last production in which Joyce was involved that does not carry his name. The advertisement, which lists other sources by name, says 'The Astronomical Occurrences have been written expressly for the 'Telescope' by a gentleman eminently conversant with the subject.' Aspland credits Joyce with the 'Astronomical Parts' and Elizabeth Joyce simply lists *Time's Telescope* as Joyce's. Analysis of the 'Astronomical Occurrences' reveals Joyce's literary style and much of the subject matter is strikingly reminiscent of other material by Joyce. The advertisement is dated 13 November 1813 and Joyce must have spent some considerable time in 1813 working out the dates and times of various forthcoming celestial events.

It may appear surprising that Joyce, whose rational religion stood in opposition to any type of superstition of which the predictive discourse of astrology, contained in some almanacs, is symptomatic, could have had anything to do with such a production. However, the type of knowledge contained in *Time's Telescope* was utterly consistent with Joyce's Unitarian and educational project. Furthermore, involvement with almanacs was not without precedent by eminent and scientific men. Charles Hutton, for instance, professor of mathematics at the Royal Military Academy, was the senior compiler of ten almanacs for the Stationers Company from 1786.[1]

Broadly there are two types of astrology that appeared in early modern almanacs. Judicial astrology in which star charts were used to predict future events, and natural astrology in which information about planetary motion and lunar phases was applied to physical phenomenon – for instance the phases of the moon to crop planting. Whilst judicial astrology largely disappeared from almanacs by 1805, natural

---

1   Perkins, M. (1996), *Visions of the future: Almanacs, Time and Cultural Change 1775 – 1870*, Clarendon Press, Oxford, p. 29.

astrology was retained until the mid nineteenth century. As a form of knowledge natural astrology was profoundly demotic as it did not, initially at least, require a high level of education on the part of the reader and was the sort of material that appealed to the widest audience. The type of knowledge contained in almanacs was therefore popular both in the sense of being understandable by the layman, and in the broadest sense of being a form of knowledge in which all social groups could consider themselves legitimately interested. As a literary tradition therefore, natural astrology was a form of knowledge which appealed to a wide audience including the lower classes offering Joyce a ready vehicle for his concerns with education and science. Furthermore, Joyce involvement in meteorology through his years of writing the meteorological reports for the *Monthly Magazine* may also have interested him in almanacs in which weather predictions featured. *Time's Telescope* is notable for being the first almanac in which tables of barometer readings appeared.

Where most of Joyce's other writings were targeted at particular reading audiences – middle class children of specific ages, teenagers, young men and attenders at Humphry Davy's lectures – his writing in *Time's Telescope* assumes a very general readership. The Astronomical Occurences are partially compiled from his own writings and many of the explanations use material he had previously published. The monthly entries are surprisingly long and follow a very similar format, opening with general and interesting remarks on particular celestial phenomena, and presenting a historical and mildly sensationalist account of the way the phenomena have been understood. For instance the December entry starts under the subtitle 'Of the Nature and Uses of Comets' and points out that before 'the light of knowledge', comets were considered 'the harbingers of awful convulsions' and many 'wild and extravagant notions have been entertained respecting them'. He recounted how 'Even a century ago the famous Whiston' had considered comets the 'abode of the dammed' and how Whiston thought a comet 'alternately hurried its wretched tenants to the terrifying extremes of perishing cold and devouring fire'. He then delivered a Newtonian and physical account of the tails of comets formed from rising 'vapour' through the process of 'rarefaction' and centrifugal force.

> Now the ascent of vapours into the tail of the comet, he [Newton] supposes occasioned by the rarefaction of the matter of the atmosphere at the time of its being in the perihelion. The ascent of the vapours will be promoted by their circular motion around the Sun.

One of the striking features of Joyce's narrative here is how he uses a quite chatty sensationalist style, designed to appeal to a popular readership, as a platform for imparting some quite difficult information. This is a deliberate pattern and he was clearly trying to educate his readers at the same time as interest them. He introduced Newton's idea that comets may 'recruit the Sun with fresh fuel' and goes on to explain resistance of the solar atmosphere and increasing gravitation. He explored the idea that 'Comets have been regarded as the cause of the deluge' and went on to discuss attractive powers, the rotary motion of the globe and centrifugal force. He did not hide any features of celestial mechanics on grounds that they would be too difficult or inappropriate for the production in general and he found a way of explaining phenomena in language which is kept as simple as possible; he imparted information in a style that assumed that the reader would be able to follow his reasoning.

In each monthly entry, after three or four pages of introductory historical material and observations, he presented a number of tables which predicted the times of the sun and the moon's rising and falling, and the alterations to clocks necessary to keep time in line with the earth's rotations. He also recorded any interesting phenomena calculated to take place. For instance in December he included data predicting the passage of eclipses of the moon and of Jupiter's satellites. He then gave a lecture on astronomical subjects in which material that he had used in his *Dialogues*, *Letters* and his encyclopaedia entries on astronomy, were recycled under such titles as, 'Of the Georgian Planet, and of Comets'. Where Joyce had worked heavily on presenting a very accessible opening and providing predictive information in his middle sections, these closing sections rely heavily on his previous works. Such differences in the way Joyce placed his energies show his experience and skill in handling a new project. He shaped and designed his openings for a general readership, he worked on providing interesting information in line with the genre of almanacs, and he then filled the gaps with a re-arrangement of his own material. This was a formula for dealing with a new literary task achieved through his years of compilations and jobbing authorship. For the efficient execution of his craft, Joyce had to apply his practised skills effectively and economically through the twelve monthly sections.

The Lives of the Admirals

Both Aspland and Elizabeth Joyce record Joyce's work on a new edition of John Campbell's *Lives of the Admirals* (Barrington, 1812, 1st ed. 1750). Very little is known about Barrington and very little can be said about Joyce's work on this project which was published by Barrington in 1812 and by John Stockdale in 1813. The original editor employed to update the work was Henry Redhead Yorke, who was, like Joyce, involved in political radicalism in the 1790s but who later became an arch Tory.[2] Yorke had been urged to do the work by Richard Valpy, the headmaster of Reading School, early in 1812 but Yorke became ill and died in early January 1813. Joyce was probably invited to complete the task but it is impossible to determine which were Joyce's contributions. It is perhaps a fitting end to an account of Joyce's individual books that there is very little that can be said.

---

2 DNB, Yorke entry.

Chapter 17
Overview of Joyce's Works

Joyce's educational works share many distinctive features. They were all created from a combination of the commercial imperatives of the market-place, the interests of the various publishers with whom Joyce worked, and Joyce's own material needs. They all contain and express Joyce's Unitarian belief in a rational world which reveals the beneficent designs of God. They were all founded on the premise that true knowledge of the natural world would bring humanity to a closer and more honest relationship with God, and they were all optimistic in the sense of presupposing that, with the right education, human society would progress to a more harmonious and egalitarian future.

Yet his works also reflect the eclecticism and experimentalism of publishing speculations in a growing market-place for books. They all reflect the influence of publishers, Joyce's own designs, and the expansion of the educational sector of the market and each of the works reflects a different balance of factors. With Johnson, Joyce's works reflect an older perspective on education influenced by Joyce's employment with the aristocratic Earl Stanhope and the educational experimentalism of Rousseau, Edgeworth and Priestley. With Johnson, Joyce was able to exercise literary freedom in narrative construction. He adopted and used the established conventions of the literary forms of the dialogue, the letter and the catechism, which he transformed to his own purposes. He used 'dialogues' not in the sense of literary vehicles to prompt speculation, but as vehicles of didacticism; he used 'letters' as individual lessons; and he mixed up the symbolic power of the religious 'catechism' with the pedagogic flexibility of the dialogue. He was not alone in using these forms of writing elastically to produce new literary products, but he was clearly one of the first nineteenth century writers to develop them to popularise science.

With Phillips, Joyce's works reflect the hard-nosed but imaginative profiteering of a publisher who seized the opportunities of the new market and created new educational products. Phillips expanded the range of educational publications with considerable success. His educational works were less literary than those of Johnson and were built on his own commercially driven formulas. Joyce's commissions with Phillips followed clearly defined prescriptions: Phillips's 'grammars' and Joyce's *System*, were textbooks written to a formula directed at the target markets of both schools and home learners, while the *Wonders* and the *Book of Trades* were fashioned for general markets and were respectable general reading. Joyce gained little long-term material benefit from his works with Phillips but he learnt how to adapt to, and fulfil, the demands of a range of projects and he gained a reputation as an editor through his work on *Gregory's Dictionary*.

With the large firm of Longmans Joyce had two roles – of employee and of author. He was involved with encyclopedia projects – Rees's, Nicholson's and Kendall's – where he was employed to do specific literary tasks. Longmans also accepted two of Joyce's own productions – *Familiar Introduction* which was a very general, cheap and inoffensive compendium, and *Systematic Education*, which was overtly Unitarian and expressed Joyce's educational programme. The corporate publishing house of Longmans generated large projects in which he could fulfil the functions of both editor and contributor and enabled him to consolidate his reputation as an able and respectable literary worker.

Joyce was clearly well known to London publishers as an adaptable writer who could fulfil a role in their speculative projects. His work with H.D. Symonds, Sherwood Neely and C.J. Barrington, in which Joyce engaged in a variety of speculations none of which carried his name, were projects that forced Joyce to write in particular styles and adapt himself to quite different literary formats to those he employed in his educational writings.

Conclusion

In telling a story it is necessary to build patterns that at least have the appearance of coherence. In telling the story of Joyce's life and work, I have traced links between his social circumstances and his intellectual outlook. I have used his biography to navigate the histories of dissent, radicalism and educational publishing in order to create just such a coherent patterns. The pictures I have drawn create Joyce's biography against the background of political radicalism and the social vision of Unitarianism, but such pictures can only be partial in their attempt to describe the real compromises of Joyce's life. The image of consistent and high principled heroism that might be suggested by his actions in the early 1790s and his life-long dedication to the Unitarian cause, is challenged by his acquiescence in the commercial and social exigencies that circumscribed his life. The economic realities which influenced writer-publisher relations sometimes led Joyce to write on the basis of speculative estimates of potential markets, rather than on the basis of his elevated social vision. Joyce espoused and aspired to a sense of social respectability, yet it was the very standards of respectability that served to partially alienate him and that created some of the compromises he had to negotiate.

Such contradictions are the stuff of life and impossible to escape. Joyce's life is no exception. His grip on his own principles loosened or tightened according to the demands of the situation and his power to influence it. As a young man invigorated with millennial hopes of the French Revolution, enthused by the company of fellow radicals and horrified by what he saw as the abuses of government, he challenged the most powerful forms of authority. A very different image emerges if he is pictured sitting at his writing desk producing Richard Phillips's latest publishing speculation in which a pseudonym was used and a pedagogy – rote learning – was deployed which ran counter to his own educational philosophy. Indeed in his day-to-day life of a jobbing writer, he may well have had to forego any sense of moral purpose in his concern to secure sufficient income. Yet despite such contrary images, there are a number of features revealed in his personal and intellectual deportment, that suggest a consistency of human fibre and purpose.

Joyce did not possess a brilliant intellect in the sense that Priestley or Price or Burke or Coleridge did. He didn't attain a level of intellectual dexterity with which to develop innovative insights and move ideas and understanding significantly forwards. He was a worker, a craftsman who turned his skills, acquired through his artisan upbringing and trade apprenticeship, to craft knowledge for public consumption. The sense of guidance over the learning process, the use of pedagogical devices adapted and changed for different circumstances, and the dogged perseverance to complete the task, are characteristic of Joyce's craftsman-like engagement with life.

His unswerving belief in divine providence provided him with a system that he held and prosecuted with focused dedication. There is no evidence in any of his writings that he ever doubted God's existence or His providential design of the physical universe. The completeness of his religious belief does not mean that he was intellectually unable to consider counter arguments, but that it provided him with an explanatory framework with which to understand the world. For Joyce, the mysteries of life were answered in the mind of God and this simple formula cast out atheistic challenges or contrary evidence as both pernicious and unnecessary. These two features of Joyce's disposition – a craftsman's practical engagement with life and a complete belief in God – provide the basis of his mindset.

For a considerable portion of Joyce's literary production it is possible to identify the tenets of Unitarianism – particularly in his writings for the Unitarian publisher Joseph Johnson and in his last book, *Systematic Education*. The link between his Unitarianism and his writings for other publishers however, is not so clear. Joyce's editorial and literary skills were the services sought by Richard Phillips, Longmans, H.D. Symonds, Sherwood Neely and C.J. Barrington. His skills as a literary project worker were marketable and secured him his livelihood in the world of metropolitan publishing. In such circumstances, and in the face of the commercial reasoning to which he had to adapt, he could not afford to maintain his earlier Unitarian agenda.

Joyce's Unitarianism conferred an authenticity to his social persona and established a sense of moral purpose in his negotiations with the book trade. Indeed his Unitarianism combined with his radical past made him a minor celebrity and secured his entry to the offices of publishers. In particular, his involvement in the Treason Trials, which turned out to be a test of the 1792 Libel Act and the jury's, rather than the judge's, right to decide whether writings were seditious or not, was a major landmark in publishing history. For the publishing world Joyce had been instrumental in securing a freedom which benefited the whole industry. The Treason Trials, symbolically at least, had served to delimit the range of governmental control and censorship of the press and preserved the literary freedom within which publishers could operate. Some publishers may therefore have been grateful to Joyce and were disposed to employ him on relevant projects.

Joyce was writing at a time when the English book trade was undergoing major transformations. When it was changing from being dominated by small independents such as Joseph Johnson and Benjamin Flower to large corporate enterprises such as Longmans. One feature of this period was the increasing importance of potentially lucrative sections of the market for books. Popular education was one such developing market in which writers did not require a high literary and artistic reputation. In the marketing of educational books, publishers had much more licence to create and control projects in which books were published anonymously or pseudonymously and were increasingly created as much from publishers' estimations of the market, as from authorial intention. This type of literary enterprise therefore conferred relatively more power in the hands of the publishers to direct the form and content of individual works. This was particularly true of Sir Richard Phillips, whose speculations provided Joyce with considerable employment. The expansion of the market created space for the development of new ranges of literary products and Joyce was well placed to share in such an expansion.

Joyce had many personal contacts in the publishing industry. His working relationship with Joseph Johnson in the production of Unitarian tracts secured Johnson's support. His relationship with Richard Phillips was forged through their mutual radical past. With Longmans, one of the partners, Joyce's fellow Unitarian Owen Rees and Joyce's former tutor, the encyclopedia editor Abraham Rees, maintained Joyce's strong links with the firm. His connections were important in securing him work, but his radical reputation was also important in establishing credentials interesting to certain publishers. Joyce's reputation however, was a double-edged sword. It worked in his favour to the extent of helping him to obtain work, but against him in that marketing considerations sometimes prevented the use of his name, leaving him frustrated that his reputation did not benefit from his labour.

Joyce's writings represent a compromise between his Unitarian views, the requirements of his publishers and the developing market for books. His Unitarian inheritance, received largely through Priestley, provided a mechanics of learning based on Lockean categories and Hartleyian associationism. This inheritance generated a pedagogy with which Joyce could apply his craft skills but his licence to direct literary projects to a manifestly Unitarian vision was crucially determined by his relationship with publishers in which his status was sometimes as an independent writer and sometimes as an employee. For Johnson he could produce works that reflected his Unitarian views. For Phillips he had to write according to commercial formulae and with Longmans he had to find a niche within a large corporate enterprise.

Infused with the conviction of divine providence, Joyce was optimistic. He believed that if people were educated to use their powers of reason they would more fully appreciate God's work and would build a fairer and better world. The major domain in which reason could be successfully applied was science, and it was to science that Joyce focused his educational efforts. Consistent with traditions of Unitarianism, he combined an intellectual form of theology with the optimistic elements of the Enlightenment programme and the power of scientific method. Joyce was a populariser of science not only because it provided a market he could exploit – although that was increasingly the purpose of his publishers – but also because he profoundly believed scientific education would lead people to a better understanding of God. Joyce had been trained for the pulpit and his intention from the 1780s had always been to obtain a ministry. Unable to fulfil his first calling, his educational activities enabled him to develop a different form of ministry, but one which was nevertheless concerned with moral guidance and the cultivation of human relationships with God. For Joyce, a closer relationship with God was achieved by cultivating an attitude of rational piety and both understanding and using scientific reasoning.

Joyce's personal history had taken him through a period of intense social change and political challenge to the authority of the government. Despite the defeat of radicalism through the early 1790s, he always sought to drive people towards his vision of a more equitable society. In this respect, his mature educational vision was as informed by political principles as were his activities as a political radical in the early 1790s. Education was, and remains, political, in the sense that it is a site for the reproduction of cultural values over which there is vested and conflicting political interest. Joyce's educational work took place in a period when the power and necessity of education was becoming increasingly recognised at all levels of society. Yet Joyce's works largely avoided the defensive fire of his Establishment and conservative critics. He produced books whose price, at the point of sale, kept them out of reach of the lowest classes of readers and they were therefore unlikely to be seen as a dangerous extension of knowledge downwards in the social hierarchy. The scientific content of his writings and the narrative structures he used could not be readily challenged on political grounds as they flattered the middle class values of industry and respectability. Indeed most of his works use narrative forms, for instance the *Scientific Dialogues*, which given its aristocratic setting and dialogue between a tutor and the sons of an aristocrat, served to re-inforce respectable values.

Between his earlier activities in the Society for Constitutional Information and his later educational works, Joyce appears to have extended his expectation of the time necessary to achieve his Unitarian vision of a better society. Like many others disillusioned by the promise and then horrors of the French Revolution, Joyce realised that the process of education had to be more gradual than he had originally thought. The Society for Constitutional Information had always been more gradualist and intellectual in its outlook than the working class London Corresponding Society which had urged immediate representative democracy but caught on the wave of optimism in liberal intellectual circles following the outbreak of the French Revolution and responding to signals of support from other reform groups, the Society for Constitutional Information in the early 1790s had briefly seen its goals as achievable in the near future. In the event, from the time of the September massacres in 1792, liberal, and particularly Unitarian, sentiment was pushed back to a more removed sense of paternal guidance over the social programme in which the goal of a more equitable society was placed much further into the future.

The initial audience to whom Joyce's literary products were directed was ring-fenced by economic boundaries in the form of book price. As the market for books increased and as the technologies of book production improved, the capacity for large print-runs of lower priced books yielding sufficient profit for publishers increased. Joyce was working at a time when publishers were just beginning to exploit such markets. Educational books, traditionally cheaper than other forms of writing, were one of the obvious markets to exploit. In the growing industry of the production of educational materials Joyce was one of the first professional educationalists to obtain a living from writing science books.

Joyce made no pretence of owning the ideas he crafted, although he became responsible for them as they appeared on the page. There is a clear sense in which the books he produced were the product of his own work. His craft was the craft of teaching and his art was the pedagogical formulation of a Unitarian vision. He worked over a huge range of subjects to which he adapted to under the pressure of circumstances. He possessed the ability to adapt to circumstances, to fulfil the demands of the project in hand and to construct a new product from a range of materials.

Joyce was not a grand theorist. He did not engage the philosophical difficulties over the nature of reason, the existence of God, the paradox of predestination and human freewill or the problems of democratic government. But he didn't need to. His craftsman style and his rational piety gave him an assured sense of purpose with which to live his life. The commercial imperatives of the publishing world, the contradictions of political and social reality and sense of alienation from the Unitarian community no doubt confused, dismayed, challenged and compromised him. But his religious and optimistic engagement with the world provided him with the answers that gave his life sense and meaning.

List of Joyce's Published Works

Evidence that these titles were composed by Joyce comes from a number of sources. The most important are Robert Aspland's memoir of Joyce, which gives a comprehensive list of Joyce's works, but which has some gaps and errors in dating, and the partial memory of Joyce's wife Elizabeth as recorded by Joyce's daughter in a letter to her sister. Supplementary evidence is gleaned from the recollections of Joyce's contemporaries, close study of bibliographical information, advertisements, prefaces and title pages. In the following list of Joyce's titles, Joyce has been identified as author where two sources confirm his authorship and where any available supplementary evidence is consistent.

Note that unless otherwise stated, Joyce's works were published in London.

1. *An account of the author's arrest for "Treasonable Practices"* (Printed for the author, 1794).
2. *A Sermon preached on Sunday, February the 23rd, 1794: to which is added an appendix containing an account of the author's arrest for treasonable practices* (Printed for the author, Nov. 1794),
3. *Analysis of Paley's view of the Evidences....* (Benjamin Flower, 1795).
4. *Analysis of Adam Smith's Wealth of Nations* (Cambridge: Benjamin Flower, 1797).
5. *Institutes of Natural Philosophy* (Johnson, 1799, 1st ed., 1785). [Ascribed to W. Enfield]. Also printed as, *A Short Introduction to Magnetism & Electricity and the First Principles of Chemistry* (1799).
6. *Shakespeare's Seven Ages of Man Illustrated* (H.D. Symonds, 1800).[Anon].
7. *Scientific Dialogues Intended for the Instruction and Entertainment of Young People: in which the first Principles of Natural and Experimental Philosophy are fully explained* (Johnson, 1800–03)
8. *An Easy Grammar of General Geography* (Phillips, 1803). [Pseud. Goldsmith J.]
9. *Geography on a Popular Plan Illustrated* (Phillips, 1803). [Pseud. Goldsmith J.]
10. *Courage and Union in a Time of National Danger*, ('Published at the desire of several persons who heard it', 1803).
11. *Book of Trades or Library of Useful Arts* (Tabart, 1804). [Anon]
12. *An Analysis of Paley's Natural Theology or Evidences of the Existence and Attributes of the Deity Collected from the Appearances of Nature* (Cambridge: Flower, 1804).
13. *Wonders of the Microscope or An Explanation of the Wisdom of the Creator in Objects Comparatively Minute, Adapted to the Understanding of the Young* (Tabert & Phillips, 1805). [Anon]
14. *Wonders of the Telescope or Display of the Starry Heavens Calculated to Promote and Simplify the Study of Astronomy* (Tabert & Philips, 1805). [Anon]
15. *Dialogues in Chemistry intended for the Instruction and Entertainment of Young People In Which The First Principles Of That Science Are Fully Explained. To Which*

are added *Questions And Other Exercises For The Examination Of Pupils* (Johnson, 1807).
16. *Dictionary of Arts and Sciences* (Phillips 1807) [Under Gregory G.]
17. *An Easy Grammar of Natural and Experimental Philosophy for the Use of Schools* (Phillips, 1807). [Pseud. Blair Rev. D.]
18. *A System Of Practical Arithmetic Applicable to the Present State of Trade, and Money Transactions, Illustrated by Numerous Examples Under Each rule; For the Use of Schools* (Phillips, 1808).
19. *A Key to Joyce's Arithmetic Containing Solutions and Answers* (Phillips, 1808).
20. *The British Encyclopaedia or Dictionary of Arts and Sciences* (Longmans et al., 1809). [Under Nicholson W]
21. *Familiar Introduction to the Arts and Sciences for the Use of Schools* (Longmans, 1810).
22. *Letters On Natural And Experimental Philosophy Addressed To A Youth Settling In The Metropolis* (Johnson & Co., 1810).
23. *Kendall's Pocket Encyclopaedia or a Dictionary of Arts, Sciences and Polite Literature. Compiled from the Best Authorities* (Longman, Hurst, Rees, Orme & Co., J. Harris, Scathherd & Letterman, Peacock & Bampton, Wilkie & Robinson & R. Baldwin, 2nd edn., 1811). [Joyce's update]
24. *Dialogues on the Microscope intended for the Instruction and Entertainment of Young Persons, Desirous of investigating the minuter parts of creation* (Johnson & Co., 1812).
25. *Catechism of Nature for the use of Children* (Johnson & Co., 1812, 9th ed.).
26. *A Sketch of the History and Proceedings of the Deputies Appointed to Protect the Civil Rights of the Protestant Dissenters to which is added a Summary of the Laws Affecting Protestant Dissenters* (Samuel Burton, 1813). [Anon.]
27. *Systematic Education* (Longmans, 1815). With William Shepherd and Lant Carpenter.
28. *The Subserviency of Free Enquiry and Religious Knowledge, among the Lower Classes of Society to the Prosperity and Permanence of a State* (For the author, 1816).

Works in Which Joyce Was Significantly Involved

The New Testament an Improved Version (A Society promoting Christian Knowledge and the practice of virtue, by the distribution of Books, 1808).
Time's Telescope for 1814; or a Complete Guide to the Almanac: Containing an Explanation of Saints' Days and Holidays, is *Time's Telescope* (Sherwood Neely, 1814). [Anon]
Imperial Review 1804–5
Lives of the Admirals (Barrington, 1812). [Ascribed to Henry Redhead Yorke]
Series 2 of *Tracts* (1805) published by the Unitarian Society.

Known Publication in the *Monthly Repository*

Vol. 3, Jan., Feb., Mar., Dec., 1807 and vol. 4, Feb. 1808. Reports on the proceedings of the Commitee to prepare a Unitarian version of the New Testament.

Vol. 3, Jan. 1808, p. 12. Joyce's review of Corry.

Vol. 8, April 1813, pp. 561–577. Joyce J., 'Memoir of the Rev Hugh Worthington.

Vol. 10, 1815, p. 260. Joyce, J., 'On Unitarianism'.

Vol. 11, Mar 1815, p. 35. First of a series of essays on Natural Theology – continues each month for 13 months.

Obituary notices Hannah Joyce, vol. 11, Mar. 1816, p. 110.

                    Joshua Joyce, vol. 11, April 1816, p. 244.

Index

Adams Daniel 48
Aiken John 136, 153
Arianism 22–30
Aspland Robert 7–8, 86–8, 95, 119, 144, 151, 156, 170, 172

Barbauld Anna Laetitia 73, 75, 123, 148
Bell Andrew 101
Belsham Thomas 72–82, 113
Benson Revd. J 4
Bentham Jeremy 24
Blair David [pseud.] 120, 151, 181
Bonney John 42, 55
British Convention 45–9
Broadhurst Thomas 27–9
Burdett Francis 75
Burke Edmund 29, 32, 39, 41, 50, 58, 61, 65, 66, 176

Carpenter Lant 68, 158, 165, 181
Cartwright Major John 17, 42
Catlow Samuel 151
Cheshunt 3–10, 77
Chevening 32–7, 58, 67–81, 99
Church and King Mobs 45
Coleridge Samuel Taylor 73, 136, 175
Collins A. S. 99–100, 138
Collins Wilkie 122
Common Council of London 15
Commonwealthman 17–18
Condorcet Marquis de 34–5
Congers 153–62
Copyright 74, 103–4, 138, 151, 159
Corrie John 158
Corry W. 87, 182
Crown and Anchor Tavern 48, 61

Daubeny Revd. Charles 83
Davy Humphrey 118, 121–2, 134
Disney John 72, 80, 81, 92
Dr. Williams's Library 9, 27, 118
Dundas Henry 53, 48, 51

Edgeworth – Richard and Mary 124, 174
Enfield William 118–19, 170
Essex Street Chapel 16–18, 21, 43, 46, 72, 75, 80, 85, 92–3, 118

Fagg Captain 69
Farmer Hugh 80–81
Feathers Tavern Petition 24
Flower Benjamin 109–11, 135, 176, 170
Fox Charles James 26, 40, 43–4
Frend William 70
Fulton Robert 71

Gagging Acts 60, 65, 109
Gilray James 35, 59
Godwin William 26, 32, 73–4, 90, 102
Goldsmith Revd. J [pseud.] 138, 150–51, 180
Good John Mason 153
Gordon Riots 16
Grafton Duke of 95
Gregory George 153, 155, 181
Gregory Olinthus 122, 153
Grenville Lord 34–5
Grenville Louisa 34, 71
Griffiths J.W. 3, 22

Habeas Corpus 46, 52
Hackney College 18, 26–33, 40–41, 72, 76
Hackney Gravel Pit Meeting 32
Hall John 132
Hansard Luke 71
Hardy Thomas 48, 54, 59, 107, 110
Hartley David 21, 67, 73, 86, 124
Hazlitt William 26
Heber Bishop Reginald 122
Henry William 25
Herschel William 120, 131
Highgate 75
Hinckley John 82
Holcoft Thomas 42, 48, 55, 73
Hollis Thomas Brand 17, 26

Holt Daniel 76
Home Office 41
Hume David 87
Humphreys H. 36
Hunter Rowland 126, 129
Hutton Charles 170

Imperial Review 89–90, 171

Jackson Francis 69
Jebb John 17
Johnson Ebenezer 82
Johnson Joseph 16, 19, 30, 41, 73–4, 70–71, 86, 101–6, 118, 123–4, 128–9, 136, 153–6, 173, 186–7, 180–81
Joyce Joshua 18, 43, 54, 180
Joyce Hannah – also listed as Ridyard Hannah 12, 53, 55, 59, 72, 74–5, 137

Kendall Edward Augustus 144
Kentish John 70
Kippis Andrew 28, 41, 73
Kyd Samuel 55

Lamb Charles and Mary 73
Lancaster Joseph 101, 149
Lardner Nathaniel 30, 70, 83
Libel Act (1972) 41, 60, 176
Lindsey Theophilus 16–17, 21, 40, 52, 55–6, 72, 80–83,108
Locke John 23, 41, 67, 86, 124
Lofft Capel 17
London Corresponding Society 33, 46–8, 53, 62, 55, 107, 178
Longman Thomas N. 103, 156
    Publishing firm 20, 106, 138, 149, 151, 155–6, 158–9

Mansfield Street 37, 49
Martin James 46
Martinet Johannes Florentins 114–16
Miles Mr 35
Mill James 122
Mill John Stuart 122
Millenarianism 21–2, 46
Monthly Magazine 136, 144, 153, 171
Monthly Repository 6, 9, 16, 18, 20, 30, 54, 75–7, 81, 83, 86–7, 94, 167, 181
More Hannah 113

Morgan George Cadogan 26
Muir Thomas 107–8

Newcome John 81
Newton Isaac 21, 31, 121, 189
Nicholson William 108, 123–4, 155, 157–8, 181

Paine Thomas 24, 32, 34, 38, 43, 45, 56, 60, 66, 100–102, 168
Painters and Glaziers 12–15
Paley William 86, 88,110–11
Palmer Thomas Pysche 86, 107–9
Parkes Samuel 125
Patronage 11, 25, 99–105
Payne Joseph 122
Pepper John Henry 122
Phillips Richard 73, 91–105, 136–56, 161, 173, 175–7, 180
Pinnock William 122
Pitt William 34–5, 43, 46, 48, 50, 61–70, 76
Place Francis 54, 96, 110
Playfair Professor 131
Post Office 41
Presbyterian Fund 27
Presbyterians 3–6, 10, 22, 27, 35
Price Richard 17–32, 39–43, 50, 52, 60, 66, 73, 78, 80, 175
Priestley Joseph 11, 17, 21–6, 30, 35, 40, 45, 50, 52, 56, 60, 67, 73, 78, 80, 83, 86, 90, 104, 109, 119, 124, 136, 166, 168, 173, 175, 177
Privy Council 46, 48, 51–2, 76

Rathbone William 89
Rational Piety 78–9, 177, 179
Rees Abraham   28, 73, 156, 177
Reeves John 45
Reform Society 32
Revolution Society 32, 38–42
Richter John 42
Ridolfi Marquis 131
Ridyard Hannah – also listed as Joyce Hannah 18, 30, 71, 73, 87, 90, 92–3, 155
Rights of Juries 44, 55, 58, 93, 95
Robinson Henry Crabb 73, 76
Rochefoucauld Duc de 35, 39
Rosslyn Hill Chapel 75
Rousseau – JJ 124

Rowe John 185
Royal Institution 102, 125, 134
Rutt J.T. 76, 81

Salters Hall 19
Scottish Martyrs 45, 47, 60, 107
September Massacres 66, 178
Sermons 19, 30, 39–60, 86–7, 92–95, 146, 148, 180
Sharp William 42
Shepherd William 9, 11, 15, 19, 45, 53, 55, 68–77, 89–90, 108, 137, 158, 165, 181
Skirving William 60, 107–9
Smith Adam 42, 122, 166
Smith J. A. 122
Smith William 42, 122, 166
Society for Constitutional Information 17, 38–49, 55–65, 75, 100, 107–8, 118, 136, 178
Society for the Supporters of the Bill of Rights 17
Socinius Faustus 22
Spies 33, 41, 45, 48, 54, 59, 62, 85
Stanhope
    Charles Lord 17, 29, 31–44, 48–62, 66–7, 69–72, 88, 99–100, 106–7, 114, 121, 173
    Charles 34, 79, 123, 125–6
    Ghita 33, 34, 37, 39–40, 52, 70–71
    Grizelda 70
    Hester 34, 37, 58, 70–71
    James 34, 70, 123, 125–6
    Lucy 34, 70
    Mahon 51–2, 67, 88
    Phillip Dormer 150
Strand 12, 16, 61

Surprize Transport 47, 107–8
Symonds H.D. 106, 114–15, 117, 174, 176, 180

Tabert Benjamin 7–8, 170
Taylor Thomas 20, 29
Test and Corporation Acts 10, 23, 26, 32
Thelwall John 48, 58
Thomson Thomas 125–6
TookeJohn Horne 42, 48–9, 54, 59, 61, 65–6, 9, 72–3, 76, 78, 109, 116, 176
Towers Joseph 27
Treason Trials 41, 44, 48, 54, 59, 61, 66, 69, 72–3, 76, 78, 109, 116, 176
Trimmer Sarah 143–4

Unitarian New Testament 81–6, 181
Unitarian Society 38, 40–42, 56, 80–82, 85–6, 93, 100, 171
Unitarianism 16, 18–23, 30, 66, 78, 83, 86, 102, 113, 153, 163, 165, 175–7, 180

Valpy Richard 172
Vidler W 81, 92

Wakefield Gilbert 26, 83
Walker C V 122
Webbe Francis 69
Willis Mr. 12
Windham William 58–9
Woolcombing 5–8, 142
Worsley Samuel 10–11
Worthington Hugh 18–22, 27, 30, 79, 86, 180
Wyvill Christopher 17

Yorke Henry Redhead 172, 181

For Product Safety Concerns and Information please contact our EU
representative GPSR@taylorandfrancis.com
Taylor & Francis Verlag GmbH, Kaufingerstraße 24, 80331 München, Germany

www.ingramcontent.com/pod-product-compliance
Lightning Source LLC
Chambersburg PA
CBHW051413290426
44108CB00030B/1579